HOW TO BE A LEARI ... .
IN HIGHER EDUCATION

Filled with practical guidance for those working in and interested in the emergent field of Learning Development, this must-read book encapsulates what it means to be a Learning Developer and how to thrive in this role.

With carefully constructed contributions which explore different aspects of the role, this edited collection is comprehensive in its approach. Alongside practical advice, it is underpinned by theoretical and epistemological insights to provide a bridge between theory and practice.

Organised into five key parts, it is arranged in a way that reflects the journey that practitioners take into and through Learning Development, from their initiation into the field, through professional development, to becoming an established expert. It covers key topics such as:

- the basic principles of working in Learning Development
- the theoretical and practical foundations of the field
- how to engage more critically with the role
- how to become an active contributor to the field through research and publication
- the as-yet unrealised possibilities of Learning Development

Capturing a diverse array of voices, experiences, and perspectives, this book is an essential guide for both new and established practitioners concerned with student Learning and Development.

Alicja Syska is a hybrid academic at the University of Plymouth, UK. She is a Learning Developer for the Faculty of Arts, Humanities and Business alongside teaching and research roles in Education and History.

Carina Buckley is the Instructional Design Manager at Solent University, UK. She is an AdvanceHE Principal Fellow and a researcher in the field of Learning Development.

HOW TO BE A LEARNING DEVELOPER IN HIGHER EDUCATION

Critical Perspectives, Community and Practice

Edited by Alicja Syska and Carina Buckley

Routledge
Taylor & Francis Group

LONDON AND NEW YORK

Designed cover image: Getty Images

First published 2024
by Routledge
4 Park Square, Milton Park, Abingdon, Oxon OX14 4RN

and by Routledge
605 Third Avenue, New York, NY 10158

Routledge is an imprint of the Taylor & Francis Group, an informa business

British Library Cataloguing-in-Publication Data
A catalogue record for this book is available from the British Library

ISBN: 978-1-032-56008-3 (hbk)
ISBN: 978-1-032-56007-6 (pbk)
ISBN: 978-1-003-43334-7 (ebk)

DOI: 10.4324/9781003433347

Typeset in Galliard
by SPi Technologies India Pvt Ltd (Straive)

The Open Access version of Chapter 15 and Chapter 21 was funded by University of Reading.

CONTENTS

ILLUSTRATIONS

Figures

Tables

CONTRIBUTORS

Steph Allen is a senior lecturer in Learning Development and Academic Integrity, having worked at Bournemouth University since 2002. She is a Senior Fellow of the Higher Education Academy. Her interests focus on quality education, and reduced inequalities through academic integrity.

Ryan Arthur manages Learning Development at Birkbeck College, University of London. He is a Fellow of Advance HE. His research interests include the BME Award Gap, decolonisation, and disruptive pedagogies.

Gordon Asher is an academic proofreader and editor, independent scholar, and Learning/Researcher Developer. He worked, for over a decade, in Learning Development at UWS and Strathclyde University. Much of his work focuses on UK HE's present and future – within a framing of 'working in, against, and beyond the neoliberal university'.

Ed Bickle is a lecturer in Learning Development at Bournemouth University, a position he has held since 2017. He is a Fellow of the Higher Education Academy and a Certified Learning Development Practitioner (CeP).

David Biggins has a strong interest in technology enhanced learning and led the academic development of a TEL toolkit. He champions the use of TEL amongst colleagues, has led learning analytics projects, and continues to research the positives and negatives of using data for the benefit of staff and students.

Silvina Bishopp-Martin has been a Learning Developer at Canterbury Christ Church University since 2012. She is currently aligned to the education courses of the Faculty of Arts, Humanities and Education. Her research interests include professional identity, critical discourse studies, critical pedagogies, and academic literacies. She is an ALDinHE Certified Leading Practitioner and an Advanced HE Fellow.

Kevin Brazant is a Learning Developer at London Metropolitan University. He is a University Teaching Fellow Award recipient, a Senior Fellow with the Higher Education Academy and a Leading Certified Practitioner with the Association of Learning Developers in Higher Education. His research interests include the degree awarding gap, anti-racist practice, decolonisation, and the application of digital content creation as part of an inclusive pedagogy.

Steve Briggs is currently Director of Learning and Teaching Excellence at the University of Bedfordshire. He is a chartered psychologist, National Teaching Fellow (2020), and PFHEA. Steve was previously Co-Chair of the Association for Learning Development in Higher Education where he led work related to professional development and recognition.

Carina Buckley is the Instructional Design Manager at Solent University, where she is responsible for ensuring an active and inclusive learning environment. She has a PhD in Archaeology, and is a Principal Fellow of AdvanceHE, a member of the *JLDHE* editorial board, and an ALDinHE Certified Leading Practitioner.

Tom Burns, SFHEA, CeLP, is a member of the ALDinHE Mentoring Working Group, senior lecturer, University Teaching Fellow, and CATE. Together, Burns and Sinfield are co-authors of *Teaching, Learning and Study Skills: A Guide for Tutors* and *Essential Study Skills: The Complete Guide to Success at University* (5th edn 2022).

Ursula Canton is a senior lecturer in Academic Writing at Glasgow Caledonian University and a Learning Developer at the Royal Conservatoire of Scotland. Her teaching is shaped by her research into the evaluation of teaching and writing, the writing process, and academic and professional literacies.

Kate Coulson is the Head of Learning and Teaching Enhancement at the University of Northampton. She is a strong advocate of Learning Development and the impact it can have on student outcomes. Kate was awarded a National Teaching Fellowship in 2022 for her work in developing and championing Learning Development practice.

Emma Davenport is a University Teaching Fellow and Head of Student Experience and Academic Outcomes for the School of Architecture, Art and Design at London Metropolitan University. Emma's research interests include academic writing as social practice, thematic analysis, the material culture of HE, and digital education.

Jennie Dettmer is an academic skills tutor in the Business School at the University of Hertfordshire. She is a qualified dyslexia tutor, holds an MA Education (SEND and Inclusion), is a Senior Fellow of AdvanceHE, and co-chairs LearnHigher and the ALDinHE Neurodiversity/Inclusivity Community of Practice.

Sunny Dhillon is a lecturer in Education Studies at Bishop Grosseteste University (BGU). He previously worked as a Learning Developer at BGU and the University of Leeds (2016–2021). His academic background is in Spanish and Philosophy. His research interests are primarily in Nietzsche and The Frankfurt School.

Jason Eyre is a senior lecturer in Learning Development at De Montfort University, Leicester. He holds a doctorate in philosophy of Education from the UCL Institute of Education.

Lee Fallin works as a Lecturer in Education Studies at the University of Hull. He has ten years of experience working as a Learning Developer for the University Library and is an ALDinHE Certified Learning Practitioner. His interests include learning spaces/communities, inclusive digital practice, research methodologies, and geographies of place.

Louise Frith has been a Learning Developer for over 20 years. She currently works at the University of York teaching academic writing skills to postgraduate students. Louise has published three books: *Professional Writing Skills for Social Workers* (2021); *The Students' Guide to Peer Mentoring* (2017); and *Mindfulness and Wellbeing for Student Learning* (2023).

Nicola Grayson is an academic developer at the University of Salford. She is a Senior Fellow of the HEA and was an editor for the *Journal of Learning Development in Higher Education*. Her primary areas of expertise include measuring impact, co-creation, researcher support, and community building.

Debbie Holley is Professor of Learning Innovation at Bournemouth University, where she leads innovation in research, teaching, and professional practice. As a National Teaching Fellow, she is a passionate educator and has research interests in digital frameworks and the affordances of technologies such as augmented reality, virtual/immersive realities, and mobile learning.

Sonia Hood is the Study Advice Manager at the University of Reading. She has worked as a Learning Developer since 2006, after a successful career in Marketing. She completed an EdD in 2019, researching self-efficacy beliefs and academic writing. She has an interest in university transitions and levelling the playing field.

Nahid Huda is a Learning Developer at London Metropolitan University, UK and is a Fellow of the Higher Education Academy. Her research interests are in academic reading circles and integrating academic literacy practices within the taught curriculum.

Ian Johnson is a Learning Developer of eight years' experience. His doctoral research examines the value of LD work to its stakeholders and its implications for LD professional practice. He has particular interest in LD's dual 'embedded yet third space' function. Ian's educational background is Applied Linguistics and English Language Teaching.

Emma Kimberley is a Learning Development tutor at the University of Northampton. She is interested in the affective context of academic literacies.

Georgia Koromila is a study adviser at the University of Reading. She worked at the Graduate School of International Development, Agriculture and Economics in supporting international students' transition to UK higher education. Georgia holds a doctorate in Archaeology (2016, University of Reading) and is a strong proponent of interdisciplinarity.

Aaron Kuskopf Undergraduate student studying Creative Writing and English Literature

Anne-Marie Langford is a Learning Development tutor at the University of Northampton. She joined HE from a career in Heritage Education. She is enthusiastic about creating learning opportunities for a wide range of students, critical thinking, co-creation, and digital learning.

Shelene Macintosh Undergraduate student studying Education

Marian Mayer (she/they) is Principal Lecturer in Learning Development and a Senior Fellow of the Higher Education Academy. She has been an LD practitioner since 2004. Her research areas include transformative education, widening participation, and challenging neo-liberalism in Higher Education.

Chandrika McDonald Undergraduate student studying Education

Edward Powell is a study adviser at the University of Reading, where he also contributes towards the university-wide decolonising of the curriculum working group. He received his PhD in Postcolonial Literary and Cultural Studies from the University of Leeds in 2015.

Christie Pritchard is the Head of Academic Development at the University of Plymouth, a Senior Fellow of Advance HE, and an associate professor of Higher Education. She is also the co-chair of the Association for Learning Development in Higher Education (ALDinHE) and a Certified Leading Practitioner of Learning Development.

Steve Rooney is a Learning Developer at Aston University. He works with students and staff across all programmes, but with a particular responsibility for supporting learning in Health and Life Sciences disciplines. He continues to enjoy a long-standing, active involvement with the Association for Learning Development in Higher Education (ALDinHE).

Oliver Selic Undergraduate student studying Fashion

Sandra Sinfield, SFHEA, CeLP, is a member of the ALDinHE Steering Group, senior lecturer, University Teaching Fellow, and CATE. Together Burns and Sinfield are co-authors of *Teaching, Learning and Study Skills: A Guide for Tutors* and *Essential Study Skills: The Complete Guide to Success at University* (5th edn 2022).

Tracy Slawson is a senior lecturer in Learning Development at De Montfort University, Leicester.

Jarelle Smith is a Learning Developer at London Metropolitan University. His experience in psychological therapy informs his approach to building cohesive and supportive learning environments in Higher Education. His main areas of interest are in social psychology and social cognition.

Alicja Syska is a hybrid academic, combining the roles of Learning Development Advisor with lecturing posts in Education and History at the University of Plymouth. She has a PhD in American Studies, is a Senior Fellow of Advance HE, a co-lead editor for *JLDHE*, and an ALDinHE Certified Leading Practitioner.

Kirstie Tucker Undergraduate student studying Interior Design

Helen Webster has worked in Learning Development since 2006 and is a National Teaching Fellow, SFHEA and CeLP. She is Academic Skills

Educational Development consultant at Oxford University. Prior to this, she was Head of Learning Development at UEA and Newcastle universities and Senior Consultant at AdvanceHE. She blogs about Learning Development as @Scholastic_Rat.

Karen Welton is a Learning Development Adviser at Arts University Plymouth. Her MA Education research centred on the juxtaposition of dyslexia as a [dis] ability in HE. She facilitates communities of practice for neurodivergent staff and students and also co-chairs the ALDinHE Neurodiversity/Inclusivity Community of Practice.

Maura Burns Zaragoza Postgraduate Biological Sciences

FOREWORD

John Hilsdon

On a wet, chilly Saturday
I sat down
to tap out patterning
preparation perhaps
and now some hundreds of words are here
not generated by
any AI
or chatter-bot
black box
probabilistic prophet
but rather by
a real being
flesh and blood
a sometime learner-teacher
looking back in wonder
from where they came and how
hoping what they say
will make some sense
to friends at the chalkface
striving still
building, writing
talking, listening
recomposing
dreams of the possible
dramas imagined and calculated states
paving paths and opening gates
aspiring to
university

The need for this book arises not just from its role in charting the continuing history of Learning Development (LD) or the explication of its origins (some of that was achieved in Hartley et al., 2010) but, more importantly, in exploring further the persistence and powerful influence of the underpinning ideas of LD. This powerful influence is best demonstrated by LD practitioners in their commitment to work *alongside* students to make sense of the academic contexts and tasks facing them on courses of study, and their ingenuity in finding ways to help make success in higher education (HE) a real possibility for learners from all backgrounds.

Thinking back to the early days of LD in the UK, and the excitement surrounding initiatives such as the establishment of the LearnHigher Centre for Excellence in Teaching and Learning, it would be easy to drift into nostalgia. But, despite the dominant forces determining that university contexts and processes continue to be shaped largely in market rather than human terms, the deep sense perceived by many that education is not just a 'service', and still less a commodity, remains a powerful motivating impetus. To be a Learning Developer was, from the outset (and perhaps now is even more so), to envision university education as a social and collective enterprise to equip us and to inspire us, and an engine to drive our efforts in confronting the (literally) burning global problems threatening our very survival.

The idea of a university as a place for the pursuit of universal knowledge, and open to all who are able to study, is a liberal idea often associated with a mid-nineteenth century treatise by Cardinal John Henry Newman, and developed in the 1960s in the UK government's Robbins report proposing a widening of access to, and participation in HE. Leading into the 21st century, the subsequent, massive expansion of HE in the UK and some other countries, was, however, shaped by a neoliberal turn in economic and social policy, enjoining marketisation and commodification of all aspects of teaching and learning. Despite this straitjacket, the liberal idea continues to inspire many of those seeking to participate in learning communities as learners, teachers, and researchers.

The rise and evolution of LD can be attributed to a combination of factors. Firstly, the neoliberal policies and practices in HE which brought such new (and, ironically, usually non-academic) posts into being, and secondly the collective commitment of those employed in such posts to interpret, critique, and reinterpret their remit to 'deliver' their work with students. Unpacking and exploring the complex interrelations between these two strands is a key purpose of this book, along with relating the impact of LD so far and imagining its future in a landscape characterised by increasing complexity and challenge for students.

LD has such an important role to play in this effort to reclaim universities as real-life learning communities because our field has at its heart a focus on learning as a network of social and developmental processes, rather than as a set of mechanistic or disembodied skills to be transferred from teachers to students. If anything distinguishes an LD approach, it is this insistence on starting out from the position of the learners, involving them and offering them an invitation to join in on their own terms, and to comment in their own language, on where they find themselves. Under these conditions students can engage more fully with the (often mysterious and challenging) language, tasks and practices of their subjects of study, but, more importantly, they have opportunities to critique and recreate such practices for their own use in carrying forward the torch of learning and attending to the urgent practicalities of our times.

The challenges to a commodified and uncritical version of HE are increasingly evident as we enter the third decade of the century and debate grows over the role of Artificial Intelligence and the uses of Large Language Models in education, adding to ambiguities about the notions of authorship and academic integrity or ownership of academic products. Similarly, questions about whether and how to 'decolonise' the curriculum combine with a renewed focus on participation amid 'culture wars' over what constitutes legitimate and valuable knowledge. The increased indebtedness of students and rising uncertainty about future employment prospects, along with the casualisation of jobs, places further economic pressure on those from less-affluent backgrounds and threatens to undermine the standing (and the implied neoliberal purposes) of university education. Furthermore, the post–Cold War world order seems close to collapse just at a time when international cooperation is needed urgently to address impending human-made environmental catastrophes.

Given such instability and turmoil in our times, there are innumerable trials facing the would-be learning developer, just as there are for all students and education workers. But to work alongside students as they try to make sense of it all, to give them new opportunities to ask questions about what they are doing, and why, and to forge a path together: what a fabulous and uniquely creative way to spend your time!

ACKNOWLEDGEMENTS

Like most people on this planet, we both always wanted to write a book one day. What we didn't know was that it would be a collective endeavour, edited and nurtured into being by the two of us in a creative collaboration. We now cannot imagine having done it any other way. Curating this collection and writing together was not so much an act of two people working towards a common goal, but an immersive, rewarding, *flow*-imbued act of co-creation that helped us discover the essence of collaboration itself: the doing *with*, *alongside*, and *between* each other.

We could not have accomplished it without all the people who cheered us on and supported this hopeful venture along the way. Firstly, we are grateful to all our contributors who responded with such enthusiasm to our invitations to be part of this collection, and whose voices we gladly created a platform for. Their generosity with both their time and ideas made it a pleasure for us to edit this volume. We might even do it again!

Big thank you to all our colleagues in the global Learning Development community for the support, excitement, and faith in us to deliver a book that they had been hoping for. It would not have come into existence without you.

The Association for Learning Development in Higher Education and our home institutions – the University of Plymouth and Solent University – have nurtured us as scholars and as Learning Developers, which in no small part has laid the foundation on which this book has been built.

We also thank our editors at Routledge, Sarah Hyde and Lauren Redhead, for giving us a very positive first book experience. Their receptiveness and encouragement smoothed the path towards publication for us.

Finally, we want to express much gratitude to our closest ones, Kate and Chris, for their love and patience, incessant support and reassurance, and for gracefully tolerating all this time we spent locked away working on the book.

The book may now be in existence, but it only comes alive once someone picks it up. We are grateful to you, the reader, for doing so, and would like to encourage you to get in touch with us and share your thoughts on it. This is an open conversation.

INTRODUCTION

Alicja Syska and Carina Buckley

> *I love being a Learning Developer.*
> *(This is the first job where I've been able to say that!)*
>
> *(Survey participant)*

Every day, thousands of students across institutions of higher education find themselves immersed in a conversation about some seemingly impenetrable aspect of their learning, be it writing an essay, understanding an assignment, sitting an exam, or articulating ideas in a presentation. The person they are talking to and seeking guidance on these esoteric academic practices from is a Learning Developer – a practitioner whose role is to help the student unpeel the layers of academic expectations and discourses, develop their skills, and reflect on their learning. There is nothing predictable about that conversation; each Learning Developer will approach it differently, and each student will take away from it what they will. But what connects all these encounters is a love of learning, a deep need for scholarly engagement, and a set of values that foster spaces encouraging students to be the best they can be and to make the most of their learning.

Learning Development (LD) is a unique field of practice. Student-centred and driven by the desire to make higher education (HE) more inclusive and less mystifying, it has grown from a loose collection of dedicated, like-minded practitioners, to an expansive territory that has been relatively successfully charted but not yet fully defined and settled. Partly this is due to the wide array of trajectories into and through LD, via pathways that encompass a variety of job titles, responsibilities, structural positions, and institutional cultures, but which do not necessarily have a clear route of progression or promotion, if any.

DOI: 10.4324/9781003433347-1

As a result, most Learning Developers, including ourselves, learned how to do the job – and even understand what kind of job it was – by trial and error, finding our way eventually to a wider and growing community. There we encountered colleagues and spaces for conversation and collaboration, encouragement for research, conferences at which to share that research, and the confidence to transform our intuitive practice into genuine praxis.

Part of our goal with this book was to explore and map this rugged ecosystem and to provide a platform for a multidirectional articulation of what it means to be a Learning Developer in today's higher education. Thus, the book has been assembled and curated from fragments of experience, an array of concepts, and a slew of practices that form what we know as the Learning Development community. It is a community of practice in Wenger's sense (1998), as it is nurtured by what brings us together rather than what sets us apart. The values that connect Learning Developers allow the community to exist despite the lack of an agreed definition of what LD is. Such a definition was attempted in the first book on Learning Development – Hartley et al.'s *Learning Development in Higher Education* (2011), which brought together the nascent ideas of a fledgling field. Since then, various publications have explored and challenged these original ideas, including lively debates over whether LD is a mindset or a professional practice, what pedagogies it should be guided by and what definitions best capture its ethos. Even though it is not common practice, in response to this continued dialogue in our edited collection, we chose to spell 'Learning Development' in uppercase as a way of inducing a sense of momentary 'oneness' in the midst of these debates, while acknowledging that Learning Development as a field and a practice is constantly in formation, moving with the murmuration of its members, ever shifting, caught in the 'not-yet-ness' (Gale and Wyatt, 2022) of being, and always becoming. LD is brought to life by the community, in the process of *sympoiesis*, or 'making with' (Haraway, 2016); the community which – in line with Spinoza's philosophy – is less interested in what it is than what it does and how it is enacted.

The title of the book, *How to Be a Learning Developer in Higher Education*, is therefore a provocation, rather than an invocation; an opening rather than an answer; an invitation to a conversation rather than an edict on how in fact to *be* a Learning Developer. Here, we will lean on Wenger again, whose words resonate with our approach: 'A perspective is not a recipe; it does not tell you just what to do. Rather it acts as a guide about what to pay attention to, what difficulties to expect, and how to approach problems' (1999, p.9). Our goal was to capture – not petrify – the diversity of voices, experiences, and perspectives of those who practise LD at this particular moment in time. To emphasise the importance of the community, most of the authors in this volume (including ourselves) consulted colleagues before writing their chapters. We sent out ethically approved surveys, conducted short interviews, and carried conversations that would allow us to represent the diverse LD voices as best as we can.

We also commented on each other's chapters in the process of internal review, generating a community collaboration where authors' words and ideas intermingle and shape each other's work. In a way, together we took the pulse of LD as it existed in 2023, even if it still provides only a small insight into this rich, vibrant, ever-changing, and eclectic field and community.

In spite of the fluid and emergent nature of the contents of this book, careful thought went into its structure. In an effort to capture the breadth of topics, perspectives, and concerns, we opted for short chapters rather than exhaustive analyses, and gave our authors strict word counts and focal points to convey often very complex processes and ideas. To make space for creativity, reflection, and even provocation, we asked each writer to begin their piece with a sort of epigraph – in the form of a statement, story, or anecdote – that captures the essence of their work and reveals something about the motivation for it, thus helping the reader to register the tenor of each chapter. The book is organised into five parts that reflect a practitioner's journey into and through Learning Development, from their initiation into the field to becoming an established expert in LD. Thus, the first two parts explore the theoretical and practical foundations of the field, addressing the basic principles of working in LD: its theory and praxis. They are followed by two parts that invite practitioners to engage more critically with their work and to explore ways in which they can become active contributors to the field through research and publication. The final part probes more advanced levels of the role including the as-yet unrealised possibilities of LD. While we create no compulsion for completing this journey in a prescribed way, we open up opportunities and offer encouragement to engage with the field on multiple levels and with a wide range of goals in mind.

The book is meant as a companion for the Learning Developer's journey; however, it need not be read in a linear way. We encourage our readers to dip in and out, begin in the middle or end, and be guided by their interests and needs when engaging with the material. While multiple entry points into the book exist, taken together, it proposes a way of thinking about LD and the role of Learning Developers in higher education that reflects the dynamic nature of the field and its inhabitants. Indeed, we do not end with a conclusion but rather an attempt to open up the conversation to yet more voices and perspectives, so we can continue to build the field of Learning Development together.

What we hope our readers will take away from this book is a sense of support – if you are a new practitioner; an inspiration – if you are well established and looking for novel ways to do good work in LD; and inside knowledge and information – if you are curious about this extraordinary field of practice. Regardless of your reasons for picking up the book, by reading it and engaging with its ideas, you are participating in the actualisation of the field and its sympoietic process of becoming. Welcome to LD.

References

Gale, K. and Wyatt, J. (2022) 'Making trouble with ontogenesis: Collaborative writing, becoming, and concept forming as event', *Qualitative Inquiry*, 28(1): 80–87.

Haraway, D. J. (2016) *Staying with the trouble: Making kin in the Chthulucene*. Duke University Press.

Hartley, P., Hilsdon, J., Keenan, C., Sinfield, S. and Verity, M. (eds) (2011) *Learning Development in Higher Education*. Basingstoke: Palgrave MacMillan.

Wenger, E. (1999) *Communities of practice: Learning, meaning, and identity*. Cambridge: Cambridge University Press.

PART I

Becoming a Learning Developer

Ideas and Identity

The collection opens with an examination of theoretical and epistemological issues that underpin the field of Learning Development. In Part I, five chapters guide the reader through the conceptual landscape of LD, interrogating how we conceive of ourselves as Learning Developers within it. It begins with an invitation from Tracy Slawson and Jason Eyre to consider theory as a thoughtful way into practising the field, one that acknowledges the deep intertwining of what we do with who we are. The foundations of the field are then explored in more detail in Chapter 2. Ian Johnson and Silvina Bishopp-Martin focus on the foundational concepts that inform LD pedagogy, which is explored in the context of student agency by Steve Rooney in Chapter 3. The situated nature of LD means, for him, understanding who gets to participate, what they are participating in and how, a theme continued in Chapter 4's sketch of a potential route towards expertise. Carina Buckley and Louise Frith present a networking model for the development of a professional identity rooted in community and enacted through socially situated relationships. Finally, Nicola Grayson and Alicja Syska investigate what it means to inhabit the in-between spaces of academia, balancing an LD role with one in a discipline, and the challenges and rewards such hybrid work can bring.

DOI: 10.4324/9781003433347-2

1

THEORY IN LD

We Are All Players

Tracy Slawson and Jason Eyre

> *I am working with a student on her essay. She is explaining to me how she is responding to the assignment brief:*
>   *'Oh, and it says I need to have a theory. I was thinking of using Marxism. But maybe Feminism would be a better theory to use? What do you think?'*
>   *My mind turns over. What do I think?*
>   *What does it mean to 'use a theory'? What does theory even mean? As a Learning Developer, what theory am I 'using' in my work?*
>   *I smile at the student as I consider my response…*

Introduction: What Is Theory?

Before we begin to answer the fundamental question of what theory is, it might be useful to pose another question first, which is: why does theory matter at all to a Learning Developer? Our answer is this: if we are to engage effectively in the day-to-day practices of our work as Learning Developers, and if we are going to do so in accordance with our professional values, then we need to be able to think clearly about what it is we are doing and what we are trying to achieve, not just in the present but in the future as well. The capacity not only to act and do things but to act and do things thoughtfully is fundamental to effective Learning Development practice. This chapter is devoted to making the case for theory in LD.

Theory comes to us from the Latin *theoria*, itself derived from the Ancient Greek θεωρία. At its root, the word means the action of viewing, contemplation, sight, spectacle, and speculation (*OED*, 2023). In its essence, then, theory implies a separation from the object of its attention, a standing aside or apart from something so that we might view and consider it in a way we cannot if we are too close or immersed in it. It is a process of distancing and

DOI: 10.4324/9781003433347-3

looking. Indeed, the word 'theory' shares a common lineage with the English word 'theatre', which is perhaps an appropriate way of emphasising the idea of theory as a form of 'spectacle', seeking to set something before our gaze so that we might consider it with some distance or objectivity. Unsurprising then that we often talk of a 'theoretical lens'.

The notion of theory as a form of 'distancing' and 'seeing', and this separation of what we see and consider from what we actually do, goes back at least as far as Aristotle and other philosophers of Ancient Greece. Indeed, it is perhaps Aristotle who is partly responsible for giving theory such an intimidating and aloof reputation. He draws a distinction between *theoria* – which he labels the noblest form of human activity (contemplation) – and two other activities: *poiesis* and *praxis* (Kraut, 2022). According to Aristotle, *poiēsis* (to make) is the act of producing something distinct, in the way an artisan or craftsman might; importantly, what is produced is something distinct from its human producer, and in Learning Development we might encounter such a thing when we consider our 'outputs' – the tangible products of our efforts that we can use to justify our time and resource. Think of the small-scale projects we engage in which require such 'outputs' (reusable learning objects, reports, and online resources), and which need to be produced as efficiently as possible.

Aristotle also distinguishes *theoria* and *poiesis* from *praxis* – our actions and their value and consequences – our practices. Rather than the exercise of a technical skill, as with *poiesis*, *praxis* consists of the application of our practical reason in accordance with our values. An example of this would be when we use our professional judgement as Learning Development practitioners in designing a teaching session, for example, or determining what to focus on in a student tutorial.

From a Learning Development perspective, then, we can see two consequences of this influential understanding of theory. Firstly, an emphasis on its distinction from the practices and products of our professional lives; and secondly, a consequent elevation of theory into a rarefied space, untouched by such practicalities. It is easy to see how in the context of contemporary higher education, in which our practical judgements and our technical 'outputs' are valued so highly, theory might therefore come to be seen as aloof, indulgent, and perhaps somewhat irrelevant in the professional context of LD work, where we are exhorted at all turns to be 'productive'. If there is nothing measurable or quantifiable in this conception of theory, where then does its value lie?

However, Aristotle values theory as the most divine of human activities. He identifies human beings with their theoretic reason, so that to choose *theoria* is to choose the life peculiarly appropriate to being human. In a higher education system that is product-oriented and output-driven, holding on to Aristotle's idea and lifting ourselves up to occupy this 'rarefied' space of theory can be seen as a humanising act, a means by which we can exercise our agency and autonomy.

Theory in Practice

Arguably, much of the literature and research on education that informs Learning Development practice is grounded in the fields of sociology and psychology, with the evidence base that informs effective teaching and learning practice in higher education (and therefore much of LD practice too) largely based on empirical studies in those fields. 'Theory' in educational research grounded in these disciplines tends towards a more (social-) scientific orientation, being primarily in the service of empirical enquiry and perceived scientific objectivity (Cohen, Manion and Morrison, 2007, pp.12–14). Furthermore, research and enquiry in the literature on Learning Development itself is often small-scale, empirical, and practically focused. Case studies of practice, a focus on 'what works', and the evaluation of projects and initiatives predominate, reflecting perhaps the value we place on practical outcomes, and an interplay between the 'outputs' of work-based research that has been conducted with few resources (akin perhaps to *poiesis*) that seeks to improve our professional practice (our judgements and practical reasoning, *praxis*). When we encounter theory in these contexts, it is sometimes rather cursory, in the form of ready-made theoretical constructs and frameworks that at best serve to provide a shared language or common ground to aid in the understanding of complex ideas. Theory may also be employed to lend authority to empirical work, and we must be wary of accepting this authority simply because impressive-sounding (and exclusory) theoretical language is being wielded in this way (hooks, 1991).

Theory nevertheless plays a key role in empirical research. Rather than being distinct from the empirical, the theoretical effectively 'book-ends' any given study based on observation or data collection. For example, looking at the world helps us to formulate the initial research questions that we may seek to answer, or to provide a framework for understanding a 'problem' that we are seeking to address, shaping the nature of our investigation. From an empirical perspective, then, one way to think about theory is in terms of 'hypothesis formation' as distinct from method (the mode of investigation), and hypothesis testing (the empirical research itself; Gorelick, 2011). Theory also plays a role at the other end of any given empirical study or case study analysis, where an author will attempt to interpret and discuss their findings through the use of theoretical concepts (for example, Foucault's understanding of power, Bourdieu's concept of the *habitus*, or Lave and Wenger's idea of 'communities of practice') in order to better make sense of their meaning and implications.

There is, therefore, a dual 'predictive/interpretive' function of theory in empirical research and case study analysis, and this is perhaps the conception of theory most familiar to those from a scientific or social science background. However, theory also finds its own mode of expression in the research literature in the form of non-empirical studies, where there is no data collection, and which is grounded not in empirical observation but on the application of reason alone, guided perhaps by some kind of conceptual framework for thinking (that is, some kind of theory), and adopting methods appropriate to this mode of enquiry. This kind of theoretical writing is the mainstay of philosophy, for example, but other disciplines will make use of entirely theoretical approaches too. In many ways, the depth of engagement with a topic might be richer in a theoretical study than an empirical one, where the analysis and interpretation of findings might be brief and cursory. We can therefore think of theoretical writing and thinking as a way of taking things further, taking up where an empirical study might have left off, and helping to develop the questions that might inform the next generation of empirical studies, in a kind of virtuous circle.

This interplay of the theoretical and the empirical can be illustrated in the well-known example of Lea and Street's seminal 1998 paper 'Student Writing in Higher Education: An Academic Literacies Approach'. The authors' research is based on case study interviews, and Lea and Street clearly outline their position with respect to theory:

> Our research, then, was not based on a representative sample from which generalisations could be drawn but rather was conceived as providing case studies that enabled us to explore theoretical issues and generate questions for further systematic study.
>
> (Lea and Street, 1998)

Here we see an exemplar of theoretical work, where the value of the research is based not on the definitiveness of the real-world evidence, but on the thinking it inspired. This in turn spawned and inspired a range of theoretical and empirical studies that have had an enormous impact on everyday practices. Indeed, at the time of writing, the paper has been cited over 3,800 times (according to Google Scholar), and has been so influential on the emergent field of LD that it spawned an entire special edition of the *Journal of Learning Development in Higher Education* in 2019 devoted to its influence.

Theory as Practice

We can think of theory, then, in a much broader and more creative sense than simply as an adjunct to the empirical: stepping back from our work can simply *help us think*. Theory, and perhaps more importantly, *the act of theorising*, can be viewed as a useful tool for the reflective practitioner (Schön, 1991).

We have seen the common lineage of theory and theatre, with all of its connotations of distanced contemplation. 'All the world's a stage, and all men and women merely players' runs the line in Shakespeare's *As You Like It*. Indeed, the theatre/theory may set a spectacle upon the stage for our detached consideration, but we would do well to remember that we are players upon that stage ourselves. There is no true separation between the play and the players, and no audience that is not also upon the stage they are viewing. Our lives and our practices are implicated in our consideration of them, and our thinking about practice is a practice in itself. We might talk of the practice of theory as much as the theory of practice.

British educationalist Jon Nixon (2004) links theorising in this way with the exercise of professional judgement, and identifies three aspects of theory that are relevant for Learning Developers:

> Theory, in other words, faces outwards in three different directions: towards the analytical interpretation of intent and action; towards the speculative evaluation of alternative courses of action; and towards the explanatory justification of the principles underlying practice. Analytical interpretation, speculative evaluation, and explanatory justification are, to shift the metaphor, the vanishing points at which the lines of theory and practice meet in the landscape of professionalism.
>
> (Nixon, 2004, p.34)

Nixon's linking of theory with professionalism highlights the varied ways the theoretical is integral to our practice. If we are to analyse and interpret our actions, or evaluate alternative courses of action, or explain or justify the underpinnings of our practice, all of these acts are theoretical in nature. To be theoretical is to be the actor upon the stage who adopts the perspective of the audience – however briefly – in order to better understand their own role. This reflexive self-understanding is crucial if our actions as professional practitioners of Learning Development are to be anything other than reactive and unthinking. Habits of thought can be protective, permitting us to do our work without continually having to devise appropriate actions from first principles; but to dwell in the habitual brings the risk that our practice becomes stale, unresponsive, and routine (Eyre, 2020, pp.82–84).

The 'thoughtfulness' that theory enables is, Nixon argues, a hallmark of professional judgement, and the relational nature of professionalism itself entails a *moral responsibility* for our actions and a capacity to enact professional judgement in our dealings with others in a responsive and thoughtful way (Nixon 2004, p.30). The professional practice of Learning Development is no different. It does not occur in a vacuum, characterised as it is by our relations with colleagues, students, academics, administrators, and so on. We have a responsibility to act in those relations *thoughtfully*, and according to the values that guide our profession. Our capacity to theorise is, then, crucial to our professional integrity, and closely linked with our values as Learning Developers. To do so, we need to develop our capacity to engage with theory as an integral part of our practice, and to do so in line with our professional values.

Theory Informing Learning Development

Alongside common practices and shared values, Learning Development has been informed by various complementary theoretical strands. John Hilsdon explains the choice of the term 'development' in the name 'Learning Development':

> Whichever theoretical stance towards learning one adopts, there is agreement – particularly within the dominant constructivist and phenomenological approaches favoured in texts about HE ... that learning depends upon an array of complex social and psychological factors, and that knowledge of learning cannot simply be transferred like an object from one person to another. For this reason 'development' was seen as so vital among our group.
>
> (Hilsdon in Hartley, et al., 2011, p.18)

Later in the same chapter Hilsdon notes the following (full references reproduced for those interested in following these threads):

> A growing number of those adopting a learning development perspective emphasise more holistic approaches... In so doing, we draw upon theoretical work on literacies (Lea and Street, 1998), social identity (Ivanič, 1998) and pedagogy (Lillis, 2001; Meyer and Land, 2006; Haggis, 2006).
>
> (Hilsdon in Hartley et al. 2011, pp.22–23)

We can see in these brief selections that a number of theoretical strands have been woven together to form the theoretical foundations of the profession. Each of the identified strands has its own theoretical and philosophical lineage – the constructivism of Lev Vygotsky; the phenomenology of Husserl, Merleau-Ponty, Sartre, and Heidegger. Looking more closely at the authors of the works Hilsdon cites in the second quotation, we find that in addition to the original and influential theoretical work of the authors themselves, the academic literacies of Lea and Street have been informed by constructivism, but also by work on the marketisation of higher education, social and critical linguistics, critiques of sociocultural theory, and the multi-modal semiotics of Günter Kress; we find that Meyer and Land make use of notions of threshold concepts and liminality; we note that Lillis draws in part on Mikhail Bakhtin's work on dialogue, and that Haggis also has an interest in the dialogic, citing the likes of Paulo Freire and David Bohm. We can add to this growing list the extensive engagement with the emancipatory project of Critical Pedagogy by a number of foundational authors in Learning Development (notably Sandra Sinfield and Tom Burns); and then there is the work by John Hilsdon drawing on Foucault and concepts of institutional power (Hilsdon, 2018). And we have only barely begun to scratch the surface.

The point we wish to make about *theory* at this juncture is that the theoretical foundations of Learning Development are varied and eclectic. Patterns and themes can certainly be found (for example, emancipation, construction of learning, dialogue, and social learning), but the constellations that are drawn will depend on what sources the reader selects, and where their particular interest lies. Moreover, as well as drawing lines across the various sources for the filaments of theory, the reader might also choose to dig down, to see where the roots of particular theories are emerging from – the epistemological and philosophical earth from which they have sprung.

While complex, the range of possibilities for theory in Learning Development are not infinite, nor are they entirely contingent on individual tastes and predilections. Nixon draws attention to Hannah Arendt's observation that thoughtfulness is a public endeavour. We do not think alone; our thought – and our engagement with theory – is 'always deeply social, regardless of the isolated circumstances of the individual thinker' (Nixon, 2004, p. 33). There is, then, a kind of normativity associated with theory in the professional community of Learning Development that seeks consistency and compatibility, and which, when successful, generates a form of consensus across the professional community, alongside points of contention and debate which serve to further fuel our thought. The most useful and relevant theoretical perspectives to draw on remain open to discussion. Colleagues will no doubt have plenty to say about the sampling of theoretical currents listed above, infuriating omissions, and baffling inclusions, and Learning Development is all the richer for such thoughtful and thought-provoking dialogue.

Conclusion: Thinking the New – (Re)creating Learning Development

In this chapter, we have drawn attention to the long-standing idea, perhaps commonly held, that theory is distinct from practice. At its root, theory involves a form of distancing and contemplation that enables us to view our practices as separate from ourselves as practitioners. We have argued, however, that *what we do* and *what we think about what we do* are not so clear and distinct, but deeply entwined and implicated. Theory has utility in empirical and practice-based research, but also in its own right as a means to form questions, guide enquiry, and interpret our findings in a way that gives us meaning and which in turn influences what we do. Furthermore, we have made the case that theory is an integral part of professional practice, the means by which we might take responsibility for a thoughtfulness that is guided by (and in turn, shapes) our values. Learning Developers do not practise in isolation but as part of a professional community which was established on the basis not only of common practices and shared values but also from a range of complementary theoretical traditions. Its evolution since, and into the future, depends in large part on our continued engagement with theoretical thinking and thoughtfulness.

Not all of this thoughtfulness has to have an aim or an objective. For Learning Development to continue to evolve and respond to the shifting environment of higher education, it will need to be continually refreshed by new thinking, new thoughts. As such, Learning Developers themselves will have to take on the burden and responsibility for just sitting and thinking about things with no predetermined aim; for reading books for inspiration and insight; for talking to one another as a community about what we have done, what we have seen, what we have felt, and what we have imagined. We all have a part to play. This will require us to somehow create the spaces to do this work; not indulgent or aloof, but important, integral, and vital. It will sometimes take courage to stand up for this space, in the face of instrumentalist imperatives to be productive. But we need theory: our practices depend on it.

References

Cohen, L., Manion, L. and Morrison, K. (2007) *Research Methods in Education*, 6th ed. Abingdon, Oxon.: Routledge.

Eyre, J. (2020) *The Crisis of Practice: Deleuze and the Idea of Learning Development in UK Higher Education*, PhD Thesis. University College London. Available at: https://discovery.ucl.ac.uk/id/eprint/10102621/1/Eyre__Thesis.pdf (Accessed: 31 January 2023).

Gorelick, R. (2011) 'What is theory?' *Ideas in Ecology and Evolution*, 4: 1–10.

Haggis, T. (2006) 'Pedagogies for diversity: retaining critical challenge amidst fears of "dumbing down"', *Studies in Higher Education*. 31(5): 521–535.

Hartley, P., Hilsdon, J., Keenan, C., Sinfield, S. and Verity, M. (2011) *Learning Development in higher education*. London: Palgrave Macmillan.

Hilsdon, J. (2018) *The significance of the field of practice 'Learning Development' in UK higher education*. PhD Thesis. University of Plymouth. Available at: https://pearl.plymouth.ac.uk/handle/10026.1/10604 (Accessed: 31 January 2023).

hooks, b. (1991) 'Theory as liberatory practice', *Yale Journal of Law and Feminism*, 4(1): 1–12.

Ivanič, R. (1998) *Writing and Identity: The Discoursal Construction of Identity in Academic Writing*. Amsterdam: John Benjamins.

Kraut, R. (2022) 'Aristotle's Ethics' in *Stanford Encyclopedia of Philosophy*. Available at: https://plato.stanford.edu/entries/aristotle-ethics/ (Accessed: 30 March 2023).

Lea, M. and Street, B. (1998) 'Student writing in higher education: An academic literacies approach', *Studies in Higher Education*, 23(2): 157–172.

Lillis, T. (2001) *Student Writing: Access, Regulation, Desire*. London: Routledge.

Meyer, J.H.F. and Land, R. (2006) *Threshold Concepts and Troublesome Knowledge: Issues of Liminality*. London: Routledge.

Nixon, J. (2004) 'What is Theory?' *Educar*, 34: 27–37.

Oxford English Dictionary (2023) 'Theory'. Available at: https://www.oed.com/view/Entry/200431 (Accessed: 30 March 2023).

Schön, D. (1991/2016) *The Reflective Practitioner: How Professionals Think in Action*. London: Routledge.

2

CONCEPTUAL FOUNDATIONS IN LEARNING DEVELOPMENT

Ian Johnson and Silvina Bishopp-Martin

> *It's seldom in doubt that academic colleagues deem Learning Development valuable. It's asking them 'valuable why or for what?' that can bring on the blank looks or befuddled answers. Working in the field, we know the vital, unique contribution that we make. It's incumbent on us to help others understand it too, so everyone can benefit. We must fight the good fight for who we are, what we do and why we're here ... fight it fast and fight it together. It's for everyone's good that we're here.*

Introduction

The journey into Learning Development (LD) work can be disorientating. One contributor is the eclectic entry routes, meaning the field employs practitioners with myriad attributes and experiences, including language or subject teaching, advice or guidance, learning technology, or specialist learning difficulty support (Webster, 2022). Equally, universities' naming, location, deployment, and explanation of LD roles vary widely (Murray and Glass, 2011; Johnson, 2018). Professional entrants might easily conflate their university's lack of clarity about LD with there being no manifesto for 'doing' LD. However, to sustain that belief is fallacious, given the strongly contrary evidence that the role is unique and makes distinct contributions to today's higher education (HE) sector.

This chapter crystallises the foundations for new and established practitioners alike, by drawing together theory- and practice-based insights about LD. It firstly explores the underpinnings for Learning Developers' praxis and orientation inherent in its history and values of the UK professional association, ALDinHE. It then distinguishes LD, theoretically and practically, from related fields such as English for Academic Purposes (EAP) and from mischaracterisations

DOI: 10.4324/9781003433347-4

that it functions exclusively to develop study skills or remediate deficits. The chapter then summarises the tenets that demarcate LD work. We place LD as making unique contributions to academia, related to both emancipatory learning and subject-disciplinary communication. We therefore map out the vital professional territory that LD occupies – what it means, at any career stage, to *do* LD and to *be* a Learning Developer.

Historical, Value-driven, and Theoretical Foundations

The conceptual foundations of our praxis have roots captured in Hilsdon's (2011, p.14) seminal definition of LD as 'a complex set of multi-disciplinary and cross-disciplinary academic roles and functions, involving teaching, tutoring, research, and the design and production of learning materials, as well as involvement in staff development, policy-making and other consultative activities'. Hilsdon's formulation characterises a broad church, further delineated as any work that emphasises 'examining how students experience and make sense of academic practices'. This primary focus on understanding HE *as the student experiences it*, or learning to walk in students' shoes, is the crucial delineating hallmark of LD. Practising in this spirit clearly requires the full remit of praxis components outlined by Hilsdon. Not every LD role description would contain mentions of teaching, staff development, research, and disciplinary boundary-crossing (Johnson, 2018). However, these practices are inherent to forming an awareness about how students experience academia, then fostering it in one's own and others' pedagogic praxis.

The edited collection in which Hilsdon's contribution appeared grew from within the LearnHigher Network. Established through government funding as a Centre of Excellence in Teaching and Learning, LearnHigher represented the first formal cross-UK LD collaboration, encompassing 16 institutions whose practitioners attended the initial conference in 2003 (Hartley et al., 2011). ALDinHE was established in 2007 within the ongoing evolution of LearnHigher's remit. As ALDinHE expanded to over 100 institutional members by 2023, it increasingly focused on codifying the profession. A keynote at the 2017 ALDinHE conference (Buckley and Briggs, 2017) led to the formulation of five community-driven values to guide the ethos of LD work.

The ALDinHE values (Table 2.1) underpinned the pathways to practitioner and leading practitioner certification (Briggs, 2018), which have currently accredited over 100 Learning Developers (ALDinHE, 2023), and which provide benchmarks against which professional LD practice in the UK can now be measured.

The values centralise a commitment to social justice – to working in partnership with students, in pursuit of their academic emancipation. By definition, the values rely upon tenets from the Academic Literacies (AL) theory. As first pinpointed by Lea and Street (1998), AL theory holds that students

TABLE 2.1 ALDinHE's values

	Value
1	Working in partnership with students and staff to make sense and get the most out of HE
2	Embracing and respecting diverse learners through critical pedagogy and practice
3	Adapting, sharing, and advocating effective Learning Development practice to promote student learning
4	Commitment to a scholarly approach and research related to Learning Development
5	Critical self-reflection, ongoing learning, and a commitment to professional development

should not be regarded as possessing deficits, or being unsuitable for HE. Rather, it proposes that the HE system inherently places students in 'alienating' territory (Lillis, 2001) whose negotiation requires considerable scaffolding. Assuming this mantle can leave Learning Developers as outsiders to, even outspoken critics of, the system that employs them (Hilsdon, 2018). Nonetheless, by occupying that space in concordance with the goal of walking in students' shoes, Learning Developers play a vital, distinctive role.

Also notable in the values are the professional commitments to collaboration, scholarship, and research. In 2021, we wrote alongside eight colleagues about our experiences of aligning as an online community of practice concerned with research by and into the LD field (Bickle et al., 2021). We concluded that while research was seldom contractually expected of Learning Developers, creating opportunities to research within and about our profession was inherent to a values-driven LD praxis. We explore the scholarship of LD further in Chapter 17 of this volume.

Despite the positive points of coalescence in LD praxis evident in the values, it remains inescapable that LD is not yet consistently understood across the HE sector (Verity and Trowler, 2011), certainly not in a sense that satisfies its practitioners (Johnson, 2018; Webster, 2022). Therefore, as we move to document the distinctive identifiers of LD, we necessarily also tease out what LD is not, yet might be misconceived as being.

'Doing' and 'Being' in Learning Development

People as Producers, Not Texts as Products

A cornerstone to LD praxis is an appreciation of its foundations in AL, which itself has epistemological and methodological roots in anthropology (Lillis, 2001). Critically, these origins set LD apart from surrounding professional fields. Coffin and Donohue (2012) use this foundation to distinguish LD from EAP. They argue that whereas LD is intrinsically focused on people in the production process, EAP's underpinnings in Systemic Functional Linguistics (SFL) mean it traditionally grants primacy to end products. Texts, for example, may be provided to students as aspirational language and stylistic models to emulate in their writing. Whilst EAP instruction has been argued to be traditionally normative (Harwood and Hadley, 2004), the position has been somewhat challenged by alternative EAP approaches that encourage students to focus on textual genres (Swales, 1990; Wingate, 2015) or engage more critically with texts (Benesch, 1993; Pennycook, 1999). However, the departure point for the LD movement is that a critical orientation has been in its DNA since inception. This is partly attributable to its anthropological and AL roots, and partly to LD having always sought to make HE accessible for a highly diverse student population. LD thus seeks to create spaces where norms can be discussed, negotiated, even opposed, where textual practices are 'a challenge for students and teachers' alike (Coffin and Donohue, 2012, p.72). Within LD spaces, students' worlds meet and sometimes collide with those of the academy, yet the direction towards solutions is not inevitably one-way.

Skills Teaching Alongside Content, Not in a Vacuum

Through the AL lens in which lecturers and students negotiate and co-create knowledge (Ivanič and Lea, 2006), LD can be regarded as the teaching of skills through pedagogies conjoined to a student's disciplinary studies. Maldoni and Lear (2016) advocate that a curriculum-based approach of embedding, integration and team-teaching best showcases the connections between academic skills, disciplinary content, and assessment. This position suggests that Learning Developers must prioritise how such teaching can be seamlessly integrated into disciplines, not strive for complete dissociation from skills teaching itself. Wingate (2006, p.457) equally argues that 'learning how to study at university cannot be separated from subject content and the process of learning'. She furthermore highlights two false premises of discipline-independent study skills delivery: firstly, that it views students who require such instruction as intrinsically being in deficit or not acclimatising; and secondly, that by decoupling learning processes from subject knowledge, the model errantly leads students into beliefs that a superficial approach towards learning will suffice. However, despite the LD field's long-standing efforts to dissociate from both the deficit and the study skills models, these ideas remain steadfast. The tendency is visible in how universities characterise their LD provision (Richards and Pilcher, 2020), and how LD has been represented by certain authors to maximise an audience – as a relatively generic curriculum of trans-disciplinary skills. A key priority for the LD field is thus to effect changes in these territories, towards those where skills and content instruction cohabit.

Working <u>with</u> Disciplinary Instructors, Not <u>as</u> Disciplinary Instructors

The essence of LD work is its ability to focus on facilitation of learning while standing apart from marking as a form of gatekeeping. This nuance is not captured when representing LD activity via the study skills model and positing that the acquisition of skills and subject knowledge are inseparable (Richards and Pilcher, 2020) or that no staff should teach study skills without also having a subject-content teaching remit (Richards and Pilcher, 2021). That stance is highly problematic, given the reticence (Ivanič and Lea, 2006; Hallett, 2021) or lack of confidence, experience and/or knowledge (Murray and Nallaya, 2016; McNaught et al., 2022) among subject lecturers to deliver skills-building instruction. Additionally, Learning Developers oscillate between fulfilling several unique functions for students, classified as 'interpreter', 'coach', 'dialogue partner', 'listener', and 'intermediary' (Gravett and Winstone, 2019, p.727). Arguably, Learning Developers can assume these personae precisely because of their dissociation from certain traditional tasks of subject lecturers, notably summatively marking work. Should the divides between subject lecturers and Learning Developers collapse wholesale, the operational space of LD could be compromised. Once staff members assume judging or gatekeeping functions as opposed to facilitation, their work ceases being LD (McIntosh and Barden, 2019) in the spirit of Hilsdon (2011) or the ALDinHE values.

More promising results have been documented (Gornall, 2019; Hallett, 2021) when subject academics and Learning Developers collaborate on subject-based delivery that blends content and skills through methods relatable by students to their experiences and to assessment requirements. Jacobs (2005) argues that Learning Developers can uniquely view academic disciplines from an insider-outsider perspective, making for a powerful combination. The insider element can be gained through their background and/or professional immersion in the discipline, the outsider element through appreciating how students approach studying therein. Positive outcomes are achieved when Learning Developers and subject academics co-work with the aim of unmasking the often tacit communication practices of disciplines; disciplinary meta-knowledge is then surfaced and transferred, augmenting and accelerating students' induction into the subject community.

More than a Mindset

The ALDinHE values have raised discussions about whether 'Learning Development' is a mindset adoptable by any academic professionals, or whether it is its own distinct field, profession, pedagogy or even discipline (Webster, 2020). When outlining the LD practitioner certification processes, Briggs (2018) documented his experiences of the LD community having sympathy for both the mindset and profession positions. While Syska and Buckley

(2022) favour the latter, they stress the futility of entering too deeply into the profession, field, pedagogy, or discipline debate. Instead, they emphasise that LD staff can better expend efforts by working to cultivate perceptions of LD as distinct, valuable activity in its own right. We would argue that the positions advanced by Briggs (2018) are simultaneously possible, with caveats: firstly, that 'lowercase' learning development is a mindset that can be taken on widely, but, importantly, only in the continued presence of 'uppercase' Learning Development professionals driving that process.

In summary, the features that distinguish our professional field from those surrounding it, and those that we must self-advocate for, are that we are person- and process-centred, not product-centred; we develop tailored learning processes within disciplinary fields, not a vacuum; we act in a non-judgemental space that facilitates, not gatekeeps; and we bridge tacit disciplinary expectations, not normatively, but through combining insider and outsider perspectives of disciplines. The next section locates these ideas within two theoretical formulations of LD. These combine previous literature with the unpublished research contributing to our two complementary doctoral theses: Bishopp-Martin's on the professional identity of Learning Developers, and Johnson's on the value of LD to stakeholders.

What Is Learning Development? Two Theoretical Perspectives

A Third Space

Although conceiving LD as a third space is not novel, it befits the arguments made across this chapter, and the characteristics of LD work collated herein. Third space is popularly applied to HE to characterise the burgeoning 'hybrid' professional roles, usually centred on student support, that are neither traditionally academic nor administrative but rather combine both (Whitchurch, 2008). Although Learning Developers tend to accept third space status relatively willingly (Bickle et al., 2021), greater depth on why can be gleaned by looking backwards to Soja's characterisation:

> [in third spaces] everything comes together ... subjectivity and objectivity, the abstract and the concrete, the real and the imagined, the knowable and the unimaginable, the repetitive and the differential, structure and agency, mind and body, consciousness and the unconscious, the disciplined and the transdisciplinary, everyday life and unending history.
>
> (Soja, 1996, p.57)

Soja's definition widens the possible meanings of a third space, and appears apt for LD. It suggests additional angles such as viewing third spaces as gaps between the students' worlds inside and outside university, and between them and their lecturers. The spaces are secure ones where students can negotiate their identities by consulting a Learning Developer in capacities such as those mentioned above from Gravett and Winstone (2019). They allow Learning Developers to work toward goals such as enhancing mutual understanding about students' and lecturers' teaching, learning, and assessment practices. Students arrive into HE with unique experiences, and face myriad tacit expectations to negotiate a pathway through university compatible with their experiences and worldviews. The third space intersection allows for reconciliation of these matters between student and university, exactly as AL theory advocates. A potential problem in framing LD as a third space is how to accommodate the integral role of research and scholarship in the profession. Such duties are atypical of third space contracts: a status quo that we would advocate that Learning Developers must strive to transform. Effective practice within third spaces is possible only through scholarship-informed understanding of the very teaching and learning practices that occur there.

Disciplinary Insider-Outsider and Community Builder

LD professionals should maintain necessary boundaries from other academic activity, such as undertaking summative assessment of students' work. However, it is through knowledge of how assessed work is communicated, scaffolded, marked, and fed back that Learning Developers stand to have their strongest impact (Gravett and Winstone, 2019). It is therefore vital that the LD profession claims these expertise territories, which involves departing from its 'palpable reluctance' (Webster, 2022, p.181) to do that.

Assessment, feedback, and learning are, nonetheless, profoundly discipline-specific (van Heerden, Clarence and Bharuthram, 2017). Therefore, visions of Learning Developers as resident experts in these processes augur well for their physical or 'epistemological' location (Hathaway, 2015) inside disciplines. Studies have shown how such institutional architecture can work alongside the third space of LD, with each element enhancing the other. Gornall (2019) situates Learning Developers as 'literacy brokers' acting to bridge linguistic, cultural and textual divides. Her paper demonstrates how they could assume positions as experienced figures who ease students' transitions into discipline-based communities of practice; it also draws synergies with the third space framing and its associated values. Examples of the highly regarded impacts of Learning Developers' work include helping to pre-empt students' potential challenges in understanding course content, and deconstruction of academic expectations and assessment rubrics via social pedagogies (Gornall, 2019). The possibilities for Learning Developers in realising the value of the third space are enhanced by a disciplinary location, with time devoted to understanding and unpacking its communicative practices and assessment expectations.

Conclusion: So What Are We Fighting For?

The ALDinHE values provide a manifesto for LD work, impressing that it should be student-centred, collaborative, social justice-motivated, and scholarship-informed. The LD professional field must seek not only to practise as such, but to educate others about how it practises. Pursuing that goal can enhance consistent understanding, hence the value that LD is held in, and ultimately its practitioners' professional statuses, identities and career pathways. Without these efforts, all these ideals are potentially jeopardised (Malkin and Chanock, 2018). This chapter allows us to add to the defining characteristics of LD work. Firstly, it is primarily focused on person and process, not product. Secondly, it works distinctively at disciplinary margins, with feet both in and out, to bridge gaps. Finally, it should always be facilitative, not judgemental. Thereby, LD can be both a third space and a distinct tranche of expertise that work seamlessly with discipline-based academic colleagues and students. We therefore advance a firm argument that while lowercase 'learning development' can be a mindset, uppercase LD is much more: a distinct professional niche. Learning Developers must fight for that niche by self-advocating consciously and collectively. Worthwhile battles include highlighting the intrinsic necessity of research to our praxis, gaining optimal institutional locations and culture around the work, and obtaining the mechanisms to ensure that the staff and student perspectives can mutually inform. Whether you are on day one of your LD career, or far further down the road, these challenges might seem daunting. However, adopting a mission statement to appreciate and discuss HE as your students truly experience it should stand you in firm stead as an LD professional.

References

ALDinHE (2023) *Home.* Available at: https://aldinhe.ac.uk (Accessed: 3 April 2023).

Benesch, S. (1993) 'ESL, ideology, and the politics of pragmatism', *TESOL Quarterly*, 27(4): 705–717.

Bickle, E., Bishopp-Martin, S., Canton, U., Chin, P., Johnson, I., Kantcheva, R., Nodder, J., Rafferty, V., Sum, K. and Welton, K. (2021) 'Emerging from the third space chrysalis: experiences in a non-hierarchical, collaborative community of practice', *Journal of University Teaching and Learning Practice*, 18(7): 135–158.

Briggs, S. (2018) 'Development of the ALDinHE recognition scheme: certifying the "Learning Developer" title', *Journal of Learning Development in Higher Education*, 13: 1–11.

Buckley, C. and Briggs, S. (2017) 'Community keynote: defining the future of Learning Development.' *ALDinHE 2017: The Learning Development Conference*, University of Hull, England. 10–12 April.

Coffin, C. and Donohue, J. (2012) 'Academic literacies and systemic functional linguistics: how do they relate?', *Journal of English for Academic Purposes*, 11(1): 64–75.

Gornall, L. (2019) 'Brokering academic literacies in a community of practice', *Journal of Learning Development in Higher Education*, 15: 1–18.

Gravett, K. and Winstone, N. (2019) '"Feedback interpreters": the role of Learning Development professionals in facilitating university students' engagement with feedback', *Teaching in Higher Education*, 24(6): 723–738.

Hallett, F. (2021) 'Contradictory perspectives on academic development: the lecturers' tale', *Teaching in Higher Education*, 26(1): 115–128.

Hartley, P., Hilsdon, J., Keenan, C., Sinfield, S. and Verity, M. (eds) (2011) *Learning Development in Higher Education*. Basingstoke: Palgrave MacMillan.

Harwood, N. and Hadley, G. (2004) 'Demystifying institutional practices: Critical pragmatism and the teaching of academic writing', *Journal of English for Specific Purposes*, 23(4): 355–377.

Hathaway, J. (2015) 'Developing that voice: locating academic literacies tuition in the mainstream of higher education', *Teaching in Higher Education*, 20(5): 506–517.

Hilsdon, J. (2011) 'What is Learning Development?', in P. Hartley, J. Hilsdon, C. Keenan, S. Sinfield and M. Verity (eds), *Learning Development in Higher Education*. Basingstoke: Palgrave MacMillan.

Hilsdon, J. (2018) *The Significance of the Field of Practice 'Learning Development' in UK Higher Education* [Unpublished doctoral thesis]. University of Plymouth. Available at: https://pearl.plymouth.ac.uk/bitstream/handle/10026.1/10604/2018Hilsdon10029559EdD.pdf?sequence=1 (Accessed: 3 April 2023)

Ivanič, R. and Lea, M. (2006) 'New contexts, new challenges: the teaching of writing in UK Higher Education', in L. Ganobcsik-Williams (ed.) *Teaching Academic Writing in UK Higher Education*. Basingstoke: Palgrave MacMillan.

Jacobs, C. (2005) 'On being an insider on the outside: New spaces for integrating academic literacies', *Teaching in Higher Education*, 10(4): 475–487.

Johnson, I. (2018) 'Driving learning development professionalism forward from within', *Journal of Learning Development in Higher Education*, 14: 1–29.

Lea, M. and Street, B. (1998) 'Student writing in higher education: An academic literacies approach', *Studies in Higher Education*, 23(2): 157–172.

Lillis, T. (2001) *Student Writing: Access, Regulation, and Desire*. London: Routledge.

Maldoni, A. and Lear, E. (2016) 'A decade of embedding: where are we now?', *Journal of University Teaching and Learning Practice*, 13(3): 1–22.

Malkin, C. and Chanock, K. (2018) 'Academic Language and Learning (ALL) in Australia: An endangered or evolving species?', *Academic Language and Learning*, 6(1): 15–32.

McIntosh, E. and Barden, D. (2019) 'The LEAP (Learning Excellence Pathway Framework): A model for student development in higher education', *Journal of Learning Development in Higher Education*, 14: 1–21.

Mcnaught, L., Bassett, M., van der Ham, V., Milne, J. and Jenkin, C. (2022) 'Sustainable embedded academic literacy development: the gradual handover of literacy teaching', *Eaching in Higher Education*. https://doi.org/10.1080/13562517.2022.2048369

Murray, L. and Glass, B. (2011) 'Learning development in higher education – community of practice or profession?', in P. Hartley, J. Hilsdon, C. Keenan, S. Sinfield and M. Verity (eds) *Learning Development in Higher Education*, Basingstoke: Palgrave MacMillan.

Murray, N. and Nallaya, S. (2016) 'Embedding academic literacies in university programme curricula: A case study', *Studies in Higher Education*, 41(7): 1296–1312.

Pennycook, A. (1999) 'Introduction: Critical approaches to TESOL', *TESOL Quarterly*, 33(3): 329–348.

Richards, K. and Pilcher, N. (2020) 'Study Skills: neoliberalism's perfect Tinkerbell', *Teaching in Higher Education: Critical Perspectives*, https://doi.org/10.1080/135 62517.2020.1839745

Richards, K. and Pilcher, N. (2021) *Study skills are not the answer to students' woes.* Available at: https://wonkhe.com/blogs/study-skills-are-not-the-answer-to-students-academic-woes/ (Accessed: 3 April 2023)

Soja, E. (1996) *Thirdspace.* Oxford: Blackwell.

Swales, J. (1990) *Genre Analysis: English in Academic and Research Settings.* Cambridge: Cambridge University Press.

Syska, A. and Buckley, C. (2022) 'Writing as liberatory practice: unlocking knowledge to locate an academic field', *Teaching in Higher Education*, 28(2): 439–454. https://doi.org/10.1080/13562517.2022.2114337

van Heerden, M., Clarence, S. and Bharuthram, S. (2017) 'What lies beneath: exploring the deeper purposes of feedback on student writing through considering disciplinary knowledge and knowers', *Assessment and Evaluation in Higher Education*, 42(6): 967–977.

Verity, M. and Trowler, P. (2011) 'Looking back and into the future', in P. Hartley, J. Hilsdon, C. Keenan, S. Sinfield and M. Verity (eds) *Learning Development in Higher Education*. Basingstoke: Palgrave MacMillan, 241–252.

Webster, H. (2020, May 13) *Does Learning Development have a Signature Pedagogy?* Available at: https://drive.google.com/file/d/1mq9XSbA7LXGeUWxDSX tuFQ-vXR4T9NP4/view (Accessed: 3 January 2021).

Webster, H. (2022) 'Supporting the development, recognition and impact of third-space professionals', in E. McIntosh and D. Nutt (eds) *The Impact of the Integrated Practitioner in Higher Education: Studies in Third Space Professionalism*. Abingdon: Routledge.

Whitchurch, C. (2008) 'Shifting identities and blurring boundaries: The emergence of third space professionals in UK higher education', *Higher Education Quarterly*, 62(4): 377–396.

Wingate, U. (2006) 'Doing away with "study skills"', *Teaching in Higher Education*, 11(4): 457–469.

Wingate, U. (2015) *Academic Literacy and Student Diversity. The Case for Inclusive Practice*. Bristol: Multilingual Matters.

3

THE MESS WE'RE IN

LD Pedagogies and the Question of Student Agency

Steve Rooney

> *'There's no grade because I couldn't understand most of what you had written.'*
>
> *'Oh, right… How do you mean?'*
>
> *'Well, take this sentence, for instance (I quote): "As Taiwo argues, rertiuguin morojious tarabalenu bash-fimb…" and so it goes on. I mean, what language is this?'*
>
> *'Um, mine – I created it especially for this essay.'*
>
> *'But why on earth did you do that?'*
>
> *'Well, it was in the assignment brief: "when presenting the work of others, you should demonstrate your command of the ideas by using your own words".'*
>
> * * * * * * * * * * * * * * * * * * *
>
> *This form, a constraint – Syllables set line-by-line. Free, now, to create.*

Introduction

What do Learning Developers do all day? And how? And why? We might begin to answer these questions by recalling John Hilsdon's (2013) description of Learning Development (LD) as being concerned with 'the "how we do things around here" of university life'. To help us expand further, we might turn to a certain, hugely influential, article and its oft-quoted description of higher learning as involving students 'adapting to new ways of knowing' via the development of discipline-relevant 'academic literacy practices' (Lea and Street, 1998, p.158). Our task could be defined, then, as that of calling attention to those 'literacy practices' that make participation in 'new ways of knowing' possible, and of devising appropriate pedagogical means of supporting the development of such practices. This chapter sets out to complement this broad understanding by considering how LD practice relates to questions of agency,

DOI: 10.4324/9781003433347-5

here understood as the capacity for intentional, deliberative, purposeful, reflexive action (for a recent, and trenchant, defence of this understanding of a distinctively human agency, see Malm, 2018).

Student agency, and the relationships between agency, learning, and engagement in higher education (HE), have received a fair degree of attention in recent years (see, for example: Williams, 2012; Case, 2013; Klemenčič, 2015; Stenalt and Lassesen, 2022). My aim here is to explore how viewing LD practice through a lens of student agency might help us further clarify: (a) what we think we're up to and why; and (b) why we tend to favour certain pedagogical approaches over others. Before proceeding, though, some clarifications. Firstly, the agents I have in mind here are not the atomised, non-socially situated, utility-maximising individuals of certain economists' dismal fantasies, but, rather, those complex, vulnerable, conflicted, creative, social, and relational beings who happen to actually people the world (Archer, 2000). Secondly, I recognise that the exercise of agency in directions we might wish to encourage should not be confused with agency in toto. Students may decline to journey with us for all sorts of valid reasons and may even, depending on circumstances and motivations, be deemed more critically agential for doing so. Finally, I appreciate that at least one 'elephant in the room' where ensuing discussions are concerned will be our own pedagogical agency within our varied institutional settings. Whilst detailed discussion of this question lies beyond the scope of this chapter, I will at least seek to acknowledge its salience where appropriate.

Students are Complex Human Persons (Who Knew?!)

As Zygmunt Bauman (2010, p.38) observed: 'In what we do ... we hardly ever start from a clean slate. The site on which we build is always cluttered: the past lingers in the same "present" in which the future tries ... to take root'. To take questions of agency seriously means first of all, then, to commit to getting to know students better – their hopes, disappointments, values, expectations, joys and forebodings, not to mention their existing assumptions about, and practices of, learning (Case, 2013). Yrjö Engeström's (2009) criteria for theories of learning (namely, that any theory worth its salt must attend as fully to learners' subjectivities and motivations as it does to the content of what is to be learned and how) seems to apply well to LD pedagogy. Any developmental project will likely flounder unless rooted in a respectful and sensitive curiosity concerning, to borrow Bauman's terminology, the past-informed present in which any future-oriented pedagogical labours are undertaken. This was revealed to me quite vividly early on in my career when, during a rather dry, technical conversation about reading and note-making, a student dragged me back into the messy world of actually existing human persons, by asking: 'But *who am I* to decide what's most relevant and important in the first place?'

Learning Developers should not, perhaps, need reminding of the hazards, both practical and ethical, of relying on generalised impressions about what we think we know of students' prior experiences and present capabilities. As we know, HE has a tendency to fall into habits of 'deficit thinking', particularly where students historically positioned as 'other' and so therefore frequently misrecognised as 'lacking', are concerned (Burke and Crozier, 2014). In order to check such habits, LD pedagogical practice often sets out by acknowledging and exploring the 'prior meaning-making experiences' that students bring with them (Wrigglesworth, 2019, p.18) as a starting point for discussion and negotiation around the kinds of continuities, shifts, or refinements in practice different situations may demand. In classroom settings, for example, we may often begin, where circumstances allow, by inviting students to discuss current or previously employed approaches to researching and writing assignments, engaging with taught material, or preparing for exams.

Enabling Agency: The Question of Structure

To think agency is also to think structure; to think the conditions which enable and/or constrain agency (Archer, 1995). Our activity in the world, even what we cherish as our most self-initiated, self-authored activity, is always undertaken by recourse to what is not 'ours' in any individualist or proprietary sense. As Gillian Rose (2011/1995, p.54) once observed of writing, it is 'that mix of discipline and miracle, which leaves you in control, even when what appears on the page has emerged from regions beyond your control'. Within social theory, 'structure' refers to the relatively durable social structures that work at inter-penetrating levels to condition agential possibilities, but which are themselves also sustained and reproduced, and challenged and resisted, through the exercise of agency (Case, 2013). In the conclusion, I will return to these more expansive questions regarding agency-structure relations. For now, though, my rather more parochial and immediate concerns are with how, within our everyday practice, we seek to create pedagogical structures conducive to students' learning.

Educational practitioners are perhaps more keenly aware than most of the complex and far from straightforward relationships between enablement, constraint, and agency. Our work, after all, often involves seeking to make room for student agency by creating (and, importantly, co-creating with students) what we hope will be productive and, to risk paradox for a moment, *enabling* constraints. Consider, for example, those so-called 'free writing' activities which seek to 'free' writerly agency not by removing constraints per se, but by setting their own constraints on action ('You're to do this, and not that, and you've got this much time to do it. And don't, whatever you do, stop!'). These are designed to encourage a sense of agency thought to be inhibited by other, rival constraints, not least those imposed by worries about getting it 'right'

(Li, 2007). (All this said, we should avoid the trap of complacency, here, and not assume our constraints are always of the benign and enabling variety!)

Similar types of structured enablement are also at work when, for instance, we create spaces, times, and activities designed to help students engage with various kinds of written assignment. Abegglen, Burns, and Sinfield (2021, p.77), for example, suggest educators combine a range of 'activities to *scaffold* a specific piece of writing' [my emphasis], such activities seeking, the authors continue, to '*help them* [students] *to take control* of their writing and writing practices' [my emphasis]. The phrase 'help them to take control' bespeaks an encouragement to greater agency as the guiding pedagogical rationale for the support provided and, conversely, an acknowledgement that any control taken may well hinge on what is given or withheld. These might seem obvious points to make, but as Tamsin Haggis (2006) has noted, there is a persistent misconception within HE (with which Learning Developers will be all too familiar) that meeting the need for more structured support threatens to diminish standards; to dilute cherished expectations that students develop their capacities to think and act for themselves. I don't mean to disregard these concerns entirely. I simply mean to point out that whilst it's always possible that certain supportive structures might stifle student agency, it might just as readily be the case that their absence stifles. Sometimes, and to flirt once again with paradox, 'getting out of the way' can be an obstructive move. Or, to use a well-worn metaphor, the 'freedom' of the blank canvas is an ambivalent one, as apt to debilitate as to liberate. And, to bring the metaphor closer to home, we can imagine this ambivalence deepening if our would-be painter is aware that the exhortation to 'express themselves' will also lead to their being judged according to criteria riddled with apparent ambiguities and odd, esoteric stipulations concerning what counts as a valid and praiseworthy final product.

Work on approaches to supporting academic transition to university-level study (e.g. Thomas, Jones and Ottoway, 2015; Hockings et al., 2018) has likewise emphasised the importance of providing more pedagogically robust, curricula-level frameworks of structured support designed to enable the kinds of shifts in practice and expectations students are required to make in order to become more 'independent learners' (a phrase that some, myself included, are far from enamoured with, but which does at least have the virtue of foregrounding agency). As Williams (2012, p.320) notes, learning often develops during such periods of 'disjuncture' and liminality, when existing ways of knowing and acting are called into question. A central pedagogical challenge for HE, then, is in creating those enabling structures that best support students' transitions to ways of learning which place ever greater expectations on what Heikkilä et al. (2020) describe as 'epistemic agency': a desire and willingness to assume more self-consciously agentic roles in the production of knowledge. For its part, LD brings to this challenge a pedagogical ethos and set of practices grounded in a commitment to work respectfully *with* and *alongside* students (ALDinHE, 2023; Webster, 2020). This means taking seriously the situated agency of the student and resisting tendencies to view 'the student as an object to be worked on' (Abegglen et al., 2020, p.27).

The Limitations of 'Generic Skills' (*Or*, Why Contestants on *Strictly* Don't Attend Lectures on 'Dancing Skills')

Acknowledging the situatedness of student agency can also help us see the limitations of the discourse of 'generic skills'. As Emily Danvers (2018, p.549) writes of that perennial favourite, 'critical thinking', for example: 'this seemingly benign and transparent intellectual value has multiple meanings and enactments'. The well-chosen term, 'enactments', points to a certain performativity where criticality is concerned; can students act it out in ways recognised as legitimate? The invitation to critical agency is always conditional, always contextual, always constrained by certain norms, values, expectations, and conventions. And it's an invitation received by agents who may accept, reject, or misconstrue it depending on a whole host of factors, educational and otherwise. Indeed, the same student may warm to the invitation in one context, ignore it in another, strategically decide to pretend it never arrived in yet another, and so on. Given this, the notion of generic skills seems a rather unhelpful starting point for responding to the situated, context-dependent complexities of human learning (Lave, 2009). This largely explains, I think, why so many of us argue for ever greater degrees of curricula-level engagement and why, in turn, any discussion concerning how best to support the situated agency of students is also a discussion about how we support the no-less situated agency of Learning Developers, operating within varied institutional contexts, affording varied degrees of possibility and inhibition.

The Centrality of Practice (*Or*, Why those Same *Strictly* Contestants Don't Rely on Written Guides on How to Cha-Cha-Cha)

If the aforementioned notion of 'academic literacy practices' provides a more conceptually robust, empirically veracious alternative to 'generic skills', then it also calls attention to the practical forms of knowledge with which LD tends to be concerned. Whilst pedagogical approaches based on the transmission of information, or the provision of instruction, are not without their uses where such knowledge is concerned, these uses are somewhat limited. A failure to realise this is exemplified in the apparent belief across much of HE that a proliferation of supposedly explanatory texts (assignment briefs, assessment criteria, marking rubrics, etc.) will help make assessment expectations and processes more 'transparent' and accessible to students. Such texts can certainly be effective in generating questions, and that is no bad thing, but, as we know, this points to the need for discussion, practice, and shared sense-making. On their own, and given their unavoidable levels of abstraction and opacity, these texts are unlikely to yield much by the way of genuine comprehension (To, Panadero and Carless, 2021) and still less provide any means by which students might *act* in response.

As noted in previous sections, for Learning Developers, all this signals a struggle – waged at a variety of levels, and as our own conditioned pedagogical agency allows – to devise means of assisting students in navigating assessment requirements, both in terms of what they mean for the assignments to be produced, and the kinds of practices that might underpin their production (how might they be approached, planned, researched, drafted, edited, etc.?). And this raises, in turn, the further question: what kinds of developments in students' sense and exercise of agency are we expecting/hoping they will experience, and how will we enable and support these? LD alone does not possess all the answers to these questions, of course. However, a big part of its enduring value to HE lies in its insistence that: (a) we ask them in the first place; and (b) we deploy the kinds of practice-oriented, experiential, dialogical, and facilitative pedagogical approaches most appropriate when responding to them (Webster, 2020). (Once again, though, our capacity to raise and respond to such questions will depend largely on our scope for pedagogical agency vis-à-vis, for example, the shape and design of programmes, modules, assessment practices, etc.)

Here, however, a caveat. By emphasising the need for certain pedagogical approaches in particular contexts, I am not endorsing a more general tendency, sometimes applied to HE teaching as a whole, to position the putatively 'student-centred' facilitator as the necessarily more benign and empowering counterpart to the oft-maligned 'teacher-centred' instructor. Involving students as more observably engaged participants in their own learning may turn out to be an empowering gesture, but there are certainly no guarantees in this regard. As Lesley Gourlay (2015) argues, it may just as readily be seen as a more insidious technology of control. And this leads me to some closing remarks on the always already political character of all our pedagogical endeavours.

Conclusion: The Curse of Agency?

Frantz Fanon (1961, p.29) once remarked that, in capitalist societies, education's chief function is 'to create around the exploited person an atmosphere of submission and of inhibition which lightens the task of policing considerably'. Does he mean us? Is this what we're up to? Here, I want to respond with a clear and unequivocal: 'Well, um, kind of, to some extent, inescapably, yes, but also…'. In all seriousness, though, I want to close by re-introducing some of those social-theoretical approaches to agency–structure relations alluded to earlier.

It's quite common for Learning Developers to claim that by supporting students to make sense of and respond to the challenges HE learning poses, we are helping ensure that people with diverse prior educational experiences are enabled to participate fully (ALDinHE, 2023). Further, by working to make HE a more hospitable and enabling space (open to being itself transformed, rather than assuming that the transformative initiative works exclusively in one direction), we are helping address various social injustices, commonly reproduced at curricula and institutional levels. This is valid, and laudable and fair enough, but it is incomplete unless we also ask what exactly we are supporting participation in. We might, for example, successfully enable the performance of certain forms of 'appropriate' disciplinary academic discourse, but in doing so forget to question who gets to determine what is and is not 'appropriate' and how far the criteria for such may encode the kinds of hierarchies and power relations we would otherwise wish to critique. For a lucid discussion of how some of these tensions and dilemmas are treated within the scholarship on academic literacies, see Hilsdon, Malone, and Syska (2019).

And what of the pervasive neoliberal context within which educational practice is undertaken? How do our practices, however pedagogically enlightened in their own terms, relate to the demand that HE prioritises the production of graduates who are competitive, suitably behaved, sources of 'human capital'? When (and hence the title of this section) does the exercise of agency become the student's self-regulating participation in systems that threaten to exploit, diminish, and dehumanise? How far might our practices help reinforce (even if unintentionally) individualist conceptions of agency, conducive to students' successful participation in existing structures, but at the same time preclusive of those more collective, cooperative forms of agency that might challenge these structures?

These may be discomforting questions, but LD at its best is a critical practice – never content to facilitate the orderly participation in the world as it is, but committed also to opening spaces for critique and potential transformation. In doing so, of course, we cannot step entirely outside of our own conditioning contexts, nor must we forget that we are always already implicated in what we seek to change, whatever critical perspectives we may succeed in obtaining. To borrow a formulation of Mark Carrigan's (2019) (who is not writing about educational practice as such, but whose words strike a chord resonant, I think, with every educator's predicament): 'our striving is part of the whole we are trying to apprehend from inside the mess'. This chapter certainly won't have tidied up the mess, but I hope at least to have shed some light on the kind of mess we're in.

References

Abegglen, S., Burns, T., Maier, S., Sinfield, S. (2020) 'Supercomplexity: Acknowledging students' lives in the 21st century university', *Innovative Practice in Higher Education*, 4(1): 20–38.

Abegglen, S., Burns, T., and Sinfield, S. (2021) *Supporting Student Writing and Other Modes of Learning and Assessment. A Staff Guide*. Calgary: University of Calgary.

ALDinHE (2023) *About ALDinHE*. Available at: https://aldinhe.ac.uk/about-aldinhe/ (Accessed: 5 January 2023).

Archer, M.S. (1995) *Realist Social Theory: The Morphogenetic Approach*. Cambridge: Cambridge University Press.

Archer, M.S. (2000) *Being Human: The Problem of Agency*. Cambridge: Cambridge University Press.

Bauman, Z. (2010) *Living on Borrowed Time: Conversations with Citlali Rovirosa-Madrazo*, New Jersey: Wiley.

Carrigan, M. (2019) *The Hegelian sociology of Gillian Rose*. Available at: https://markcarrigan.net/2019/03/18/the-hegelian-sociology-of-gillian-rose/ (Accessed 4 January 2023).

Case, J. (2013) *Researching Student Learning in Higher Education: A Social Realist Approach*. Abingdon: Routledge.

Danvers, E. (2018) 'Who is the critical thinker in higher education? A feminist re-thinking', *Teaching in Higher Education*, 23(5): 548562.

Engeström, Y. (2009) 'Expansive learning: Toward an activity-theoretical reconceptualization', in K. Illeris (ed.) *Contemporary Theories of Learning*. Abingdon: Routledge.

Fanon, F. (1961) *The Wretched of the Earth*, London: Penguin Books.

Gourlay, L. (2015) '"Student engagement" and the tyranny of participation', *Teaching in Higher Education*, 20(4): 402–411.

Haggis, T. (2006) 'Pedagogies for diversity: Retaining critical challenge amidst fears of "dumbing down"', *Studies in Higher Education*, 31(5): 521–535.

Heikkilä, M., Hermansen, H., Iiskala, T., Mikkilä-Erdmann, M and Warinowski, A. (2020) 'Epistemic agency in student teachers' engagement with research skills', *Teaching in Higher Education*, 1–18.

Hilsdon, J., Malone, C. and Syska, A. (2019) 'Academic literacies twenty years on: A community-sourced literature review', *Journal of Learning Development in Higher Education*, 15: 1–47.

Hockings, C. Thomas, L., Ottaway, J. and Jones, R. (2018) 'Independent learning – what we do when you're not there', *Teaching in Higher Education*, 23(2): 145–161.

Klemenčič, M. (2015) 'What is student agency? An ontological exploration in the context of research on student engagement', in M. Klemenčič, S. Bergan and R. Primožič (eds) *Student engagement in Europe: Society, higher education and student governance. (Council of Europe Higher Education Series No. 20.* Strasbourg: Council of Europe Publishing.

Lave, J. (2009) 'The practice of learning', in K. Illeris (ed.) *Contemporary Theories of Learning*. Abingdon: Routledge, 200–208.

Lea, M.R. and Street, B.V. (1998) 'Student writing in higher education: An academic literacies approach', *Studies in Higher Education*, 23(2): 57–172.

Li, L.Y. (2007) 'Exploring the use of focused freewriting in developing academic writing', *Journal of University Teaching and Learning Practice*, 4(1): 46–60.

Malm, A. (2018) *The Progress of This Storm: Nature and Society in a Warming World*. London: Verso.

Rose, G. (2011 [1995]) *Love's Work: A Reckoning with life*. New York: NYRB.

Stenalt, M.H. and Lassesen, B. (2022) 'Does student agency benefit student learning? A systematic review of higher education research', *Assessment and Evaluation in Higher Education*, 47(5): 653–669.

Thomas, L., Jones, R. and Ottoway, B. (2015) *Effective practice in the design of directed independent learning opportunities.* York: The Higher Education Academy.

To, J., Panadero, E. and Carless, D. (2021) 'A systematic review of the educational uses and effects of exemplars', *Assessment and Evaluation in Higher Education*, 47(9): 1167–1182.

Webster, H. (2020) 'Does learning development have a signature pedagogy?' *Association of Learning Development in Higher Education.* LD@3 Event (online), 13 May. Available at: https://aldinhe.ac.uk/event-resources/ (Accessed: 11 January 2023).

Williams, K. (2012) 'Rethinking "learning" in higher education', *Journal of Critical Realism*, 11(3): 296–323.

Wrigglesworth, J. (2019) 'Pedagogical applications of academic literacies theory: A reflection and case study', *Journal of Learning Development in Higher Education*, 15: 1–22.

4

THE DEVELOPMENT OF EXPERTISE AND IDENTITY WITHIN A COMMUNITY OF PRACTICE

A Networking Model

Carina Buckley and Louise Frith

> *I do not feel I learnt my job as such. It was a journey of similar experiences where one scaffolded the other. My firm belief that it's the system (and not the student) that needs to change led me to get involved with my national professional association. I always had a view that I wanted to dismantle a 'service' approach to Learning Development and embed it instead in every aspect of how my university operates, so I got involved in networks beyond my own field, to extend the ethos and knowledge of LD.*
>
> *(Research study participant)*

Introduction

The concept of professional identity, while complex, provides a framework for professionals to construct their own ideas of how to be, how to act, and how to understand their work. MacLure (1993, p.316) sees identity as a form of 'argument', through which a Learning Developer can rationalise, explain, and interpret their actions, priorities, and values in a way that allows them to reconcile their substantive self – who they believe themselves to be – with their situational self – that which is constructed via the relationships and contexts in which they are immersed (Murray and Male, 2005). Identity is therefore closely aligned to an individual's context and the networks that comprise it. Without a unifying route into Learning Development (LD), nor a standardised professional qualification recognised by employers, the 'process of adjustment' (Murray and Male, 2005, p.127) into LD may rely more on the situational self and networking and social opportunities than it does on any outward markers of progress. Some practitioners find the way smooth and deliberate, and achieve the feelings of self-efficacy and effectiveness that arise when substantive and situational selves are in alignment. However, others

DOI: 10.4324/9781003433347-6

reach an LD role via the ups and downs of temporary or short-term contracts, often having left a previous, more tightly defined field, increasing the potential for dislocation. With this background, the title of 'expert' is often troubling and troubled, feeding a negative loop of non-recognition and a precarious professional identity. This chapter therefore explores the often fluid identity of a Learning Developer and how this can be expressed and negotiated within a dynamic and networked professional community.

Working in the Third Space

Learning Development occupies the 'third space' (Whitchurch, 2008) between teaching and non-teaching. Whatever their job title – tutor, advisor, lecturer, instructor – Learning Developers work alongside students to help them make sense of higher education practices (ALDinHE, 2023), yet they travel into the role along diverse pathways, from backgrounds including English Language teachers, subject academics, and librarians. Developing a coherent LD identity is therefore a process of negotiation between these pathways, and between the individual and their professional community (Smith and Boyd, 2012). In turn, the development of expertise is based on active participation within a community of practice; theory is enacted in practice and experiences are conceptualised in interaction with others (Wallin et al., 2019). By actively engaging with a body of professional knowledge, practitioners develop a lens through which they see the (professional) world, learning what to pay attention to – or not – within a shared worldview that underpins localised priorities and structures (Penrose, 2012).

This process of participation in a Community of Practice (CoP) leads a new Learning Developer into their new LD identity. While Lave and Wenger's (1991) original CoP model envisaged novice practitioners learning through proximity to a master practitioner, we take a networking approach to CoPs, emphasising the relationships between members. These relationships develop and emerge from the tasks and practices of the role and evolve through the shared knowledge, experiences, and values (what Lave and Wenger might term the domain) of Learning Developers. We refer to this as networking capital, that is, the accumulation of knowledge and connections that allows an individual to move from a marginal role of low-networking capital to a central one of high-networking capital. We apply a staged approach to networking to the original conception of CoPs (Figure 4.1).

In this networking model, Learning Developers might start as a *Novice* in that they may occupy a marginal role within a team or sphere of influence. However, through professional-related reading and listening, they can progress to the second stage of *Functional Group Membership*, where they might begin to feel more confident in the role and how they perform it. The third stage of the model is *Networker*. This stage involves more active engagement with tasks and colleagues to exchange and experiment with ideas. As Learning

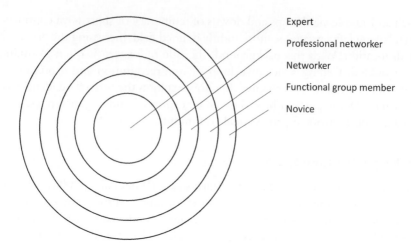

Expert

Professional networker

Networker

Functional group member

Novice

FIGURE 4.1 The five stages of networking capital accumulation (adapted from Lave and Wenger, 1991)

Developers grow in their roles, they can adopt a more confident professional identity. At this stage, termed here *Professional Networker*, Learning Developers are able to present their position on LD and engage in activities such as curriculum development and innovative approaches to learning and teaching. Finally, our model's fifth stage is that of *Expert*: the Learning Developer has a confident understanding of the LD agenda and its nuances, feels legitimised in their role, and has a clear professional position. This networked approach to professional identity suggests a staged linear approach; however, it is rarely a direct route. Learning Developers are likely to move up and down between the stages of this model many times within their professional career, due to the situated nature of LD practice.

Learning Developers' Journeys

The diverse ways in which Learning Developers can establish and construct their professional identity is best expressed by example. The lived experiences of 11 Learning Developers were captured through a series of narrative case studies collected at a workshop held at the ALDinHE conference in 2019. Each participant wrote reflectively for 30 minutes on their transition into and journey through Learning Development, the narrative approach allowing them to find the guiding structure that shaped the individual details (Szurmak and Thuna, 2013) and place events and relationships in context with each other. In this way, they constructed their own understanding of what it means to be a Learning Developer, the values that guide their substantive identity and the activities, knowledge, and practices that inform their situational self. The content of these short narratives was analysed in NVivo, drawing on the five stages of Figure 4.1 to establish how each participant experienced and moved through them.

Novice

No aspect of any of the participants' responses were categorised as novice; by attending a professional networking event, one possible way of performing their role within a community, they demonstrated an understanding of the agenda of their profession. Nevertheless, Respondent 6 noted, 'I am figuring out who I am in my new role – how I can use my prior experiences and skills and knowledge to best support students', suggesting a sense of marginality in an 'as yet unrecognised' new team. This supports the idea that institutional structural factors can impact on individual identity.

Functional Group Member

At this stage, the Learning Developer's priority might be the accumulation of relevant information about LD and drawing on the experiences of others. Respondent 10 is characteristic of this:

> To keep updated I read the [*Journal of Learning Development in Higher Education*] and follow the LDHEN [jiscmail] list. I also love [a Learning Developer's] blog and follow other Learning Developers on Twitter.

For others, the assimilation of knowledge came about through close contact with colleagues, whether that is by sitting in 'on others' teaching … organically and over time my knowledge in and of the field [growing]' (Respondent 3), or in a more ad hoc way: 'I read widely, I pick up ideas in passing on social media, conferences, random conversations' (Respondent 9).

Networking

Those moving towards more active engagement identified that 'finding shared practice, values and discourse with Learning Developers within the same team' (Respondent 1) and 'participating in the ALDinHE conferences and learning what others are doing across the sector' (Respondent 5) were central means of achieving it. These activities were further intensified for those who had the confidence to 'get involved in networks and work beyond my own field' (Respondent 3) and '[institute] a series of spaces to encourage sharing of practices' (Respondent 5). Finally, one respondent demonstrated their sense of legitimacy as a professional via their work '[setting] up a blended learning network across my organisation … [and meeting] regularly as an expert member of the Jisc student digital experience and research panel' (Respondent 4).

Professional Networker

This stage is differentiated from the previous one in that the Learning Developer feels able to take a leadership position, which may be informal, in conversations on curriculum development and learning and teaching delivery. For example, Respondent 5 describes himself as 'the bloke that is always banging on about allowing "genuine", "meaningful" forms of embedding, ... pushing on issues about change at the curriculum level'. He acknowledges that these conversations may position him 'into more of a staff educational development territory', yet they have resulted in 'being invited to take part in rethinking curricula and getting to involve members of my LD team as facilitators and catalysts for more student-centred approaches'. This experience demonstrates the social and networking capital required to move towards the centre of the model in Figure 4.1. To network professionally is to expand the role and claim a wider remit.

Expert

The final stage of Expert does not imply that those who are not engaged in setting the agenda do not have expertise; rather, it is intended to mark out those who are active in shaping the field and recognised as such. This can take several forms, such as getting 'involved in networks and work beyond my own field – so I can extend the ethos and knowledge of our field into other areas' (Respondent 3). Similarly, Respondent 4 writes that 'my networking beyond the uni is very important to my identity' as she is 'recognised in ways that do not occur within my own organisation'. To be an Expert, then, is to have confidence in how the LD role is performed and for that confidence to be recognised by others. Where that is not the case, 'erosion of self belief hampers confidence', making it necessary for a Learning Developer to 'develop a sense of myself as a professional that isn't reliant on validation from people who don't necessarily understand what my role is' (Respondent 2).

Opportunities and Challenges

Despite the challenges of legitimacy inherent in a 'third space' position, Learning Developers have numerous opportunities to work creatively and collaboratively with colleagues and students across disciplinary and hierarchical boundaries. Here we identify four contexts where Learning Developers can actively develop networks and expertise, and therefore professional identity, in the opportunities offered for reconciling their substantive and situational selves.

Inter-programme work: Working across a wide range of programmes within a discipline or faculty allows Learning Developers to see the synergies between them and potentially develop inter-programme projects, such as student conferences and student showcases. We locate this type of work at the level of *Networker*, as Learning Developers can broker relationships and collaborations and in doing so greatly enhance students' learning experiences (Freeman et al., 2021). Students have the opportunity to network with staff and other students within their school or faculty who they may not have met within the constraints of the classroom, while also enhancing their employability skills. However, these events take significant time and energy on the part of the Learning Developer and other colleagues, making the success of the event dependent on key people in particular roles.

Peer learning: Learning Developers often find themselves facilitating peer learning for students, whether a formalised and highly structured Peer Assisted Learning programme, curriculum-based and timetabled, or more informal student mentoring relationships where students are matched with a partner to work with and share their learning. Both types of peer learning have the potential to carry the Learning Developer into the *Professional Networker* stage, depending on how involved they might get in curriculum development. Other peer learning approaches to support this stage of networking might include one-off writing retreats, regular 'Shut Up and Write' sessions, and writing centres. Peer learning is often favoured in universities because it seems to be a free activity which will support students' learning and signify a strong academic community. However, to establish a peer-led learning culture within a programme takes a significant level of staff commitment and administration, and its success can often hinge on student misperceptions that it is remedial, amongst other reasons for low attendance (Connolly-Panagopoulos, 2021).

Collaborative work: Learning Developers often support academic colleagues to introduce new assessment tasks or innovative methods into teaching, providing them with opportunities to share their ideas through conferences and publications and build their own academic profile (D'Alesio and Martin, 2019). This type of activity sits firmly at the level of *Professional Networker*, over time it can lead to *Expert*. The partnerships formed with academic colleagues in schools can be long-lasting and productive on both sides, enhancing Learning Developers' professional standing, and helping academics to gain confidence and achieve recognition as teachers, through the Teaching Excellence Framework and AdvanceHE Fellowship. Collaborative work can also be pursued with colleagues in professional services, such as Librarians and EAP specialists. Although collaboration between academic and professional colleagues can be highly productive and expose new areas of work, the power dynamics need to be carefully navigated to ensure that the Learning Developer's input is properly recognised.

Project work: Learning Developers often find themselves crossing boundaries within institutions, so they can also work with students and colleagues on projects (Johnstone et al., 2019). These projects might be aimed at supporting new students' successful induction and transition into university, or at addressing current issues within higher education such as student wellbeing or students' use of AI writing tools. Learning Developers in this position are leading the LD agenda and as such can be identified as *Professional Networkers*, recognised in their institutions. These types of projects provide students with invaluable 'real world experience' of the process of project development and delivery, and enable the university to demonstrate that it is addressing contemporary student issues. The only hazard with this work, like the inter-programme work, is the time intensity of it and the possibility of running out of time to complete the project within the student's study-cycle.

Reflection: Networking

The journey to expertise can be fraught with obstacles, due to the structural changes imposed upon UK HE since the 1990s such as widening participation, employability, Brexit, internationalisation, and online learning. These shifting agendas mean that Learning Developers need to ensure they build networks that are flexible and responsive to new challenges. Growing into a professional identity as a Learning Developer is therefore an active endeavour on the part of the individual, but there are ways in which this process can be supported. This can be done in three key locations: within the LD team, through university structures, and externally through professional bodies.

Team Level

The LD team can provide a useful space for new members to discuss and reflect on their practice and gain feedback, capturing the interactivity emphasised by Wallin et al. (2019). Although there are always day-to-day practical issues to discuss at team meetings, making regular time and space for sharing practice and discussing teaching issues in a reflective way is fundamental to supporting the professional development and identity shaping for novice Learning Developers. At a team level, those new to LD should be encouraged to attend team networking events and pedagogical discussions. This enables a novice to understand their role and develop confidence and a sense of belonging within it. More experienced team members can permeate the spheres of Professional Networker and Expert by acting as a mentor (formally or informally) to novice colleagues.

Institutional Level

Internally provided professional recognition schemes such as a Postgraduate Teaching Award or AdvanceHE Fellowship are generally mandatory for new academics, but optional to people in Learning Development roles. There are two main benefits of these types of programmes: they offer an opportunity for formal learning and reflection about teaching in HE; and importantly, they provide an environment to network with the central Academic Development team and with academic colleagues from across the institution. This means that Learning Developers can share their practice with others and at the same time raise the profile of LD within the university. Many HE institutions also provide departmental teaching and learning events or conferences; participation can range from taking an active role in discussions, to co-presenting a poster up to presentation of research and in some cases involvement in the planning and hosting of the event. This is an important aspect of identity building for the individual, in the way it allows for their recognition as a Functional Group Member and then Networker within the team and the university.

External Professional Development

Attendance at national or international conferences or symposia enhances professional identity through the juxtaposition of community, knowledge, and practice. Although the resource implications can be difficult for some Learning Developers to justify, especially if they are on non-academic contracts, nevertheless the active construction of knowledge and recognition by and interaction with others which they afford bring the Learning Developer within the Professional Networker and Expert levels. Online events and the possibility of funding from professional bodies are valid ways of opening up this avenue of professional identity development.

Conclusion

We began this chapter by introducing the concept of the situational and substantive selves, which must be brought into alignment for the Learning Developer to feel authentic and at ease in their professional identity. Building a network of like-minded colleagues engaged in similar work with similar values is a vital step towards cultivating a professional identity as a Learning Developer, a situated, multifaceted, and dynamic construction based on social relations that helps us understand 'who we are' (Skott, 2019, p.471). Importantly, the situational self, as a social construction, relies on networking and recognition by others in order to develop. Identity is therefore contextualised, and, we argue, that context is fundamentally shaped by community and the networks it comprises. Our model of networking capital acknowledges the fluid nature of networks and the negotiated positions they require. By focussing on relationships, the model provides a means for Learning Developers to explore different avenues to developing their professional identity by helping them identify where they are now and where they would like to be (their substantive selves), and suggests the type of activities to undertake that will support them in reaching that stage (their situational selves). Team leaders and managers can use the model to nurture a professional identity in their colleagues through the professional development opportunities it anticipates. For despite the plethora of qualifications and certifications that are open to Learning Developers, it is professional behaviours that inculcate a professional identity, performed within a community of like-minded others, and this chapter has provided a range of ways in which this might be achieved.

References

ALDinHE (2023) *About ALDinHE.* Available at: https://aldinhe.ac.uk/about-aldinhe/ (Accessed: 31 March 23).

Connolly-Panagopoulos, M. (2021) 'Centralisation: placing Peer Assisted Study Sessions (PASS) within the wider work of Learning Developers', *Journal of Learning Development in Higher Education,* 21. https://doi.org/10.47408/jldhe.vi21.647

D'Alesio, R. and Martin, B. (2019) 'Creating an academic literacy framework to enhance collaboration between Learning Developers and subject academics', *Journal of Learning Development in Higher Education,* 15. https://doi.org/10.47408/jldhe.v0i15.539

Freeman, O., Hand, R. and Kennedy, A. (2021) 'Breaking down silos through authentic assessment: a live case analysis', *Journal of Higher Education Theory and Practice,* 21(4): 236–241.

Johnstone, K., Thomas, S. and Dodzo, N. (2019) 'Investigating the feasibility of co-production of digital media with students', *Journal of Learning Development in Higher Education,* 16. https://doi.org/10.47408/jldhe.v0i16.520

Lave, L. and Wenger, E. (1991) *Situated Learning: Legitimate Peripheral Participation.* Cambridge University Press.

MacLure, M. (1993) 'Arguing for your self: identity as an organising principle in teachers' jobs and lives', *British Educational Research Journal,* 19(4): 311–322.

Murray, J. and Male, T. (2005) 'Becoming a teacher educator: evidence from the field', *Teaching and Teacher Education,* 21(2): 125–142. https://doi.org/10.1016/j.tate.2004.12.006

Penrose, A.M. (2012) 'Professional identity in a contingent-labor profession: expertise, autonomy, community in composition teaching', *Writing Program Administration* 35(2): 108–126.

Skott, J. (2019) 'Changing experiences of being, becoming, and belonging: teachers' professional identity revisited', *ZDM Mathematics Education,* 51: 469–480. https://doi.org/10.1007/s11858-018-1008-3

Smith, C. and Boyd, P. (2012) 'Becoming an academic: the reconstruction of identity by recently appointed lecturers in nursing, midwifery and the allied health professions', *Innovations in Education and Teaching International,* 49(1): 63–72. https://doi.org/10.1080/14703297.2012.647784

Szurmak, J. and Thuna, M. (2013) 'Tell me a story: The use of narrative as a tool for instruction', *Imagine, Innovate, Inspire: The Proceedings of the ACRL 2013 Conference,* 546–552.

Wallin, A., Nokelainen, P. and Mikkonen, S. (2019) 'How experienced professionals develop their expertise in work-based higher education: a literature review', *Higher Education* 77: 359–378. https://doi.org/10.1007/s10734-018-0279-5

Whitchurch, C. (2008) 'Shifting identities and blurring boundaries: the emergence of third space professionals in UK higher education', *Higher Education Quarterly,* 62: 377396. https://doi.org/10.1111/j.1468-2273.2008.00387.x

5

HYBRID LEARNING DEVELOPERS

Between the Discipline and the Third Space

Nicola Grayson and Alicja Syska

> *I've recently had the opportunity to increase either of my roles to full time –*
> *essentially, I had the choice to stop being a dual professional and make a deci-*
> *sion which profession/career to focus on. I couldn't do it. I couldn't make a*
> *decision between the two roles – I love working both, I love the flexibility, the*
> *variety, the interest that comes from working for two separate departments. It's*
> *a tricky balancing act sometimes but I wouldn't do it any other way.*
>
> *(Anonymous hybrid practitioner)*

Learning Developers who practise alongside an academic role as 'hybrid' professionals occupy a unique position in higher education: comfortable in both
the academic and professional worlds. This distinctive location involves constant boundary crossing as they negotiate the challenges and advantages of
straddling both academic and professional spheres, moving within and beyond
'third space' (Whitchurch, 2013). This chapter confronts the challenges of
conceptualising hybrid practitioners as a distinctive group operating within the
Learning Development (LD) community and shows a range of ways in which
such intermingled roles can inform and enrich the respective practices. It
attempts to capture how, at the core of the hybrid practitioners' identity, lies a
capacity to switch between the established contexts and hierarchies related to
discipline-specific work and the third space of Learning Development.

   Having over a decade of experience of working as hybrids, in authoring this
chapter we build on our personal journeys and enhance insights from our
experience with stories from our colleagues elicited via an informal community
survey. Themes extracted from these narratives are harnessed to communicate
the advantages and the challenges of crossing the boundaries of multiple roles,
sometimes in multiple institutions, and to present hybrid practitioners as

DOI: 10.4324/9781003433347-7

'boundary spanners' (Fitzgerald et al., 2013) who possess a unique dual or even manifold perspective on working in higher education (HE). We elucidate the movement between such roles to conceptualise the spaces hybrid practitioners must occupy and be able to transgress. Through the lenses of identity (which cannot be fixed), practice (which must be adaptive), wellbeing (in relation to the necessity to spread oneself across boundaries), future prospects (which in some ways open up and in other ways are limited), and our sense of belonging (with reference to splitting loyalties), this analysis reveals and affirms the richness of experience, the value of contribution, and the uniqueness of insight that hybrid Learning Developers can offer the wider LD community and HE as a whole, while acknowledging the challenges and tensions involved in hybrid work.

Capturing the Ineffable: Conceptualising the Hybrid Practitioner's Role and Identity

Increased cultural hybridity of contemporary societies (Werbner and Modood, 1997; Bhabha, 2012), and parallel changes to the ways of working in HE more specifically, have been extensively documented (Whitchurch, 2013; McIntosh and Nutt, 2022; Smith et al., 2015). Being a hybrid practitioner aligns with post-essentialist concepts of identity (Foucault, 1970), which understand it as fluid, interactive, culturally conditioned, and context dependent. Those who routinely switch between roles and cross institutional and disciplinary boundaries construct their identity by drawing on 'the regions of experience' (Melucci, 1997) derived from their respective roles and enacting them in everyday practice. This switching, or 'boundary spanning' (Fitzgerald et al., 2013), involves seemingly opposing dynamics, including continuity and change, being an insider and an outsider, at times simultaneously, and often accommodating the both/and and either/or states of being and meaning making. Such identity is open to constant re-positioning, re-configuration, and re-negotiation, 'as agents weave together the various elements of experience in managing their own identities' (Barry et al., 2006, p.281). Hybrid practitioners, in this respect, are both a reflection and a consequence of contemporary society and the modern university.

What exactly do we mean by 'hybrid practitioners' and what variations exist within this professional positioning? Hybrid professionals/academics are sometimes referred to as 'blended' (Whitchurch, 2013; Quinney et al., 2017) or 'integrated' (McIntosh and Nutt, 2022) and while these terms work to describe the idea of mixing roles and identities well, we feel that the term 'hybrid' is in fact the most neutral, inclusive, and capacious. While 'blending' implies inseparability of the end compound and 'integrating' has assimilationary connotations, being a 'hybrid' seems to allow for shifting from/to and between independent but – crucially – complementary areas of work. Thus, we would identify Learning Developers who also work as academic lecturers or librarians as hybrid practitioners, but not those who combine their role in HE with unrelated professional activities such as a salesperson or a bookkeeper. Hybrid practitioners in the context of LD are those who combine their role with another related role within the orbit of HE, including, but not limited to, academic lecturers, demonstrators, librarians, EAP (English for Academic Purposes) tutors and Educational Developers, in any contractual combination or proportion. We also assume that the roles held in a given combination are interrelated but characterised by separate institutional cultures, and that the hybrid state results in, or at least has the capacity to build bridges and productive connections between the areas of work involved.

A number of scholars working in different fields and intellectual traditions have developed sophisticated ways of thinking and writing about identity switching and 'shape shifting' (Barry et al., 2006), which we draw on to better understand the effects of this cross-pollination on our daily LD/academic practice. 'Weaving' together her two identities as a daughter and 'a woman of color', Maria Lugones (1987, p.3) proposes the concept of 'world-travelling'. Her definition of a 'world' is very broad and inclusive, allowing for subjectivity, flux, and the discomfort of incompatibility. She encourages an exploration of how we inhabit our worlds, often at the same time, and how we can 'travel' between them while retaining our distinctiveness to/in each and striving to be 'at ease' in them by adopting their norms, language, history, and community. Through this travelling, we become 'ambiguous beings', simultaneously constructing our worlds and being constructed by them. Echoing Lugones's theorisation, Gloria Anzaldúa (1999, p.101) calls for a 'tolerance for ambiguity' when fashioning our self-identity. She writes about 'crossing over' or being 'sandwiched between two cultures' that results in a new 'consciousness of the Borderlands' that offers us 'a more whole perspective'.

While we do not attempt to compare the experience of hybrid working to the complexities of racialised and gendered identities (although they are often enmeshed within hybrid workers' realities), these rich metaphors help us conceptualise our journeys in creative and productive ways. We can see ourselves as 'world travellers', 'ambiguous beings' with 'dual identities', who bridge the worlds we inhabit by skilfully navigating their boundaries and mastering the often-conflicting discourses and internal contradictions involved in this state of 'in-betweenness' to create fertile spaces for dialogue and coexistence. In shining a light on this space, we follow Anzaldúa's advice to first 'take inventory' (1999, p.104) of our in-betweenness. In order to explore what we bring to each role, what challenges we face and how we can productively respond, we will now shift the focus of our discussion from theory and abstract concepts to lived and embodied (Merleau-Ponty, 2013) experience.

To set the stage, both of us began our careers in HE as academic lecturers on a mix of part-time, fixed-term, and casual contracts – in Philosophy (Nicola) and History (Alicja) – before taking on the additional role of Learning Developer (Nicola since 2013 and Alicja since 2015). At the time of writing, Nicola has left the hybrid space and moved on to a full-time post in Educational Development, and Alicja has accepted an additional fractional lecturing post, thus straddling three fields: LD, History, and Education. While our journeys differ, we have extensive experience of working as hybrids and the colleagues who responded to our informal questionnaire share similar trajectories that enrich our perspectives.

Boundary-Spanning, World-Travelling, and Bridge-Making: The Advantages of Being a Hybrid

The most striking epiphany we both experienced when it comes to our respective transitions from teaching in the discipline to teaching in LD was the realisation that we had been covert Learning Developers all along (for similar reflections see Pollard, 2023). The values of LD (ALDinHE, 2023) and its student-centred approach felt almost natural to us (which may be why we were drawn to LD in the first place), although even if initially we did not fully appreciate the skills required to support students to think critically across different fields and to understand their struggles to articulate knowledge effectively. Moving in and out of our subject specialism and to and from the LD role enabled us not only to gain better insight into our students, but also to educate ourselves on the importance, power, and relevance of issues such as inclusive practice, curriculum design, student engagement, peer learning, and assessment design. These in turn enriched our disciplinary teaching and created opportunities to spread innovative findings about good practice among our academic colleagues. Indeed, one of our respondents confided that in traversing the jobs, 'sometimes I'm the first person to see a combined way forward' in addressing problems which benefit from the input of both perspectives.

Dual roles create space to synergise ideas and perspectives that would not otherwise be possible or readily accessible (D'Alesio and Martin, 2019). Building bridges brings opportunities for team teaching and research collaborations, finding solutions to problems concerning NSS (UK National Student Survey) ratings and contributing to improving institutional approaches to promoting student belonging or co-creating learning communities. Moving between the roles not only feels like travelling through the respective worlds where we gather memories, tools, inspiration, and ideas, but also gives us a unique view of those worlds; as one respondent put it, when working as a hybrid 'you see the bigger picture' – the 'borderlands' effect. Through switching between two disparate, yet interrelated, spaces we forge a perspective that merges and combines our insights, expanding our networks to bring greater exposure to colleagues and practices across HE.

While our academic roles reveal to us the conditions that give rise to problems reported by students who engage with us in the third space, the LD relationships provide access to the learning struggles we may not have access to as academics because the existing power dynamic sometimes prevents these students from confiding. Working 'behind the scenes' thus offers privileged insight into otherwise closely guarded information, while working as an academic allows for greater development of consistent and longer-term relationships with learners. Whereas delivering LD sessions often results in students treating us as a kind of 'messiah' guiding them to demystify secret knowledge, as academics we tend to experience more 'frostiness' brought on by students being challenged to the point of discomfort (Dhillon in Buckley and Syska, 2022). While academics may feel exasperated by some student behaviour (especially instances of breaching academic integrity), Learning Developers may tend to idealise students and see only 'their side' of issues. So, boundary-spanning hybrid work, with its inherent outsider/insider access and an ability to take us out of our silos, helps to understand complex learning contexts better and to see students' worlds more holistically. Ultimately, holding these dual roles can make us both better academics and better Learning Developers while preventing the feeling of being 'stuck' in one perspective.

Juggling on a Tightrope: The Difficulties Involved in Hybrid Work

While the 'in-betweenness' inherent in hybrid work affords privileged insights and undisputable benefits for us, our students, and the colleagues we work with, it also poses clear challenges that make the role a real test of one's ability, self-image, and resilience. Juggling multiple jobs and responsibilities may be physically and emotionally exhausting, and the necessity to divide one's time and resources requires exceptional time management skills alongside great flexibility and ability to prioritise. Hybrid practitioners' workloads often spill into one another and – if serving different institutions – may require mastering different digital platforms, coordinating unconnected calendars, and navigating disparate work environments. Even splitting roles at the same university does not guarantee that the daily 'switches' go smoothly or that contractual hours are respected. As one of our respondents commented, 'I appear to be "available" full time' in both roles'. Another consistently used one emphatic word, 'circus', to describe their sense of being pulled in different directions.

In the current culture of overwork (Kucirkova, 2023), juggling roles may create undue pressures on hybrid practitioners, resulting in working overtime to meet often competing expectations and demands in ways that are not always noticed, appreciated, or rewarded. One hybrid colleague combining fractional contracts was made to feel guilty by their head of department for being 'the only person who is not over 100% of workload', a comment that did not take into account the impact or cost of the daily switching and multitasking

(Sum and Ho, 2015) involved in managing compounding roles. The hybrid insights are sometimes also exploited as a valuable resource, as in the following statement: 'Some of the overworking is because sitting in both teams means I have a good overview of everything that's happening. I end up being the logical person to do crossover tasks which weren't originally really part of my role'.

Straddling different worlds may have a profound impact on one's mindset and identity, mostly by creating a sense of not belonging to either but rather 'tightroping' between the fields. The conceptual fluidity of dual roles is not always seen as a blessing. Some colleagues mourn 'a loss of identity' at stepping away from their primary discipline and losing what they felt they were 'known for'. Advancements made in one sphere sometimes come at a cost to the other, although it is important to remember that the interrelated nature of hybrid work may also result in unexpected gains in expertise and fruitful research collaborations. An additional upside of a 'portfolio' career is that it can protect hybrids against academic precarity – a growing problem exacerbated by the coronavirus pandemic, particularly for women (Docka-Filipek and Stone, 2021). As one respondent noted: 'I was at risk of redundancy in one of my roles a little while ago. Knowing that even if things did go badly, I at least still had 0.5 FTE of a job was reassuring'.

Some of the most painful challenges involved in hybrid work seem to relate to the nature of the worlds it attempts to span. Academic and professional cultures differ and at times may exist in a state of tension (Magruder, 2019; McInnis, 1998), which hybrids need to skilfully navigate. When the hierarchical conceptions of academic roles are set against professional roles it can subject the hybrid to unequal treatment. When asked to share a critical experience that could be described as negative, respondents told us some jarring stories, including being undermined by academic colleagues in front of their students, being visibly perceived 'in a subordinate way', or having their expertise disregarded and being treated like a junior colleague, despite having greater accomplishments both in teaching and publishing. On the other hand, colleagues in professional services may sometimes distance themselves from us if we are perceived as representing that 'incomprehensible' world of academics. The us versus them divide between academic and professional services is present but not impermeable, and we have both experienced many fruitful and supportive relationships with both professional and academic colleagues.

Where Do We Go from Here?

Even though hybrid work reflects the nature of our fragmented, flexible, and fluid modern world, in many ways universities are not designed to accommodate hybrid roles. There are no 'in-between' categories to describe or classify what we do, as institutional processes are not prepared to deal with 'alternative selves' (Thomas and Davies, 2002). One respondent noted, 'at my institution I am officially identified by my most dominant contract and my other roles can only be "added" in the explanatory text on my university profile'. In having to choose the side of ourselves we share in different professional contexts, because there is no accommodation for the whole picture, we risk presenting a reductive view of ourselves and our work. This limits the extent to which we can communicate the truth of what we do and have accomplished, and may reinforce our position as outsiders, even though we often have more 'insider' knowledge than others.

This lack of a clear space for hybrids to occupy manifests itself in limited opportunities for professional connection and progression. Our respondents agreed that dual professional networks with space to share stories and seek advice would be an invaluable way to relieve some of the tensions involved in straddling roles. The irony is, of course, that setting up and moderating such groups takes time and resources, which are already stretched for those working across multiple roles. Similarly, hybrid practitioners often lack clear progression routes, which is a well-recognised issue for Learning Developers in general (Johnson, 2018). If combined with an academic contract, these routes may be clearer, but the effort required to meet promotion criteria is sometimes disproportionate to the size of the contract, and the reality of juggling fractional contracts may result in an inability to meet publishing demands or undertake leadership roles.

Hybrid working can be both liberating – our influence expanding along with increased access to diverse students, teaching and learning experiences – and frustrating, especially when hierarchies trump collegiality and we struggle to communicate our value and place. From boundary-spanning, world-travelling, and bridge-making to juggling on a tightrope and managing unrealistic expectations, we do it all in a variety of imaginative ways, which are very personal to everyone who inhabits a hybrid role. Both of us feel that stretching ourselves across boundaries in ways we did not think possible has not only allowed us to see better and reach further, but also helped us progress in our careers. To harness Anzaldúa's words by way of conclusion, 'Because the future depends on the breaking down of paradigms, it depends on the straddling of two or more cultures' (p.102). Hybrid spaces are filled with opportunity, and it is up to us to make the most of them. We hope that this brief introduction to the world of hybrid work in HE will inspire our readers to consider their experience in a new light and to make their own stories known.

References

ALDinHE (2023) *Values*. Available at: https://aldinhe.ac.uk/about-aldinhe/ (Accessed 14 May 2023).

Anzaldúa, G. (1999) *Borderlands/La Frontera: The New Mestiza*. 2nd edn. San Francisco: Aunt Lute Books.

Barry, J., Berg, E. and Chandler, J. (2006) 'Academic shape shifting: Gender, management and identities in Sweden and England', *Organization*, 13(2): 275–298. https://doi.org/10.1177/1350508406061673

Bhabha, H. K. (2012) *The Location of Culture*. London: Routledge.

Buckley, C. and Syska, A. (2022) *The Learning Development Project Podcast, Episode 5: Sunny Dhillon: Pedagogies of Discomfort and the Neoliberal University* [Podcast]. 24 November. Available at: https://aldinhe.ac.uk/networking/the-ld-project-podcast/ (Accessed 20 January 2023).

D'Alesio, R. and Martin, B. (2019) 'Creating an academic literacy framework to enhance collaboration between Learning Developers and subject academics', *Journal of Learning Development in Higher Education*, 15. https://doi.org/10.47408/jldhe.v0i15.539

Fitzgerald, L. Ferlie, E., McGivern, G. and Buchanan, D. (2013) 'Distributed leadership patterns and service improvement: Evidence and argument from English healthcare', *The Leadership Quarterly*, 24(1): 227–239. https://doi.org/10.1016/j.leaqua.2012.10.012

Foucault, M. (1970) *The Order of Things*. London: Routledge.

Johnson, I. P. (2018) 'Driving Learning Development professionalism forward from within', *Journal of Learning Development in Higher Education*. Special edition. https://doi.org/10.47408/jldhe.v0i0.470

Kucirkova, N. I. (2023) 'Academia's culture of overwork almost broke me, so I'm working to undo it', *Nature*, 614(7946): 9.

Magruder, E. D. (2019) 'Degrees of marginalization: "Adjuncts" and educational development', *New Directions for Teaching and Learning* (159): 55–64.

McInnis, C. (1998) 'Academics and professional administrators in Australian universities: Dissolving boundaries and new tensions', *Journal of Higher Education Policy and Management*, 20(2): 161–173.

McIntosh, E. and Nutt, D. (eds) (2022) *The Impact of the Integrated Practitioner in Higher Education*. Abingdon: Routledge.

Melucci, A. (1997) 'Identity and difference in a globalized world', in T. Modood and P. Werbner (eds) *Debating Cultural Hybridity: Multi-Cultural Identities and the Politics of Anti-Racism*. 2nd edn. Bloomsbury.

Merleau-Ponty, M. (2013) *Phenomenology of Perception*. Routledge.

Pollard, E. (2023) 'On academia, critical pedagogy and "coming out" as a third-space practitioner', *Journal of Learning Development in Higher Education*, 27. https://doi.org/10.47408/jldhe.vi27.927

Quinney, A., Lamont, C., Biggins, D. and Holley, D. (2017) 'Optimising disruptive approaches: extending academic roles and identities in higher education', *Journal of Learning Development in Higher Education*. https://doi.org/10.47408/jldhe.v0i12.417

Smith, J., Rattray, J., Peseta, T. and Loads, D. (eds) (2015) *Identity Work in the Contemporary University: Exploring an Uneasy Profession*. Vol. 1. Springer.

Sum, J. and Ho, K. (2015) 'Analysis on the effect of multitasking', *2015 IEEE International Conference on Systems, Man, and Cybernetics*. Hong Kong, China, 204–209. https://doi.org/10.1109/SMC.2015.48

Thomas, R. and Davies, A. (2002) 'Gender and New Public Management: Reconstituting Academic Subjectivities', *Gender, Work and Organization* 9(4): 372–397.

Whitchurch, C. (2013) *Reconstructing Identities in Higher Education: The Rise of 'Third Space' Professionals*. Abingdon: Routledge.

PART II
Being a Learning Developer
Praxis

This part moves on to consider how LD concepts, pedagogies, and identities are enacted within and through a Learning Developer's activities, across six chapters that focus on particular aspects of working with students. Chapter 6 opens with an outline of the ways in which students might encounter LD structurally within the institution. The London Met Collective of Tom Burns, Kevin Brazant, Emma Davenport, Nahid Huda, Sandra Sinfield, and Jarelle Smith map the diversity and variety of LD practices and encourage their formulation as liberatory and collaborative. In Chapter 7, Jennie Dettmer and Karen Welton apply these principles to the empowerment of students, particularly those who are neurodivergent. Subsequently, Ursula Canton illuminates the way Learning Developers tend to engage with teaching writing – seen as a social act and concerned with helping students find their voice and their place within a discourse community of higher education. This student-centred approach continues in Debbie Holley and David Biggins's discussion of how the affordances of technology might support an equitable, values-based, digital future for Learning Development in Chapter 8. Christie Pritchard then introduces the possibilities for LD in creating transformative, even transgressive, learning spaces in Chapter 9, arguing for the power of personal interactions in creating room for learning. The part closes in Chapter 10 with the return of the London Met Collective in collaboration with their students who present a personal perspective on LD as a fundamental part of their university experience.

DOI: 10.4324/9781003433347-8

PART II
Being a Learning Developer

Praxis

6

A DAY IN THE LIFE

What the Learning Developer Does

Tom Burns, Kevin Brazant, Emma Davenport, Nahid Huda, Sandra Sinfield and Jarelle Smith

> *I was asked to deliver a 'skills' session to a group of second years. I went into the room – the students were dotted about in ones, occasionally twos. They all had their coats on. They did not know each other's names. These students had not arrived in that classroom. Arguably, they had not arrived on the course.*
>
> *(LD staff member)*

Higher Education institutions (HEI) require a responsive, thoughtful, and action-orientated approach to Learning Development (LD) to support the aspirations of all students, including increasingly diverse and international student bodies, enabling them to become the graduates they wish to be (Abegglen et al., 2019). In practice, LD works with students and staff to improve study outcomes, module delivery, and/or to re-shape learning, teaching, and assessment (LTA) practice across whole institutions. Our identities as Learning Developers are therefore complex and dynamic, rooted in daily practices and values. Looking through the lens of LD practice, this chapter will provide insight into what LD does to support student development.

Whilst LD is essentially liberatory (Freire, 2007/1970), this chapter is not about the pedagogy of LD, which is discussed elsewhere, but about the daily practice that enacts this pedagogy through tutorials, workshops, feedback, collaboration, and staff development – all designed to promote students as actors with agency within their studies. There is no one job description for what LD does; the role can be different in every institution in which we exist; indeed, it can be different within a single institution. Our intention is to help new Learning Developers understand the diverse ways of enacting the role and

DOI: 10.4324/9781003433347-9

explore how to work with students and staff to take forward their own practice and their own development.

Where Is Learning Development?

> Every day is different, in terms of the work I do, and I love seeing how the everyday practices become the building blocks of systemic changes in the university.
>
> (LD staff member)

Learning Development in practice can be enacted in a variety of ways and from a variety of locations. LD might be situated within professional service departments like libraries or within some form of Academic or Learning and Teaching Development unit, and operate within or across the disciplines. There are hub and spoke models, totally centralised models and, more unusually, spoke models operating without a centralised hub. Dispersed 'spokes' may sit within Departments, Schools, or Faculties, answering to Heads of School, Deans, or Heads of Student Experience rather than a head of LD or of Learning and Teaching. One benefit of being within an academic unit is that the head of LD may also sit on university committees so that they can feed in information on the nuances of LD practice and values, which is not about deficit fixing or remediating 'problem' students but about working to promote student success via more equitable, critical, and socially just practices. This may involve challenging systemic injustices and inequity in education generally – and perhaps in the university itself.

Learning Development Online

The pandemic really threw universities into hyperdrive regarding their approach to digital learning: there was literally an overnight pivot to online learning, teaching, and assessment (LTA). LD tutorials, workshops, and other forms of support had to adapt. For some, the online was seen as conducive, even encouraging, of didactic transmissive teaching; but LD works with and alongside students to develop ownership, agency, and mastery. Generally, it is not good practice for the student to send in work to be 'corrected' or commented upon by an invisible, all-knowing LD wizard, even during a pandemic. So LD responded creatively, for example, by running socials and study cafes online where students met not just to talk about their work, but to socialise, bond, and belong as well.

Case Study: The Online Writing Social

A key aspect of LD work is helping students with their academic writing, and this continued online. Given that online learning can be experienced as isolating and detached (Pavlov et al., 2021), rather than writing retreats, online 'writing socials' are an effective alternative, and we tested this idea at London Metropolitan University. Socials are structured writing groups that create space for students to work alongside each other on their assignments. They provide great opportunities to alleviate anxieties about writing and for students to positively identify with their writing selves (Davenport, 2022).

> It was quite interesting because you first needed to understand what exactly you will write. And then after you've written it, you needed to explain what exactly you wrote to another person. So yeah, I think this was extremely helpful for me.
>
> It is great that all the group starts to write at the same time, this way it encourages you to write along. I like the time cap, so you really write something in that time.
>
> For me it is to be in a community-space-moment where I can learn from reliable people, specific methods and receive different suggestions that I never had before, and apply in the session itself! Save time and focus training, is the perfect combination.
>
> (Writing Social participants)

The pandemic may be receding, but many of us find ourselves navigating a new digital landscape, deciding which of our services should remain online to continue to offer flexibility to the student. Offering online one-to-one appointments to students has made it easier to accommodate students' needs. For example, for many students, childcare arrangements become less of an issue as the online appointment affords the student the opportunity to work from home. At the same time, Learning Developers talk about the power of the face-to-face space to promote perhaps bonding and belonging and cohort identity (Leathwood and O'Connell, 2003). Sometimes it can feel like the LD space is the only one where students can honestly and openly discuss their learning. What this highlights is how important it is for Learning Developers to be aware of, and curious about, the way in which the social and cultural landscape constantly shapes the form and function of learning in the university.

How Learning Developers Enact LD

> I used to go to all the staff events that I could – Research seminars, L&T Fora, brown bag lunches – and introduce myself and say how happy I would be to work with staff to develop resources or sessions for their students.
>
> (LD staff member)

Enacting LD involves various roles within HE, making it an inherently inclusive activity. Learning Developers can be positioned both within and outside of a subject area; they can be found in centralised teams focussed on professional development and digital education; they can be integrated into existing academic roles such as lecturers or senior management. As such, Learning Development is one of the most rewarding, challenging and stimulating of jobs. It is also, arguably, a diverse practice, drawing on a range of disciplines and approaches, which means enacting it can take many forms. In this section we will present different aspects of LD work from assignment support to integrating LD into the curriculum.

Assignment Support

> It can be useful to communicate to students that academic writing is not about sounding 'smart' by using sophisticated vocabulary; this can lead them down the primrose path of writing with thesaurus and completely losing themselves in the process.
>
> (LD staff member)

For many students, succeeding in academia can be anxiety-inducing; there are so many ways to feel 'not good enough' (Smit, 2012; Manavipour and Saeedian, 2016). One way that we tackle this is by offering assignment support sessions with a Learning Developer who is there to work alongside the student to help them better navigate, understand, and succeed in HE, with all its mysteries and occult practices (Burns and Sinfield, 2004). This assignment support can happen one to one, in a group or in writing cafes.

Students access an LD tutorial to better understand what is required in an assignment. They want to know whether the strategies they are using to study and answer assignment questions will work, and they want to know how to do it 'right'. The job of LD is not to provide the answer, but to create the space where the student comes to discover answers for themselves. This can happen through reflective conversations, by directing attention to particular aspects of the question or to specifics in the assignment brief.

Providing formative feedback on draft work helps orient students to HE practices in focussed ways. These exchanges can be powerful and empowering; the focus on the student's work and the 'third space' (Hilsdon, 2018) nature of the relationship – where the Learning Developer is not assessing the student but working with them – creates a special relationship that bolsters motivation and improves academic performance (Halawah, 2006; Zepke & Leach, 2010).

How LD Tutorials Work

Typically, students are encouraged to arrive at their tutorial with specific items to discuss and develop: an essay or presentation plan, draft writing, and hopefully the relevant module handbook. The students need to know they are not coming for the answer, as this can lead to over-reliance on academic support staff and hinder the students' independent learning; they are coming to take control of their own learning. The student may not always know what the issue really is – many times they say they want proofreading (which typically we do not do) – but a glance at the work reveals perhaps that they have not understood the question, or that the work itself has not been structured to answer the question well. Here a sensitive conversation is necessary to help the student understand what is needed to meet the learning outcomes.

Workshops: Extracurricular

A stalwart of LD work is the extracurricular workshop offered as a 'one-off' or a coherent programme that students can choose to attend – not to 'fix' the student (Lillis and Turner, 2001), but to help them learn how to learn, which typically they will not have been taught in school. These are usually taught sessions covering topics such as reading, note making, writing, presentation strategies, revision, and exam techniques, and will be active and interactive so that students are drawn into experiencing and reflecting on the strategies that they will need to both understand and thrive at university.

Some Learning Developers 'bundle up' workshops like these, for example as Preparation for HE programmes that students elect to attend before they arrive at university. These are popular with incoming first years, with students who feel that their grades do not reflect their effort, and with international students who want to orient themselves to HE study in the UK. The premise of courses like this is that no one is born knowing how to learn or how to study (Burns and Sinfield, 2004; Burns and Sinfield, 2022), but there are strategies and approaches to active learning that they can learn, to promote criticality, enjoyment of learning, and study success.

Workshops: Embedding and Integrating LD

> So I was invited in to run a session on the essay. I asked the students what they wanted to know and built the whole session by answering their questions. It was great.
>
> (LD staff member)

One way that we as Learning Developers work with both students and staff is to embed a workshop in the curriculum. Here the Learning Developer might deliver a relatively generic workshop on presentations, note making, academic reading, group work in a subject session. The subject-based context makes these sessions arguably more effective and meaningful (Hill and Tinker, 2013).

Integrating LD is a refinement on embedding; here typically the Learning Developer and subject staff member negotiate timetabled space to take forward the learning on the module via a carefully crafted and integrated 'skills' session. This could include a tailored workshop on the assignment or focus on the academic reading required for a particular assignment.

Integrate, Integrate, Integrate

Integrating practice creates a positive learning environment for both students and staff. Where students may have expected to passively receive knowledge and make sense of it away from the taught sessions, they now understand that they are active participants in their learning, co-constructing knowledge with their peers and staff. The staged processes of reading or writing development integrated into a subject session demystify the learning process and allow students the space to raise questions about academic literacies as well as content related ones. There is no separation of skills and knowledge-making; the two unfold in a relational way. Responses from students to such integration are overwhelmingly positive. Furthermore, there is a feeling of accomplishment and a recognition by all that there are practical tools they can take away from the session and repurpose as part of their ongoing practices (Huda, 2022).

Case Study: Academic Reading Circles

One example of integration involves the use of academic reading circles (ARC), developed into a workable model suited to the needs and demands of a widening participation university (Huda, 2022). The structure of the ARC allows students to work in individual and group capacities whilst reading from different lenses: summariser, connector, highlighter, and visualiser. Each activity is scaffolded to unravel the reading process for the student, making reading an accessible endeavour that can be enjoyed as well as being experienced as meaningful.

> This strategy helped me to understand the text better. Group discussions helped me to gain new knowledge. I learnt how to read the texts with a purpose, the different ways to read an article and what to look out for when reading a certain text.
>
> (Student participant)

In a short space of time, an integrated ARC model can take students through a learning curve that perhaps would have seemed impossible before. Many students start the session without any analysis of the text they have been asked to read. However, through engaging in the different reading roles required by an ARC, students develop knowledge and understanding of the text, and are able to demonstrate critical analysis. What is perhaps the most revelatory aspect in delivering this model is that both students and lecturers witness progression in real time and that difficulties around reading are dispelled by discussion and co-constructing understanding, using the ARC scaffolds embedded within the session.

Producing Resources

A key element of LD work is to discover or make resources. These can be the resources we use in our own teaching – to scaffold a workshop for example – or resources that we develop for students to use on their own, or even resources for subject staff to use with their students. A Learning Developer might also develop their own specific resources that contextualise academic conventions within module content, enabling students to meaningfully make direct links between the two and enact Angelo's (1993) principles of Higher Learning. With every interaction, whether it is the one-to-one tutorial or the classroom setting of a workshop, resources may be factored in to support the learning process. They can be used to speak to specific aspects of academic skills or literacies; they can also capture the learning experience within a workshop; they help to reframe concepts and ideas in a way that is accessible; and they provide another datum point for the students, allowing them to cross-reference the information against any guidance notes provided by module leaders. Moreover, they are the physical/digital remnants of the learning and teaching process that students can keep and consult as and when they need to.

Resources also refer to tools that you might use within workshops, tutorials, and presentations. These include Padlet, Mentimeter, virtual learning environments such as Moodle and Weblearn, as well as Kelso or World Cafe. We used to have a supply of one-page resources and longer workbooks that we would fish out of the filing cabinet when running drop-ins or writing cafes and resources that we might devise and develop and put online. If developing an online site yourself, look around at other universities' sites and see how they do it. One that has impressed us recently is the one from Manchester Metropolitan University which uses the web to advertise all their services, to offer accessible resources and teaching videos. The best tip is to make time and space to play with the different tools to see what they can do, and work out how you might like to experiment with using them in your practice.

Contributing to Strategies and Projects

> The Learning Developer does not need to know all the answers to successfully develop a meaningful and engaging project that can grow as more resources are developed and more staff pass through the process.
>
> (LD staff member)

Learning Developers sometimes have opportunities to contribute to wider university initiatives and strategies. We may get called upon to develop resources to integrate academic skills in the curriculum or to run sessions for staff on designing out plagiarism. Projects like these feel relatively comfortable and familiar to us. However, a good way to have reach and impact as a Learning Developer is to volunteer to participate in or lead a big strategic project, even where we may not feel comfortable as 'experts'. The guiding principles for such projects include: gathering a creative team and collaborating to put together a set of made and/or found resources; planning a programme of conversations with staff on the topic; seeding each conversation with prompt resources; holding the conversations in a safe space and not recording it; and building an institutional community of practice with participants to take forward real action (Brazant, 2022; Brazant, 2023).

Conclusion

We always knew that LD could be the practice of freedom (hooks, 2014), albeit one constrained to peripheral and extracurricular roles, often squeezed within too tight curriculum spaces, or managed by university strategic targets, which can make our job feel hard, even impossible. This chapter was written to offer a dialogic space in which to consider some of what our fellow LD practitioners currently do, to offer opportunities for the mapping of LD practice in all its variety and highlight where it might differ in form and content. We hope that this has been only the start of a longer conversation about what Learning Developers do and how they might enact the values of the field through their practice (ALDinHE, 2023).

References

Abegglen, S., Burns, T. and Sinfield, S. (2019) 'It's learning development, Jim – but not as we know it: academic literacies in third space', *Journal of Learning Development in Higher Education*, 15. https://doi.org/10.47408/jldhe.v0i15.500

ALDinHE (2023) *Values*. Available at: https://aldinhe.ac.uk (Accessed: 21 April 23).

Angelo, T. A. (1993) 'A "Teacher's dozen"'. *AAHE Bulletin*, 45(8): 3–7.

Brazant, K. (2022) 'Making space for campus colleagues to think about race as part of pedagogy', *Times Higher Education*, March. Available at: https://www.timeshigher education.com/campus/making-space-academic-colleagues-think-about-race-part-pedagogy (Accessed: 21 April 2023).

Brazant, K. (2023) 'Disrupt the discourse: applying critical race theory as a conceptual framework for learning and teaching', *Equity in Education & Society*. https://doi.org/10.1177/27526461231163325

Burns, T. and Sinfield, S. (2004) *Teaching, Learning and Study Skills: A Guide for Tutors*. London: Sage.

Burns, T. and Sinfield, S. (2022) *Essential Study Skills: The Complete Guide to Success at University*. London: Sage.

Davenport, E. (2022) 'The writing social: identifying with academic practices among undergraduate students', *Investigations in University Teaching and Learning*, 13.

Freire, P. (2007 [1970]) *Pedagogy of the Oppressed*. Translated by M.B. Ramos. New York: Continuum.

Halawah, I. (2006) 'The impact of student-faculty informal interpersonal relationships on intellectual and personal development', *College Student Journal*, 40: 670–678.

Hill, P. and Tinker, A. (2013) 'Integrating learning development into the student experience', *Journal of Learning Development in Higher Education*, 5: 1–18.

Hilsdon, J. (2018) 'Learning Development: pedagogy, principles and progress', *ALDinHE 2018: The Learning Development Conference*, University of Leicester, England, 26–28 March. Abstract available at: http//www.aldinhe.ac.uk/events/leiceister18.html (Accessed 11 August 2019).

hooks, b. (2014) *Teaching to Transgress*. Abingdon: Routledge.

Huda, N. (2022) 'Towards the setting up and evaluation of academic reading circles. A critical commentary on academic reading practices in higher education', *Investigations in University Teaching and Learning*, 13: 1–19.

Leathwood, C. and O'Connell, P. (2003) "It's a struggle": the construction of the "new student" in higher education. *Journal of Education Policy*, 18(6): 597–615.

Lillis, T. and Turner, J. (2001) 'Student writing in higher education: Contemporary confusion, traditional concerns', *Teaching in Higher Education*, 6: 57–68.

Manavipour, D. and Saeedian, Y. (2016) The role of self-compassion and control belief about learning in university students' self-efficacy. *Journal of Contextual Behavioural Science*, 5(2): 121–126.

Pavlov, V., Smirnova, N. V. and Nuzhnaia, E. (2021) 'Beyond the avatar: Using video cameras to achieve effective collaboration in an online second language classroom', *Journal of University Teaching and Learning Practice*, 18(7): 228–241.

Smit, R. (2012) 'Towards a clearer understanding of student disadvantage in higher education: Problematising deficit thinking', *Higher Education Research & Development*, 31(3): 369–380.

Zepke, N. and Leach, L. (2010) 'Beyond hard outcomes: "soft" outcomes and engagement as student success', *Teaching in Higher Education*, 15(6): 661–673. https://doi.org/10.1080/13562517.2010.522084

7

DIVERSITY IN OUR EXPERTISE

Empowering Neurodivergent Students Within
Learning Development

Jennie Dettmer and Karen Welton

A nursing student arrived in tears, distraught at not having completed any work for their deadline in a week. Initially they appeared unmotivated and disorganised, but after further conversation they disclosed their dyslexia. How could you support this neurodivergent student without having an understanding of neurodivergence and the tools needed to successfully empower students? Similarly, would you expect a musician to teach you an instrument they did not know how to play? This chapter will outline some useful tools for successfully supporting and empowering neurodivergent students.

Introduction

Learning Development's (LD) resistance to its perceived alignment with a deficit model has allowed it to evolve into an aspirational service that is integral to student success. The boundaries of the field have expanded, with expectations that Learning Developers are key contributors to an enriched learning experience for all students, resulting in the need for there to be more diversity in our expertise. Learning Developers increasingly work with people who cognitively learn and process information differently than those classified as neurotypical (University of Edinburgh, 2020), due to neurodivergent (ND) students forming the largest group of disabled students in UK HE (Higher Education Statistics Agency, 2023) (see Figure 7.1 for the most common neurodivergencies).

Students often have co-occurring neurodivergencies, with challenges intersecting and overlapping. But, just like everyone else, neurodivergent people have many strengths (see Figure 7.1) because of their ND, not in spite of it, and these are equally important to understand, acknowledge, and discuss with

DOI: 10.4324/9781003433347-10

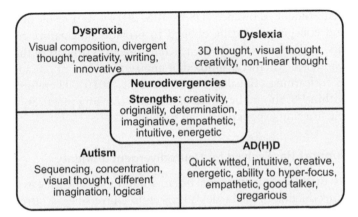

FIGURE 7.1 Co-occurring neurodivergencies showing overlapping strengths (Aquilina and Colly, 2023)

students and the wider community. When recognised and celebrated, these can positively impact confidence, self-esteem, and motivation, leading to students feeling more empowered (Welton, 2023).

As Learning Developers, our exposure to a wide cross-section of an institution's student population provides us with the opportunity to acknowledge and build on these neurodivergent strengths during our everyday interactions with students, in addition to raising awareness of the various facets of ND amongst staff members, some of whom will be neurodivergent themselves. This helps build inclusivity and foster a widespread feeling of student and staff belonging.

The Impact of Legislation Changes on Disabled Students in HE

UK legislation changes may have positively impacted the number of disabled students in HE. Legislation which first mentioned ND in the HE sector was the Disability Discrimination Act (DDA) of 1995. A disabled person was defined as having 'a physical or mental impairment which has a substantial and long-term adverse effect on his ability to carry out normal day-to-day activities' (DDA, 1995), a classification that many neurodivergencies fall within. The Act initially did not cover education, and it was not until an amendment in 2006 that the regulations were brought into HE (Jamieson and Morgan, 2008). For the first time, anti-discrimination practices were introduced into universities, as they were required to give disabled students reasonable adjustments (DDA, 1995). The DDA was superseded by the 2010 Equality Act, which uses the same definition of disability. Additionally, under the Equality Act, disabilities were classified as protected characteristics (Equality Act, 2010).

Due to the introduction of the Equality Act (2010) and technological advancements, there has been a reduction in tailored support being funded by the Disabled Student Allowance (DSA) (BIS, 2014). As a result of this, universities and colleges are legally obliged to provide anticipatory reasonable adjustments, in the form of inclusive teaching practices, to ensure that neurodivergent students (whether diagnosed or undiagnosed) are not disadvantaged by barriers to learning (Equality Challenge Unit, 2010). Therefore, all staff working within HE should be aware of inclusive teaching practices, to ensure an equitable learning experience for all students.

How LD Support Has Evolved for Neurodivergent Students

Support for dyslexic students in HE began around the same time as LD, with the 1993 introduction of the Dyslexia Projects in Universities (Cottrell, 1996). Although these services developed in parallel, there has been a tendency for a lack of synergy between LD and disability services, leading, for example, to siloing good practice. Students need evidence of a formal diagnosis in order to access support through their disability services team and financial and study skills support through the DSA. However, students may find having a diagnosis prohibitive due to costs; additionally, there is often a delay in the support being provided. This leads to those who do not disclose, are undiagnosed, are awaiting specialist support, or receive a diagnosis too late in their studies, requiring support through the LD service. Therefore, Learning Developers should have a good working knowledge of how to support this cohort of students. Sedgwick-Müller et al. (2022) have highlighted that all staff still require further training in attention deficit (hyperactivity) disorder (AD(H)D). This ND has a long waiting time for diagnosis, and contact with formally diagnosed students is subsequently limited, so a resource bank of strategies is lacking.

Attainment of Disabled Students

Another initiative for improving access and maintaining the support in HE for disabled students came into effect in 2005 with the introduction of Access and Participation Plans (APPs). From 2018 five key performance measures (KPMs) were set for universities to use in their plans, with KPM 5 detailing the 'gap in degree outcomes (1sts or 2:1s) between disabled and non-disabled students' (Office for Students (OfS), 2018, p.2). However, only 39% of universities included KPM 5 on their most recent APPs (OfS, 2022). Initially, there was a percentage point gap of 2.8 between disabled and non-disabled students, but a reanalysis of the data found that the gap had decreased to 1.4 percentage points by 2020–21. This was, in part, driven by the COVID-19 pandemic and the no detriment policies introduced by universities, and, as a result, an estimated gap of only 0.4 percentage points should exist by 2024–25 (OfS, 2022).

These figures demonstrate that measures initiated during the COVID-19 pandemic had a positive impact on the attainment gap between disabled and non-disabled students, but, with a return to face-to-face teaching practices, disabled students may no longer receive access to more inclusive learning environments, so it is questionable whether the 0.4 percentage point gap can be achieved. By retaining inclusive learning practices, such as the option of online meetings and recordings of sessions, Learning Developers will be instrumental in ensuring student equity.

The Synergy Between LD Values and Learning Developers' Work with Neurodivergent Students

Although some Learning Developers have a qualification in one or more neurodivergencies, and this is classed as desirable on many LD job role person specifications, in reality most of the knowledge is acquired through directly 'working alongside students to make sense of and get the most out of HE learning' (ALDinHE, 2023). However, it could be argued that students cannot be fully supported in this endeavour unless Learning Developers have a proficient understanding of the ways in which different people's brains work. This can be achieved in a multitude of ways, from formal training in ND, independent research, networking, and collaborative projects, to setting up neurodivergent communities institutionally and for the wider LD community, to explore and exchange ideas related to neurodiversity and inclusivity.

Due to DSA funding changes and neurodivergent students being the largest group of disabled students in HE, the boundaries of the LD role have expanded with a key requirement of 'making HE inclusive through emancipatory practice, partnership working and collaboration' (ALDinHE, 2023). Having an in-depth knowledge of ND enables Learning Developers to evaluate how extensively inclusivity is woven into the fabric of their institution to ensure neurodivergent students are not disadvantaged and, if they are, propose suggestions to change this. With increasing knowledge and experience, Learning Developers are in a unique position, as third space professionals (Webster, 2022), to enact necessary change. This can be achieved by evidencing, through examples from their own practice and a 'commitment to a scholarly approach and research related to Learning Development' (ALDinHE, 2023), the benefits of emancipatory education, not just for neurodivergent people, but for all. Foregrounding the social model of disability over the medical model in education, by acknowledging people are disabled by barriers in society, not by the challenges they may experience due to their ND, was an important step in recognising that equality reduces stigma and discrimination, thus increasing students' sense of belonging and empowerment. Addressing the institutional barriers sometimes present in HE should also positively impact student retention and satisfaction levels, key areas of institutional agendas.

Since there is no requirement for formal training in neurodiversity, some universities share the lived experiences of staff and students through good practice guides, training materials, and involvement in the annual Neurodiversity Celebration Week. Providing the opportunity for all voices to permeate HE institutions educates everyone, not just those in LD roles, so inclusion becomes more integrated and automatic, not only through practice but through 'critical self-reflection, on-going learning and a commitment to professional development' (ALDinHE, 2023). Learning Developers should never stop learning; the parameters of the role have and will continue to constantly shift with new developments in government and external policies, teaching and learning pedagogies, technology, and the expectations and needs of students.

It is accepted pedagogical practice to integrate anticipatory reasonable adjustments, as standard practice promotes equality, although it is important to remember that everyone is a unique individual and should be treated as such. There are a few small, but key, adjustments that can be made to all HE practices to make them more inclusive, such as creating accessible teaching resources, recording lectures, and using plain language in teaching (Office of the Independent Adjudicator for Higher Education, 2017).

Strategies to Empower Neurodivergent Students

A core part of the LD role is spent providing advice, guidance, and feedback to students on the academic literacy practices they are required to be proficient in. We have observed that strategies which help neurodivergent students engage in these practices are often beneficial for all students.

Confidence

Whilst neurodivergent students may benefit from strategies to overcome their academic difficulties, Learning Developers can also help to improve students' confidence in regard to their performance and assessment (Welton, 2023). According to Stankov, Morony, and Lee (2014), confidence is the best non-cognitive predictor of academic achievement. Building students' self-esteem and positivity can be achieved by finding opportunities to praise and celebrate their successes, no matter how small. Recording and reflecting on these achievements should also allow students to take credit for their own successes (McLoughlin and Leather, 2013). McLoughlin and Leather (2013) also highlight that once a neurodivergent student's strengths are identified, coupled with an achievement of their short-terms goals and positive progress, the student's self-confidence should increase. Working with students to improve their confidence should therefore have a positive impact on their academic performance.

In our LD sessions we can assist autistic students in reducing their uncertainty by, for example, creating a study schedule around their existing commitments and interests. This can help to reduce their anxiety and make their days more structured; once their anxiety is reduced and confidence increased, they are better able to focus on their studying activities (Beadle-Brown and Mills, 2018). Likewise, McLoughlin and Leather (2013) postulate that creating realistic schedules, reflecting on the successes, and rewarding dyslexic students increase both motivation and confidence. It is important to work in conjunction with students to create personalised schedules and not to make any assumptions about how and when they best study (McLoughlin and Leather, 2013).

Reading

To aid retention of information when reading, and to help with focusing on finding relevant and credible material, the active reading strategy of SQ3R (Survey, Question, Read, Recite, Review) is particularly useful. Other helpful reading tips: compile a glossary of academic and subject specific terminology including definitions and familiar synonyms encountered throughout the learning journey; text-to-speech enables material to be listened to (there are various free extensions available, for example, Read Aloud); find easy ways to engage with denser material such as using YouTube to explore the topic first; coloured overlays and reading rulers (both physical and digital) can alleviate eye strain/movement of letters; the Cornell Note Taking method provides a structure for recording information, although mind mapping can be an equally effective method, especially when combined with colour-coding (BDA, 2020).

Writing

Writing can be challenging for many different reasons: lack of experience; difficulty with structuring and organising ideas; sentence construction and grammar anomalies; inability to transfer words from the brain to the fingertips; poor motor skills; a reduction in short-term or working memory. Some methods to support writing can include: frameworks providing key headings for each section or example ideas indicating what the topic sentence of each paragraph could focus on (this not only helps with content and structure, it also means that students do not need to hold ideas in their head in any kind of sequence; they can capture them immediately, removing much of the pressure that can be caused by the fear of forgetting); mind mapping can encourage ideas to flow in an ad hoc form with colour-coding employed later to connect topics together for further consideration; speech-to-text enables thoughts to be spoken and directly translated to words via technology (BDA, 2020).

Communities of Practice

Although experienced Learning Developers are well placed to impart knowledge about ND and assist students in identifying strategies that can help make academic literacies easier to grasp and navigate, communities of practice that focus on a particular ND are beneficial to students as they encourage sharing of experiences, challenges, strategies, and strengths, leading to a greater sense of belonging (Welton, 2023). They are a very useful platform for Learning Developers to act as facilitators rather than scaffolders in the learning process which encourages an increased level of student autonomy and collegiality.

ALDinHE Neurodiversity/Inclusivity Community of Practice

In June 2021, we initiated the ALDinHE Neurodiversity/Inclusivity Community of Practice for professionals, working within the fields of neuro-diversity and inclusivity to 'adopt and share effective Learning Development practice with (and external to) our own institutions' (ALDinHE, 2023). Through engaging and lively discussions, we have shared, and built upon, existing knowledge within the key areas of terminology and identity; education and training; research; disclosure; and funding. We acknowledge the lack of neurodiversity education at many universities and the difficulty for Learning Developers, and all other student facing staff, in acquiring information and best practice examples relating to ND. It is our intention, as a community endeavour, to collate and regularly review neurodiversity resources that will be hosted on the ALDinHE website, so the diversity in our expertise can permeate throughout the wider HE landscape.

Conclusion

Throughout this chapter, we have highlighted why it has been necessary for Learning Developers to include an understanding of ND and how this specialism can have a positive impact on the learning and teaching of all university students. As discussed, neurodivergent students are the largest group of disabled students in HE due, in part, to legislation changes first introduced in 2006 when the Disability Discrimination Act 1995 was amended to include education, resulting in individual reasonable adjustments being provided. However, as evidenced by the lack of KPM 5 on the latest APPs, many universities do not have targets for disabled students and therefore it is unclear how and if they are supported in these universities.

The introduction of the Equality Act (2010), in addition to technological advancements, led to DSA financial support being reduced. Furthermore, DSA support costs and timescales have left many neurodivergent students seeking specialist support from LD. Adding to these numbers are students who are undiagnosed or unaware that they are neurodivergent. Universities are legally required to adopt anticipatory reasonable adjustments to create inclusive learning environments, ensuring that no student is disadvantaged. Some universities understand the importance of this and prioritise training for staff to ensure this is adhered to. Nevertheless, through our ALDinHE

Neurodiversity/Inclusivity Community of Practice it has become apparent that this is not the case for many. This is the reason why access to educational resources exploring ND is paramount and the justification for this being the community's principal project.

Although formal training in ND is the ideal, in reality this is not an area which many Learning Developers specialise in, due to financial and time constraints. However, an in-depth awareness of ND can be acquired through working alongside neurodivergent students to understand different academic literacy strategies. Learning Developers can also adopt and share good practice, critically self-reflect on their teaching and learning of neurodivergent students and read academic literature around the topic, suggestions that link to the ALDinHE values. This chapter has demonstrated that having diversity in our expertise is beneficial, not only to empower neurodivergent students, but for all students to thrive and succeed in HE.

References

ALDinHE (2023) *Values*. Available at: https://aldinhe.ac.uk/about-aldinhe/ (Accessed: 3 April 2023).

Aquilina, J. and Colly, M. (2023) *What is neurodiversity?* Available at: https://neuroknowhow.com/what-is-neurodiversity/ (Accessed: 30 January 2023).

BDA (2020) 'Practical Strategies for Reading and Writing' [Recorded lecture]. *British Dyslexia Association*. 01 February. Available at: https://learn.bdadyslexia.org.uk/#/ (Accessed: 01 February 2020).

Beadle-Brown, J. and Mills, R. (2018) *Understanding and Responding to Autism: The SPELL Framework: Learners Workbook*, 2nd edn, Hove: Pavilion Publishing and Media Ltd.

BIS (2014) *Higher Education: Student Support: Changes to Disabled Students' Allowances (DSA)*. Available at: https://www.gov.uk/government/speeches/higher-education-student-support-changes-to-disabled-students-allowances-dsa (Accessed: 29 January 2023).

Cottrell, S. (1996) 'Supporting students with specific learning difficulties (dyslexia)', in S. Wolfendale and J. Corbett (eds) *Opening Doors: Learning Support in Higher Education*. London: Cassell.

Disability Discrimination Act (1995) *c.50*. Available at: https://www.legislation.gov.uk/ukpga/1995/50/section/1 (Accessed: 26 January 2023).

Equality Act (2010) *c.1*. Available at: http://www.legislation.gov.uk/ukpga/2010/15/section/6 (Accessed: 20 January 2023).

Equality Challenge Unit. (2010) *Managing Reasonable Adjustments in Higher Education*. Available at: https://s3.eu-west-2.amazonaws.com/assets.creode.advancehe-document-manager/documents/ecu/managing-reasonable-adjustments-in-higher-education_1578587125.pdf (Accessed: 13 April 2023).

Higher Education Statistics Agency. (2023) *Who's Studying in HE? Personal Characteristics*. Available at: https://www.hesa.ac.uk/data-and-analysis/students/whos-in-he/characteristics#breakdown (Accessed: 30 March 2023).

Jamieson, C. and Morgan, E. (2008) *Managing Dyslexia at University*. Abingdon: Routledge.

McLoughlin, D. and Leather, C. (2013) *The Dyslexic Adult: Interventions and Outcomes: An Evidence-Based Approach*, 2nd edn. Chichester: British Psychological Society and John Wiley and Sons Ltd.

Office of the Independent Adjudicator for Higher Education. (2017) *The Good Practice Framework: Supporting Disabled Students*. Available at: https://www.oiahe.org.uk/media/1039/oia-good-practice-framework-supporting-disabled-students.pdf (Accessed: 11 January 2023).

OfS (2018) Annex D: The Development of Access and Participation Plans. Available at: https://www.officeforstudents.org.uk/media/8af8fb0f-6562-4d18-aa27-ca95552cbdf3/bd-2018-december-41-access-and-participation-annex-d.pdf (Accessed: 21 December 2022).

OfS (2022) Analysis of Access and Participation Plan Targets in Relation to OfS Key Performance Measures: 2022 Update. Available at: https://www.officeforstudents.org.uk/media/19091a2e-e1ad-4832-9207-938ef63e38d0/analysis-of-ap-plan-targets-in-relation-to-ofs-kpms.pdf (Accessed: 21 December 2022).

Sedgwick-Müller, J.A., Müller-Sedgwick, U., Adamou, M., Cantani, M., Champ, R., GudjÓnsson, G., Hank, D., Pitts, M., Young, S. and Asherson, P. (2022) 'University students with attention deficit hyperactivity disorder (ADHD): a consensus statement from the UK Adult ADHD Network', *BMC Psychiatry*, 22: 292–319.

Stankov, L., Morony, S. and Lee, Y.P. (2014) 'Confidence: the best non-cognitive predictor of academic achievement?', *Educational Psychology*, 34: 9–28.

The University of Edinburgh (2020) Support for Neurodiversity. Available at: https://www.ed.ac.uk/equality-diversity/disabled-staff-support/neurodiversity-support (Accessed: 30 March 2023).

Webster, H. (2022) 'Supporting the development, recognition and impact of third-space professionals', in: E. McIntosh and D. Nutt (eds), *The Impact of the Integrated Practitioner in Higher Education: Studies in Third Space Professionalism*. Abingdon: Routledge.

Welton, K. (2023) 'Dyslexia in higher education: enhancing student belonging and overcoming barriers to achievement through communities of practice', *Journal of Learning Development in Higher Education*, 26: 1–7.

8

TEACHING WRITING IN LEARNING DEVELOPMENT

Ursula Canton

Once upon a time the flowers on our campuses were home to fairies, who were summoned by teachers despairing about their students' writing. A few specks of their precious fairy dust brought forth elegant prose and let critical thinking flourish in an instant. One day the evil sorcerer Constructivismus put a spell on them: they turned into Learning Developers who claimed precious teaching time and said writing needed toil and graft. But sometimes, when the lamenting stops, and students and teachers forget that once there was sparkly fairy dust that would bring miraculous writing inspiration, a little magic that makes texts flourish can still happen in the classes of our all too human Learning Developers.

For some Learning Developers, their background in linguistics or other disciplines with a strong focus on language will make working on writing with students feel like home territory; for others, it will be less comfortable as they rely mainly on their own experience as writers. Yet, most of us will work with students on their writing. Sometimes we work with students on ways in which they can use 'writing to learn', for example, through note-taking or reflective writing that helps them strengthen their learning. Often, we help them 'learn to write' (Parker and Goodkin, 1987) in their assessments. Both processes are essential for successful participation in higher education (HE). This chapter provides an introduction to the teaching of writing in Learning Development for those who are beginning to develop their teaching practice in this field, while offering those more familiar an overview of relevant literature to explore further.

DOI: 10.4324/9781003433347-11

What Is Writing for Us (and What Is It Not)

Although most Learning Developers will agree that they work on 'writing' with students, they are not all working on the same things, let alone in the same way. The term 'writing' is inherently fuzzy and covers a wide range of meanings, so clarification is needed to develop our teaching, and to explain what we teach.

A first important distinction is the notion of writing as a product, that is, texts, and writing as an activity. The stability of texts, compared to the fleeting nature of the writing process, means that for a long time, research into writing focussed mainly on written texts, for example, in genre studies (Bazerman et al., 2009), as did the teaching of writing in English for Academic Purposes (EAP) (Swales, 1990) or introductory writing courses in the United States (Benson et al., 2013). Teaching students about different genres and text forms is indeed important (Wingate and Tribble, 2012), not least because they tend to focus on the product to be submitted.

Nonetheless, the writing process often takes a more prominent place in Learning Development, because we know that declarative knowledge (Biggs and Tang, 2007, p.7) about texts is not sufficient to successfully manage the process of generating texts. Sharing this focus on working with writers on writing processes is important, because it helps to avoid misunderstandings regarding proofreading, which aims at improving the product directly. Beyond pedagogical reasons, this focus reflects shifts in writing research, where interests have also shifted towards 'the relationship between the text and the activity of people in situations where texts are used' (Russell et al., 2009).

Writing processes can be considered from different angles, focussing on the individual writer and the cognitive processes involved in generating texts, or on the social interaction between writer and readers. For teaching, both are relevant, as writers have to 'reconcile psychological and social processes in every act of writing' (Bazerman, 2017, p.21), an insight that has also led to calls for greater cross-fertilisation between these often separate research traditions (Hayes, 2017, p.xiv). In the following section, I will introduce relevant aspects of both perspectives before demonstrating how their combination can inform teaching practice.

The cognitive approach to writing, prevalent in fields such as (educational) psychology, psycholinguistics, or writing studies, considers writing as 'a set of distinctive thinking processes which writers orchestrate or organise during the act of composing' (Flower and Hayes, 1981, p.366). According to Bereiter and Scardamalia's seminal study (1987), the complexity of these decision-making processes depends on the type of writing. Many simple texts can be generated by choosing relevant content and appropriate linguistic forms to fill an existing 'mould' or text form. A good example for this knowledge-telling approach (Bereiter and Scardamalia, 1987) is recipes, where writers simply have to list ingredients and then describe the process of preparing them in chronological order. Our students are all familiar with this approach, but can find it challenging to work on assignments that require the more complex approach of knowledge-transforming writing, that is, creating texts for which no pre-existing mould exists. Here writers need to negotiate the possibilities given by their knowledge of textual possibilities and their knowledge of relevant content in order to create a structure that achieves their communicative goals in a manner that is appropriate for their intended audience. The difference between these two activities is useful in helping students understand why remaining within the comfort of their usual approach is often insufficient to approach more complex assignments.

Unlike Bereiter and Scardamalia, other researchers do not distinguish different composition processes, but focus on the decision-making involved in all of them. These models commonly distinguish three different processes, although their names for them differ. The terms used by Deane et al. (2008) are probably those writers can most easily relate to: planning, drafting, and revising. Horning's (1993) labels (pre-writing, writing, and re-writing) are often used in writing textbooks, but the suggested chronological order is misleading. Although planning needs to start before writing (Alamargot and Chanquoy, 2001, p.89), which, in turn, has to start before revising, writers then switch between the three mental processes (Kellogg et al., 2013, p.161). This switching between processes has to be 'coordinat[ed] and control[led]' (Kellogg and Whiteford, 2009, p.255), so writers need to develop their 'control level' (Hayes, 2012) or 'central executive' (Kellogg, 1996; 2013).

While cognitive models help us understand the different types of activities writers need to be able to do and co-ordinate, they do not tell us what skills and knowledge writers need to do this well. A notable exception here is Grabe and Kaplan (1996). The problem is their focus on individual writers without considering the external influences that shape their decision-making. Although Hayes (1996) presents an updated cognitive model that explicitly includes social contexts, there is still relatively little research that considers both aspects (Portanova et al., 2017). This blind spot in cognitive research into writing seems to echo the attitudes students or colleagues express when they ask me for advice on 'good' writing, assuming there is a way to 'get it right' independent of context.

To address this misunderstanding in our teaching, we can borrow from other research traditions, such as discourse analysis, that are based on the premise that (oral and written) language is used to 'to scaffold performance of social activities ... and to scaffold human affiliation within cultures and social groups and institutions' (Gee, 1999, p.1). In other words, how we write shapes our interaction with others and the way others see us. From this perspective, a key aspect of our teaching is to help writers 'engag[e their readers] in appropriate ways, [to] create the social interactions which make our texts effective' (Hyland, 2005, p.ix). Focussing on interactions means looking at textual elements, as well as the sociocultural practices in which they are produced and used. In critical discourse analysis (Fairclough, 1995) this includes a commitment to critically investigate these social contexts and the silent assumptions and power relationships in them, and new literacies research (Gee, 2007) and related fields examine the role social influences play in the acquisition of literacies (e.g., Prinsloo and Baynham, 2008).

Research into 'academic literacies' in HE takes a similar critical stance: Lea and Street's (1998) canonical article clearly sets an academic literacies approach apart from both a study skills approach that sees writing as decontextualised and an acculturation approach, which assumes that writers adopt the conventions of their (discourse) environment simply through interaction with it. Academic literacies encompasses grammar and conventions, but makes them visible and questions the social structures reflected in them. Its commitment to inclusivity and diversity in HE could explain its popularity among Learning Developers. If we follow the common perception that writing problems stem from the language student writers use or do not use (Lillis and Turner, 2001), we indirectly make a judgement about these students, because language is such an important 'mediating mechanism in the social construction of identity' (Ivanič, 1998, p.18). Critically investigating the social conventions, structures, and interests that underlie dominant writing practices (Richards and Pilcher, 2018) allows us to work with students in a way that does not challenge their 'sense of identity and legitimacy as students' (Gourlay, 2009, p.187). Applying this approach to teaching means that in addition to helping students navigate the different aspects of the writing process, we need to help them navigate their place in complex social structures.

Applying This Definition to Teaching

Understanding writing as a process that creates knowledge and shapes social relationships has important implications for teaching. First of all, it means that we need to challenge the common assumptions among our students (and often colleagues) that 'it is *just* the writing' they find difficult. We need to explain that the writing process is an important step of developing subject knowledge, because transforming knowledge to create a text supports their progress from retrieval of knowledge towards analytical understanding (Marzano, 2001). Institutional structures can support or hinder this aspect of our teaching. Embedding the teaching of writing into core curricula through collaboration with subject lecturers reinforces the message that it is a complex process, closely linked to disciplinary learning. Changing less helpful structures, like short one-off consultations or big generic lectures, will often be beyond the influence of Learning Developers, but we can still see lobbying for evidence-based teaching to be part of our roles.

The need to connect the teaching of writing to students' engagement with their subjects also arises from the profoundly social nature of writing. Even if it can seem to be a solitary activity, students build their identity in their chosen fields at least partly through initially peripheral participation (Lave and Wenger, 1991) in written discourse. The degree of embedding these learning processes into their curricula can be debated (Wingate et al., 2011), but they cannot happen independently of their subject learning. A common response to institutional structures that hinder embedding writing into subject curricula is to teach only generic aspects, such as grammar or punctuation. While reducing the scope of our teaching to such a study skills approach might seem a pragmatic adaptation to circumstances, it privileges customer satisfaction over learning (Richards and Pilcher, 2020). An alternative option is to adopt Lea and Street's wider approach and find ways to help students understand how written communication facilitates social interaction in our individual teaching. Inspiration for this could come from calls to develop meta-awareness (Anson and Moore, 2017, p.353) in the Elon Statement (2015) or literature on teaching for transfer (Wardle, 2012) in the United States, as well as the concept of critical language awareness developed earlier in the UK (Clark and Ivanič, 1991).

In the following, I will present some examples of learning activities that model negotiating a place in (discourse) communities. Without disciplinary expertise, we can be mediators or guides in students' exploration of their disciplinary discourses, i.e., we need to use a pedagogy of teaching *how* rather than teaching *what*. When teaching the use of sources, for example, we cannot tell students what canonical sources in different subjects are, or what would be considered general knowledge as opposed to material that needs to be supported with sources. We can, however, use reading, recommended directly by subject lecturers or through module reading lists, and explore how sources are used in these texts with our students. Almost more important than finding answers to these questions is sharing and modelling the process of searching for them, as this enables our students to explore new discourses on their own in the future. In Lillis's terms (2001, p.158), we are establishing dialogues to 'make language visible' with individual students or groups.

Alternatively, we could remove the in-text references from excellent essays or journal papers and discuss where our students feel support from sources would be needed. Comparing their version to the original gives them a better sense of how their own choices compare to those of someone who is doing well at their level of study (good essay), or to experts in the field (journal paper). We can show them how to use the same tool for their writing by planning with two columns: one for their argument and one to add evidence, thus scaffolding the writing process in a dialogue 'aimed at populating the student-writer's text with their own intentions' (Lillis, 2001, p.158). At the same time, they learn how to do this in a manner that will meet the expectations of readers in their field, so we are talking them into specific literacy practice

(Lillis (2001) uses the term 'essayist literacy practice', but the broader label I use here covers a bigger range of subjects and text forms). These activities have been successfully used in big lectures, which shows that modelling the exploration of textual conventions and connecting them to social practices and expectations is possible in such formats. Even a class meant to focus primarily on the mechanics of referencing can maintain this focus if it derives the specific mechanisms used from the (shared) values that underpin the specific conventions, particularly transparency.

What is harder to achieve in bigger groups, because students feel less comfortable to speak in a tentative, searching way, is to challenge them to 'talk back' (Lillis, 2011) and challenge prevailing writing conventions and their underlying values. Nonetheless, 'rais[ing] critical awareness of those norms to encourage contestation' (Ganobcsik-Williams, 2006, p.11) is still possible. A good example is a class on lab reports, a highly prescriptive genre. Focussing on the reasons for textual conventions, for example, the need to be precise to facilitate replication of an experiment, gives student agency to decide themselves how much detail they want – or do not want – to provide for their readers at different points of the text. Participating in discussions on whether specific details are necessary for replication challenges them to develop greater agency as authors than following a simple checklist would do.

The examples from teaching practice described above show how Learning Developers can use a pedagogy of *how*, even with bigger groups and in subject areas with which they are not familiar. They demonstrate that we do not need to restrict ourselves to teaching generic mechanics of referencing or lists of 'dos and don'ts' for lab reports. Teaching in a way that reflects a complex understanding of writing, we can reflect the insights from writing research even within environments and for topics that make it tempting to yield to the pressures of students, colleagues, and institutions to quickly import relevant declarative knowledge.

Being evidence-based is a strong argument in favour of such an approach to teaching in itself, but it is not the only one. Teaching *how* to explore textual encounters and learn from them also fosters independent learning, a key expectation in HE (Gow and Kember, 1990). The pragmatic argument that Learning Developers cannot bring expertise in all subjects, however, can seem almost threatening – could we be replaced by others with dual expertise in writing and a discipline? The strongest way to address these worries is perhaps not the small number of people who can offer dual expertise, but the type of writing we teach.

If we see writing as a social act, we also need to consider with whom our students will and want to interact through writing. As the label suggests, most of the literature in the academic literacies tradition focuses on their writing as students. While our students' current writing challenges take place in HE, few of them aspire to becoming full members of academic discourse communities.

One way in which many of our students would contest prevailing values and conventions in academic writing, therefore, concerns the importance we attach to them. They might be central for us; for our students, they constitute a necessary step on the way to joining their professional (discourse) communities. Expanding our teaching to professional writing skills can be a form of respecting their agency in choosing their own positions as writers (Canton et al., 2018). We can strive to learn about the differences between academic and professional discourses through relevant research (Dias et al., 1999), or direct contact with industry. Nonetheless, the world of work our students will eventually enter is so diverse that it clearly defies any expectation that anyone could teach how to communicate through writing in every corner of this world from a position of expertise. We can, however, strive to prepare them for it by teaching them *how* they can engage with the new discourse they will inevitably encounter in future professional discourse communities.

References

Alamargot, D. and Chanquoy, L. (2001) *Through the Models of Writing*. Dordrecht: Kluwer.

Anson, C.M. and Moore, J.L. (2017) *Critical Transitions. Writing and the Question of Transfer*. Fort Collins: University Press of Colorado.

Bazerman, C. (2017) 'The psychology of writing situated within social action: an empirical and theoretical programme', in: P. Portanova, M. Rifenburg and D. Rosen (eds) *Contemporary Perspectives on Cognition and Writing*. Fort Collins: University Press of Colorado.

Benson, N., Corbett, S. J., Cox, A., Higgins, W., Kish, R., LaFrance, M. and Whittingham, K. (2013) 'Rethinking first year English as first year writing across the curriculum', *Double Helix*, 1.

Bereiter, C. and Scardamalia, M. (eds) (1987) *The Psychology of Written Composition*. New York: Routledge.

Biggs, J. and Tang, C. (2007) *Teaching for Quality Learning at University. What the Student Does*. 3rd edn. Maidenhead: Open UP and McGraw Hill.

Canton, U., Govan, M. and Zahn, D. (2018) 'Re-thinking academic literacies. A conceptual development based on teaching practice', *Teaching in Higher Education* 23(6): 668–684. https://doi.org/10.1080/13562517.2017.1414783

Deane, P., Odendahl, N., Quinlan, T., Folwes, M., Welsh, C. and Bivens-Tantum, J. (2008) 'Cognitive models of writing: writing proficiency as complex integrated skills', *ETS*. Available at: http://www.ets.org/research/policy_research_reports/publications/report/2008/htxo (Accessed: 12 February 2023).

Dias, P., Freedman, A., Medway, P. and Paré, A. (1999) *World Apart. Acting and Writing in Academic and Workplace Contexts*. New Jersey: Lawrence Erlbaum Associates.

Elon Statement on Writing Transfer (2015) Available at: http://www.centerforengagedlearning.org/elon-statement-on-writing-transfer (Accessed: 28 November 2022).

Fairclough, N. (1995) *Critical Discourse Analysis. The Critical Study of Language*. Harlow: Longman.

Flower, L. S. and Hayes, J. R. (1981) 'A cognitive theory of writing', *College Composition and Communication*, 32(4): 365–387.

Ganobcsik-Williams, L. (ed.) (2006) *Teaching Academic Writing in UK Higher Education. Theories, Practices and Models*. Houndsmill: Palgrave.

Gee, J. P. (2007) *Social Linguistics and Literacies: Ideologies and Discourses*. 3rd edn. New York: Routledge.

Gee, J. P. (1999) *An Introduction to Discourse Analysis. Theory and Method*. London: Routledge.

Gow, L. and Kember, D. (1990) 'Does higher education promote independent learning?', *Higher Education*, 19: 307–322.

Grabe, W. and Kaplan, R.B. (1996) *Theory and Practice of Writing*. Harlow: Pearson.

Gourlay, L. (2009) 'Threshold practices: becoming a student through academic literacies', *London Review of Education*, 7(2): 181–192.

Hayes, J.R. (1996) 'A new framework for understanding cognition and affect in writing', in: M.C. Levy and S. Ransdell (eds), *The Science of Writing. Theories, Methods, Individual Differences and Applications*. Mahwah, NJ: Lawrence Erlbaum.

Hayes, J.R. (2017) 'Foreword', in: P. Portanova, M. Rifenburg and D. Rosen (eds), *Contemporary Perspectives on Cognition and Writing*. Fort Collins: University Press of Colorado.

Horning, A. S. (1993) *The Psycholinguistics of Readable Writing*. Norwood, NJ: Ablex Publishing.

Hyland, K. (2013) 'Writing in the university: Education, knowledge and reputation', *Language Teaching*, 46(1): 53–70.

Hyland, K. (2005) *Metadiscourse: Exploring Interaction in Writing*. London: Continuum.

Kellogg, R. T., Whiteford, A. P., Turner, C. E., Cahill, M. and Mertens, A. (2013) 'Working memory in written composition: a progress report', *Journal of Writing Research*, 5(2): 159–190.

Kellogg, R.T. and Whiteford, A.P. (2009) 'Training advanced writing skills: the case for deliberate practice', *Educational Psychologist*, 44(4): 250–266.

Lave, J. and Wenger, E. (1991) *Situated Learning: Legitimate Peripheral Participation*. Cambridge: UP.

Lillis, T.M. (2001) *Student Writing: Access, Regulation, Desire*. London: Routledge.

Marzano, R.J. (2001) *Designing a New Taxonomy of Educational Objectives*. Thousand Oaks, CA: Corwin Press.

Parker, R.P. and Goodkin, V. (1987) *The Consequences of Writing: Enhancing Learning in the Disciplines*. Upper Montclair, NJ: Boynton/Cook.

Russell, D.R., Lea, M., Parker, J., Street, B. and Donahue, T. (2009) 'Exploring notions of genre in "academic literacies" and "writing across the curriculum": approaches across countries and contexts', in C. Bazerman A. Bonini and D. Figueiredo (eds), *Genre in a Changing World. Perspectives on Writing*. Fort Collins, CO: Parlor Press.

Portanova, P., Rifenburg, M. and Rosen, D. (eds) (2017) *Contemporary Perspectives on Cognition and Writing*. Fort Collins: University Press of Colorado.

Prinsloo, M. and Baynham, M. (2008) *Literacies Global and Local*. Amsterdam: John Benjamins.

Richards, K. and Pilcher, N. (2020) 'Study skills: neoliberalism's perfect Tinkerbell', *Teaching in HE*, 28(3): 580–585.

Richards, K. and Pilcher, N. (2018) 'Academic literacies: the word is not enough', *Teaching in Higher Education*, 23(2): 162–177.

Swales, J. M. (1990) *Genre Analysis. English in Academic and Research Settings.* Cambridge: Cambridge University Press.

Wardle, E. (ed) (2012) Special Issue: Composition and transfer. *Composition Forum.* Available at: https://compositionforum.com/issue/26/ (Accessed: 20 April 2023).

Wingate, U., Andon, N. and Cogo, A. (2011) 'Embedding academic writing into subject teaching: a case study', *Active Learning in Higher Education*, 12: 69.

Wingate, U. and Tribble, C. (2012) 'The best of both worlds? Towards an English for academic purposes/academic literacies writing pedagogy', *Studies in Higher Education*, 37(4): 481–495.

9

EMPOWERING AND ENABLING

Leveraging Technology for a Student-Centred Future

Debbie Holley and David Biggins

In a research study looking at attitudes to embedding TEL, it was clear that technology was very much about person centred approaches: rather than focus on the technology, we all want to ensure the best possible learning experience for our students. Instead of being on different sides of the student support divide, Learning Developers can find advocates and supporters within the TEL communities.

Introduction

Learning Developers populate a hybridity of spaces in universities and draw across professional and academic staff in developing emancipatory practice to inform and enhance the student experience (Abegglen et al., 2019). Whitchurch, in her seminal work on third space professionals, identifies that Learning Developers practise in support of the student experience, such as tutoring, programme design, study skills, and academic literacy (Whitchurch, 2018, p.1). With Learning Development's (LD) colonisation of third spaces, the new opportunities of space and place create fluidity and flexibility in engaging with students. As such, the LD role creates myriad opportunities and challenges, some of which can be mediated through developments in technology.

This chapter is structured around the conceptual model in Figure 9.1. First, we discuss what a digital future may look like and from this distil the affordances of technology. Next, we address the challenges that constrain how the affordances can be leveraged for beneficial student outcomes, through the lens of inequality, constraints, and the student voice. The vital role that Learning

DOI: 10.4324/9781003433347-12

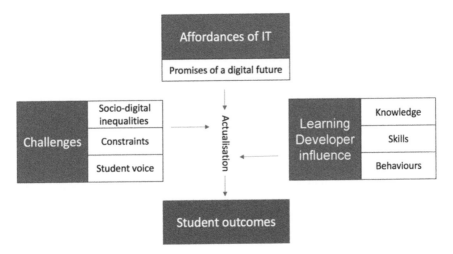

FIGURE 9.1   Conceptual framework showing the key role of Learning Developers

Developers have in influencing the actualisation of the affordances and minimising the potential challenges by using their knowledge, skills, and behaviour forms the central tenet of the work.

The Affordances of Technology and Promises of a Digital Future

The promises of a digital future are portrayed with images of smiling students, engaged staff, and seamless hybrid deliveries, beamed out from numerous university websites by those selling these promises. The lens of the Educause Horizon Report™ (2022) focuses on the impact of Learning Analytics and Big Data, the post-COVID return to the classroom, and challenges of hybrid/ online delivery to generation alpha students, expecting the best of both, and framing the debate in the wider context of the digital economy. The student view at national (Higher Education England) level can be assessed through the JISC Student Digital Experiences Insights report (2022b), which shows students wishing to have access to engaging, well-designed materials that support and enhance their learning. However, 43% of students report low-quality materials and despite many (68%) agreeing that online learning was convenient, it was the lack of community (41%) that was the key issue for many. Students turned to each other for support with digital skills, and under half (47%) approached staff. Only 33% had a formal digital skills training needs analysis. The ways in which our students access materials are changing. The OFCOM Online Nation Report (2022) points to increasing online access via smartphones with young adults (90%); and younger adults are also more likely to only use a smartphone to go online, with a third of 25- to 34-year-olds reporting this as the only way they go online.

Interestingly, the latest Jisc Teaching Insights Survey (2022a) reports 89% of teaching staff delivering at least some of their teaching from home, expressing similar difficulties as students relating to access. More than half of respondents experienced problems teaching online, and 42% cited poor Wi-Fi connection. Only 55% of teaching staff said they were supported to access online platforms and services off site, and the major platform all use, the Virtual Learning Environment (91%). The use of the VLE as a portal to authentic teaching, learning, and assessment experiences such as Virtual Reality, Augmented Reality, and Extended Reality is limited, and with the metaverse being anticipated to become the next generation of the internet, there is a disjunct between student expectations and staff offerings. The metaverse can be defined as:

> persistent 3D virtual space in which users can interact with computer-generated environments and other users. They can be viewed through conventional interfaces such as mobile phones, TVs and monitors, but also through immersive technologies such as augmented and virtual reality.
>
> (OFCOM, 2022, p.49)

Until staff develop a skill set in teaching through these fast-emerging technologies, it is difficult to see any significant breakthrough, according to the Delphi Panel of experts contributing to the State of XR and Immersive Learning Outlook Report (2021).

Challenges to Realising the Affordances of Technology

Digital inclusion is defined by the United Nations (UN) as 'Equitable, meaningful, and safe access to use, lead, and design of digital technologies, services, and associated opportunities for everyone, everywhere' (UN Round Table). In the UK, structural inequalities in access to higher education have been identified by the Office for Students in their Digital Poverty Report (2020). This cites disadvantages for those from Black and Minority Ethnic (BAME), low-income backgrounds, and students with a disability. Of particular concern was 4% of students who reported no internet access was possible; this equates to 104,000 students across English Higher Education institutions (HEIs) during the pandemic. Other studies point to education and health inequalities; work by Liu (2021) identifies intersectionality as significant with BAME females with lower social status having the lowest computer/smartphone ownership. Thus, inequality of access is complex and societal factors have influence across the lives of the excluded.

The framing of inequality ranges from work by Diaz Andrade and Techatassanasoontorn (2020, p.185), who call for a deeper critique of moving access online. Their view of digital is that we are becoming an 'enforced' digital society, which is 'the process of dispossession that reduces choices for individuals who prefer to minimise access to the internet, or even to live offline'. These authors point to technology not being benign or innocent, pointing to national governments and large technology companies displaying what Foucault (1975) would call forms of power that subject human beings to technical control. A more nuanced approach to digital inequality of access is called for by Ragnedda et al. (2022); not a dichotomy of access/no access, but a consideration of the degree to which e-inclusion improves wellbeing for individuals, community, and society. Helsper (2021) provides Learning Developers with a useful lens to understand the effect of inequalities on student opportunities and engagement. By encompassing inequalities of access, literacy, and engagement, Helsper offers contextual factors relating to the economic, social, personal, and cultural resources which can benefit/disadvantage the learner. Helsper suggests that small, bottom-up changes can create widespread improvements because all users in that group benefit. Learning Developers can work to identify the challenges faced by particular groups and then design interventions.

The barriers to innovation in the sector are well documented. The future scanning Educause Horizon Report (2019) identified a number of '"wicked" challenges'. These are defined as those that are too complex to even define, much less address. Rethinking the role of educators was identified as a clear barrier to innovation. The Jisc student experience report from 2018 showed only 54% of students surveyed considered technology embedded in their courses suitable to equip them for their future careers. Only 48% rated the overall support for effective online teaching as above average (best imaginable, excellent, or good). Forty-four per cent agreed they were provided with guidance about the digital skills needed in their teaching role, and just 14% said they were provided with an assessment of their digital skills and training needs (Jisc 2022b). And post-pandemic, staff did not perceive themselves to be well supported in terms of their digital development.

The changes in the HE sector caused by increased competition, budget constraints, and a focus on quality standards have also been fuelled by the growing influence of the student voice in education. Students rightly demand a greater say in their education, and the (England and Wales) National Student Survey's additional section with questions on the student voice has added impetus for a more strategic response from HEIs. In response to this, institutions have sought to make the student experience more engaging and collaborative with greater emphasis on activities such as co-creation, partnership, and co-production. Student wellbeing is encompassed within the student voice, and developing students' skills in becoming mindful practitioners to minimise technostress is advocated by Biggins and Holley (2022).

The Contribution of Learning Developers

In a study at one UK HEI ($n = 202$), it was found that students' knowledge and use of technology exceeded that of many academic staff (Biggins and Holley 2023). However, these findings may exclude some disadvantaged groups, and thus Learning Developers can play an important role as a conduit to facilitating nurturing staff–student partnerships. They are able to select from different pedagogic models available, choosing appropriate approaches, the available technology, and contextual information around staff and student capabilities to harness the student voice in a meaningful and effective way (Zarandi et al., 2022).

An example of this is the recent growth in the apprenticeship programmes, which has added a new model for the ways institutions interact with students. Institutions need to meet the regulatory requirements of the Office for Standards in Education (OFSTED), and helpfully, this competence-based approach sets out the knowledge, skills, and behaviours students are expected to achieve. Institutions are now recognising the different learning needs of these students, in the way that widening participation programmes have done in the past. There is an established knowledge base for Learning Developers, evidenced through a wide range of projects, developed through external funding rounds, community projects, and internal resourcing. The commitment to the open is foundational to knowledge generation. UNESCO (2012) defines this as 'teaching, learning and research materials in any medium, digital or otherwise ... [with] no-cost access, use, adaptation and redistribution by others with no or limited restrictions'. The ALDinHE repository LearnHigher is one of the few open access repositories for digital artefacts to be collated and stored for use and reuse through appropriate Creative Commons licensing (ALDinHE, 2023a).

Learning Developers have a well-articulated skill set, working in the 'third space' across academic and professional service teams, across disciplines, and across institutional boundaries. They draw upon emancipatory pedagogies framed by the human-centred work of Freire (1970), who argues that education is freedom and contends that traditional teaching styles keep the poor powerless by treating them as passive, silent recipients of knowledge. Renowned for their creative solutions, Learning Developers are able to facilitate and empower students to learn at a place and time of their own choosing, as outlined in the early work of Sinfield et al. (2004).

A seminal work on post-pandemic hybrid learning spaces draws together international perspectives. A key argument points to the blurring of boundaries and to new ways of learning that reach beyond physical and social spaces:

> Students in formal academic programs will fill gaps in their department's curriculum through online courses from other universities, congregating in

study groups that bring together local and remote peers alongside 'informal' learners. They will conduct independent research in remote laboratories and collaborate in hackathons and competitions.

(Gil et al., 2022, p.2)

Such rich and complex technology-mediated modalities of learning, formal, informal, and non-formal, individual and collaborative, face-to-face and online, have been growing intensively during the last decade, and have become part of everyday life for young students or lifelong learners. The notion of hybridity goes far beyond the concept of blending. While the former 'considers the introduction of digital elements into non-digital learning contexts (and more recently – the combination of synchronous and asynchronous modes of interaction), hybrid learning explores openly broader facets of learning coexistence' (Gil et al., 2022, p3).

Behaviours can be viewed as the practical application of one's values. ALDinHE's LD values express the aspiration to gain the most from learning in HE, being inclusive, adapting and sharing practice, pursuing a scholarly approach, and being a reflective practitioner (ALDinHE 2023b). Applying these values to technology enables the definition of behaviours that include curiosity about how technology can facilitate student learning and staff practice and to be open yet sceptical towards the promises that accompany technological developments. Learning Developers must weigh costs against benefits and consider how technology can promote and expand inclusivity and be equitable to all stakeholders (Donnolly, 2022). The history of technology reminds us that innovation can come from software and hardware developments being used in unexpected ways, which prompts us to search out innovative solutions that exploit past investments (Grinbaum Groves, 2013). Learning from others and sharing insights more widely are behaviours that enable all Learning Developers to progress much faster collectively than we could ever do alone.

Student Outcomes

The recent review of blended learning by the Office for Students (OfS, 2022) recommended that educational organisations invest in digital training support for staff and students. Less than half (48%) of respondents to the digital experience survey rated their digital support as 'above average', down from 54% the year before. In addition, only 6% of teaching staff reported being rewarded or recognised for their digital skills. Strategic policy drivers are one way in which technological innovation can occur, and a model that embraces co-creation, digital skill development, lifelong learning, and student wellbeing is the Digital Learning Maturity Model (DLMM) proposed by Holley, Biggins, and Supa (2022). Based on three years' research with key stakeholders, it comprises a strategic level with policies framing digital learning with the opportunities and challenges this raises; an operational stage that explores the tensions of the operationalisation of strategy; and a level recognising the importance of lifelong learning and digital wellbeing, gaps which both staff and students experience as they struggle with archaic HEI structures and ways of working with technology.

Within the third spaces Learning Developers inhabit, there is what Gil et al. (2022) describe as a focus on adaptive/adaptable learning spaces, that is, the flip side of passive, VLE learning spaces, and they see the hybrid blend moving ahead as opportunities for learning to become more active and diverse. Their conclusions suggest that space will be utilised in surprising ways, and the authors predict that the space design itself will facilitate students and their freedom to innovate.

A commitment to open education will ensure that digital resources are free to use/reuse for educational purposes, within the constraints of digital equity discussed in this chapter. The United Nations (2022) Sustainable Development Goal for education focuses on ensuring 'inclusive and equitable quality education and promoting lifelong learning opportunities for all'. This shared value set, agreed across the globe, matches the ALDinHE values for Learning Developers. Helsper (2021), in her work on socio-digital equity and potential solutions, reflects upon motivations, attitudes, and engagement as ways in designing forward to overcome some of the challenges to ensure no student is left behind. It is Learning Developers who possess these in abundance and can lead the way to emancipatory practices within their organisations, to empower and enable students, and to share good practice across their community and networks.

References

Abeggglen, S., Burns, T. and Sinfield, S. (2019) 'It's learning development, Jim – but not as we know it: academic literacies in third space', *Journal of Learning Development in Higher Education*, 15: 1–19.

ALDinHE (2023a) *LearnHigher*. Available at: https://aldinhe.ac.uk/learnhigher/ (Accessed: 14 May 2023).

ALDinHE (2023b) *Values*. Available at: https://aldinhe.ac.uk/about-aldinhe/ (Accessed: 14 May 2023).

Biggins, D. and Holley, D. (2022) 'Student wellbeing and technostress: critical learning design factors', *Journal of Learning Development in Higher Education*, 25. https://doi.org/10.47408/jldhe.vi25.985

Biggins, D. and Holley, D. (2023) 'Designing for student wellbeing: challenging assumptions about where our students learn', *Journal of Learning Development in Higher Education*, 27. https://doi.org/10.47408/jldhe.vi27.938

Diaz Andrade, A. and Techatassanasoontorn, A.A. (2020) 'Digital enforcement: rethinking the pursuit of a digitally-enabled society', *Information Systems Journal*, 31(1): 184–197.

Donnolly, S. (2022) 'Inclusion and learning development', *Take5*. Available at: https://lmutake5.wordpress.com/2022/03/30/take5-70-inclusion-and-learning-development/ (Accessed: 14 May 2023).

Educause Horizon Report. (2019) *Horizon Report.* Available at: https://library. educause.edu/resources/2019/4/2019-horizon-report

Educause Horizon Report. (2022) *Teaching and Learning Edition.* Available at: https://library.educause.edu/resources/2022/4/2022-educause-horizon-report-teaching-and-learning-edition

Foucault, M. (1975) *Discipline and punish.* Translated by A. Sheridan. Paris: Gallimard.

Freire, P. (1970) *Pedagogy of the Oppressed.* New York: Continuum.

Grinbaum, A. and Groves, C. (2013) 'What is "responsible" about responsible innovation? Understanding the ethical issues', *Responsible Innovation: Managing the Responsible Emergence of Science and Innovation in Society*, 119–142. Chichester, UK: John Wiley & Sons.

Gil, E., Mor, Y., Dimitriadis, Y. and Köppe, C. (2022) *Hybrid Learning Spaces.* Cham: Springer International.

Helsper, E. (2021) *The digital disconnect: The social causes and consequences of digital inequalities.* Sage Europe.

Holley, D., Biggins, D. and Supa, M. (2022) 'From tools to wellbeing: a proposed digital learning maturity model (DLMM)', in: *INTED2022 Proceedings*, 4687–4696.

Jisc (2022a) *Teaching Staff Digital Experiences Insights Survey.* Available at: https://repository.jisc.ac.uk/8973/1/DEI-HE-teaching-report-2021-22.pdf

Jisc (2022b) *Student Digital Experience Insights Survey 2021/22: Higher Education Findings.* Available at: https://www.jisc.ac.uk/reports/student-digital-experience-insights-survey-2021-22-higher-education-findings

Lee, M.J.W., Georgieva, M., Alexander, B., Craig, E. and Richter, J (2021) *State of XR and Immersive Learning Outlook Report 2021.* Walnut, CA: Immersive Learning Research Network.

Liu, B. (2021) 'The impact of intersectionality of multiple identities on digital health divide, quality of life and loneliness among older adults in the UK', *British Journal of Social Work*, 51: 3077–3097.

OFCOM. (2022) *Online Nation Report.* Available at: https://www.ofcom.org.uk/__data/assets/pdf_file/0023/238361/online-nation-2022-report.pdf

Office for Students. (2020) *Digital Poverty Risks Leaving Students Behind.* Available at: https://www.officeforstudents.org.uk/news-blog-and-events/press-and-media/digital-poverty-risks-leaving-students-behind/

Office for Students. (2022) *Blended Learning and OfS Regulation.* Available at: https://www.officeforstudents.org.uk/publications/blended-learning-and-ofs-regulation/summary/

Ragnedda, M., Ruiu, M.L. and Addeo, F. (2022) 'The self-reinforcing effect of digital and social exclusion: the inequality loop', *Telematics and Informatics*, 72, 101852.

Sinfield, S., Burns, T. and Holley, D. (2004) 'Outsiders looking in or insiders looking out? Widening Participation in a post 1992 University', in: J. Satterthwaite, A. Atkinson and W. Martin (eds), *The Disciplining of Education: New Languages of Power and Resistance*, London: Trentham Books. 137–152.

UNESCO. (2012) *Information Document on the World Congress on Open Educational Resources.* Paris. Available at https://unesdoc.unesco.org/ark:/48223/pf0000222585

United Nations. (2022) *The Sustainable Development Goals Report 2022.* United Nations. https://unstats.un.org/sdgs/report/2022/The-Sustainable-Development-Goals-Report-2022.pdf

Whitchurch, C. (2018) 'Being a higher education professional today: Working in a third space', in: C. Bossu and N. Brown (eds), *Professional and Support Staff in Higher Education*. Singapore: Springer. 1–11.

Zarandi, N., Soares, A.M. and Alves, H. (2022) 'Student roles and behaviors in higher education co-creation–a systematic literature review', *International Journal of Educational Management*, 36(7): 1297–1320.

10

TRANSFORMATIVE SOCIAL LEARNING SPACE

Christie Pritchard

> *'Excuse me, are you a student, or, erm, do you work here?' asked a student clutching hold of her draft of a written assignment. She was seeking help, guidance, but wondering if she had found the right person, the right space.*

Are You a Student?

Almost ten years ago, I was sitting alongside a student Writing Mentor at the newly opened Writing Café at the University of Plymouth. The question of whether I was a student was repeated often during those days; was it because of the informal, relaxed environment we were in? It was a café after all. Was it because we all sat together, Learning Developers and students trained to support their peers, blurring the lines between who was a member of staff and who was a student? Was it because we were not clearly positioning anyone as the expert, there was no reception desk, no lectern, no way to check in, no obvious place where the 'teacher' should be? I would argue it was perhaps a combination of all of those reasons. What was clear was that this particular student was seeking another student to talk to. They wanted to ask questions freely, using their own unfiltered language, without fear of judgement. They wanted support and guidance and were trying to navigate an informal setting that was not quite clear to them. It was situated outside of the formal teaching rooms and lecture theatres, even outside of the more traditional offering of our Learning Development (LD) unit and bookable tutorials. Much has changed over the last decade in terms of student expectations and our understanding of social learning space and how it provides opportunities to contribute to the learning process. Also, students no longer ask me if I am a student.

DOI: 10.4324/9781003433347-13

Social Learning Spaces

Since the early 2000s there has been a growing tradition and interest in learning spaces within education (Boddington and Boys, 2011a; Temple, 2008) and UK higher education institutions have invested significantly in their campuses and infrastructure, shifting the discourse from one of instruction to one of learning (Elkington and Bligh, 2019). The focus on spaces outside of formal teaching rooms became part of campus masterplans, and social learning spaces featured as a way of providing an environment for students to continue their learning. This shift in considering universities as sites of learning called upon the LD community to consider how situated, embodied learning takes place within individual, social, cultural, economic, and political contexts – or a socio-spatial practice (Boddington and Boys, 2011b). In this shift and the associated development of our campuses, Learning Developers were provided the opportunity to consider the power structures at play within and on spaces, evaluating the different affordances and constraints of different social learning spaces. They were well positioned to consider the relationship between students' learning outside of the classroom, the traditional hierarchical teaching spaces of the academy, and interactions that took place in cafes, in corridors, in the in-between spaces that are more fleeting, less scheduled, and less stable and fixed.

As learning in higher education is transitional, new knowledge and ways of knowing can unsettle our image of who we are, who we are as learners, and who we may become in relation to others; thus, the environment in which that transition takes place must play a part in our remaking (Bourdieu, 1993). Key to understanding transformative social learning and how it is entwined with the notion of space is recognising that spaces are not neutral, nor are they truly created. Of course, architects and our Estate and Facilities teams can design a space, purchase furniture, and offer it for use, but spaces cannot be *created* if we consider them through the lens of a socio-spatial practice. Rather, they are *defined* by the relationships between those who use them and the activities and practices that take place within them. They are, of course, also defined by those who do not use them but who have power and influence over them. They can simultaneously be sites of opportunity and constraint, offering opportunities for different pedagogies, and different ways of interacting. Social learning space, and transformative social learning space, therefore, has to be conceptualised in a relational way (Bourdieu, 1993; Bourdieu, 1997). The way social learning space is framed within a particular university is as important as the various ways of enacting LD within a particular space. Just as there are multiple ways of embodying and enacting LD, so are there also different ways of being within a space. Viewing social learning spaces in this way may help Learning Developers to consider that spaces emerge as learners, peer mentors, students and other actors interact within them. It is how the space is perceived, defined, and articulated by its community; it is not just the physical space itself and the furniture, lighting and decoration that adorns it. Spaces change and shift as people interact in and on it, pedagogic practices adopted influence them, and the transformation of students goes beyond student and staff evaluations of the designs and layouts.

The Writing Café

To demonstrate how social learning space is situated and embodied within a social, cultural, economic, and political context, we can look to the example of The Writing Café at the University of Plymouth. One of the key values of LD is partnership working and a collaborative approach to supporting students (ALDinHE, 2023). This is particularly true of the LD team at the University of Plymouth. The institution has a long-standing history of partnership working as part of our experiential education strategy and students as partners approach. At the time of creating the Writing Café we had an established and highly regarded Peer Assisted Learning Scheme (PALS) and multiple pan-institutional initiatives supporting students to be co-producers, co-researchers, co-enquirers, peer mentors, and ambassadors. The Writing Café was just a continuum on this trajectory, but it was also an opportunity to challenge boundaries. We founded it in 2014 as a creative and developmental space that offered peer to peer support on all aspects of academic writing, alongside Learning Developers. The project was one of co-creation with students and a partnership approach (Pritchard, 2015).

Although physical locations have changed in the decade that has since passed, the Writing Café remains a physical, and more recently a digital, open-access café in a popular and busy building on the University central campus. The original drive to establish the Writing Café was to provide a space for students to discuss their academic texts in progress and reframe the traditional notion that academic writing is solitary and isolated (Moore, 2003; Murray et al., 2008). We were trying to create a learning culture that was embodied and thus enacted a social, situated practice of learning. We did not want to just provide instrumental advice on how to improve a text according to the rules of the game, but rather question the game itself (Bourdieu, 1991; Bourdieu, 1993). Our professional insight and experience demonstrated that students were nervous about sharing their writing, often feeling unprepared for the demands of academic assignments and navigating their way through the hidden curriculum, but this was not always because they did not have the necessary capital to do so. The game is also unequal. The ethos behind the Writing Café acknowledged the contention that writing is not an easy endeavour, even for those who are particularly experienced, and that technical advice alone would not help writers to develop the combined strategies needed for their progression and development. Moore (2003, p.333) argues that even the most 'experienced academic writers encounter difficulties, challenges and obstacles in their effort to write effectively and productively' and it was hoped the Writing Café would provide the space to explore this collaboratively, in a shared environment. The historical legacy of the coffeehouse, the predecessor to the café, is rooted in a culture of community, collaboration, and social activity, and these were the values that we wanted to encourage in the Writing Café (Ellis, 2005). Whilst at the time many universities had Writing Centres, the Writing Café was the first in the sector. Where it differed from Writing Centres was the focus on recognising that the learning space was central to the learning culture we were trying to create. The LD team were keen to step into the unknown, experiment, and consider how they could keep the embodied nature of learning at the forefront of their activities, in a space that was not familiar to them in relation to how they educated students.

The team provided training, guidance, and support for students to become Writing Mentors and worked alongside them, encouraging discussions and dialogue around academic literacies and texts in progress, across the disciplines. Yet in the majority of interactions at the Writing Café the Learning Developers put the students in the position of the 'expert'. Perhaps they were not experts in the writing process, that hidden curriculum, nor experts of all of the various disciplines, but they were experts in becoming a student, and experts at knowing whether they felt like fish in water in this environment, or if they found their values and experience to be unmatched to current expectations. Learning Developers were there to help support and facilitate these negotiations between the students and the physical space whilst providing a structure to encounters, but students themselves were positioned as those with power within the space.

Over the course of the last ten years, many other higher education institutions have been interested in how we established the Writing Café, how we trained the Writing Mentors, how we convinced senior managers to invest in the initiative, how it functions on an operational level, and how we evaluate it. Whilst I will always support others to find a way to establish a service that works for them, one of the key findings I have learnt through undertaking research and analysis, through my experience of working in the social learning space and in conversation with other institutions and figures in the sector, is that no two Writing Cafés would ever be the same. Nor should they be. In fact, in relocating the Writing Café in 2019 after the original site became destined for a building redesign, we changed how it operated – not necessarily intentionally, but the environment changed as the location changed, so the relationship with its surroundings changed, and the institution, too, had changed. The many Writing Mentors over the years also changed the space, adapting and evolving to students, their environment, and the politically unstable landscape we are operating in across the sector. How the Writing Mentors understand, articulate, and envisage their roles changes how it runs. Just as no two Writing Cafés are ever the same, the same can be said for each academic year;

no two years are the same, perhaps not even the terms/semesters. Learning Developers have come and gone, as have senior leaders and managers; they have changed the way this particular social learning space is constructed within our minds, in our institutional culture and habitus, and that has impacted the language used to describe its function, purpose, and mission. Spaces of learning are not created just because we design them and offer them for use within our institutions, but the approach we take, our university culture, the team culture of our LD units, the resources available to us, our student demographics, and how we work in collaboration with students, senior stakeholders, and programme and lecturing teams. It is evident in our marketing material, the way we speak of the initiative, and the ways students hear of it. Their expectations shape social learning spaces as much as the furniture and layout we might ponder over in designs. It is truly relational.

Pushing Boundaries

Through a range of case studies, Dahl, Fihl, and Johansen's *A Comparative Ethnography of Alternative Spaces* (2013) describes individuals who look for *niches*, or *cracks* in the pockets of our culture, which allow alternative spaces to emerge. They argue that individuals who were trying to embrace ambiguity provide different possibilities for their inhabitants. This type of transgressive, transformative view of spaces can encourage thought around pushing boundaries to what we expect our universities to offer. What possibilities can we provide for our students if we think differently about social space? We can think about the type of spaces Learning Developers traditionally occupy – a library office, a traditional classroom, a tutorial room – and thus we can start to unpick how we might be able to work outside of these structures. Take a moment to think of your values as a Learning Developer; how can you create space for change? Most likely you will be able to consider areas of your role you think could be practised differently, more meaningfully, perhaps for both you and your students. It does not need to be as big as perhaps the Writing Café project may seem from the outside. How can you co-create a learning culture with your students? What opportunities do you create to learn from students, as equals? Could you ask them questions about their learning across the campus? Where do they go, and why? What spaces do you have on your campus that afford a different type of pedagogy, one that creates the culture of learning you are looking to enact?

When we first pitched the idea of the Writing Café to senior management in 2013, we did so with slight naivety to how University business worked, the cogs we were supposed to turn. I had only been a Learning Developer for six months when I became involved in leading the Writing Café project. Whilst looking for 'something different', we scouted the campus trying to identify a suitable location; depending on who you ask, it was either a rainy Friday afternoon or a sunny Monday morning. What is clear is that we were excited by the prospect of occupying a former café that had been closed due to the catering department not seeing it as financially viable. We were not interested in profit; we were interested in learning, in providing a space we thought students would want to visit to discuss challenging topics and grapple with changing identities. We were looking for an alternative space, one that might be relatively independent of the existing social and political reality of the University (Esther Fihl, 2013). We wanted to shift the collective agreement that LD was remedial support. We did not want it to be timetabled; we did not want it to be instrumental, instructional. We saw an opportunity to find a creative way to try to reframe the work of LD in line with a very clear need to evolve our support at Plymouth. We had previously occupied a Drop in Zone; student attendance was low; none of the Learning Developers really looked forward to taking on their shift there. We also knew that one-to-one tutorials were not sustainable for us. We needed to find a way to provide support across the institution, potentially reaching 23,000 students, with the all-too-well-known cutbacks we had experienced.

In opting to use our disused cafe space, we did not expect to have to take on such a role that would lead us into the arena of recruiting and advertising for catering staff, establishing coffee bean suppliers, procuring a coffee machine, and finding ways to rota a fully functioning café as well as providing the educational offer we were perhaps better suited to. Those days have long passed, and the Writing Café is much more in line with the University's wider operations, but my advice to anyone considering doing things differently within your institutions is to be prepared to take a path that is unknown, uncharted, unexpected, and unpaved. It may not be easy, it may not be smooth, but perhaps in ten years' time you too can look back with pride because you were involved. You had managed to make a mark on your university campus that would continually evolve and change, often outside of your control, but nonetheless you know that students benefit from it. In trying to establish any social learning space, be prepared to accept that it will take on a life of its own. You may step away to pursue other exciting adventures, but you will still keep a keen eye out for its development, and you never know, your paths may cross again.

Final Reflections

As has been evident in recent years, change may be the only constant within higher education, so make it personal. The Writing Café will always hold a special place in the development of my career, and my heart. It was personal. It was the first project I was involved in when I started at the University of Plymouth as a Learning Developer. It was the host of multiple international conferences, the topic I presented on at many of my first conferences, including the Association of Learning Development in Higher Education. I came along to the first conference we hosted, with my first child in a sling, not wanting to miss out on the event I had spent so long organising, thinking about, and working towards. It was the focus of my own research and the six-year-long journey of my doctorate. I was invested in the details and the design of the Writing Café, as well as the complex ways of understanding the practices that took place within it. I selected the striking Penguin wallpaper that adorns the walls in the original location, and was adamant that it remained a key visual indicator of our relocation in 2019. As I have stepped away from being a Learning Developer in the traditional sense, I have still kept a keen eye out for it and more recently saw pictures of the original Writing Café, midway through the redesign of the building, gutted and empty. Just the wallpaper and purple painted accent walls remain beside the other rubble. In a strange turn of restructures, the Writing Café now sits under my leadership again. What remains is the approach of LD, the recognition that we should challenge boundaries and advocate for social transformative learning. Whilst the Writing Café may seem to be a big project, one that I was committed to for a number of years, I hope readers can apply this advice to their own roles, smaller projects perhaps, or simply just their approach to understand their own role. My advice would be to find a creative way to promote the values you stand for. Consider your own ambitions for learning within higher education and get involved in trying to lead change, on whatever scale you are able to. Remember, too, the details matter; people relate to them. Students feel these details. Overall, leading on a project like the Writing Café truly helped me to become a Learning Developer and educator and understand my own motivation and desire for change for learning.

References

ALDinHE (2023) *About ALDinHE*. Available at: https://aldinhe.ac.uk/about-aldinhe/ (Accessed: April 2023).

Boddington, A. and Boys, J. (2011a) 'Re-shaping learning: An introduction', in: A. Boddington and J. Boys (eds), *Re-Shaping Learning: A Critical Reader: The Future of Learning Spaces in Post-Compulsory Education*. Rotterdam: Sense Publishers, xi–xxii.

Boddington, A. and Boys, J. (eds) (2011b) *Re-Shaping Learning: A Critical Reader: The Future of Learning Spaces in Post-Compulsory Education*. Rotterdam: Sense Publishers.

Bourdieu, P. (1991) *Language and Symbolic Power*. Harvard: Harvard University Press.

Bourdieu, P. (1993) *The Field of Cultural Production*. Cambridge: Polity Press.

Bourdieu, P. (1997) 'The Forms of Capital', in: A.H. Halsey, H. Lauder, P. Brown and A.S. Wells (eds), *Education, Culture, and Society*. Oxford: Oxford University Press.

Elkington, S. and Bligh, B. (2019) 'Future Learning Spaces – Spaces, Technology and Pedagogy', *Advance HE*. Available at: https://www.advance-he.ac.uk/knowledge-hub/future-learning-spaces-space-technology-and-pedagogy

Ellis, M. (2005) *The Coffee-House: A Cultural History.* London: Phoenix.

Esther Fihl, J.D. (2013) *A Comparative Ethnography of Alternative Spaces.* New York: Palgrave Macmillan.

Jens Dahl, E. F. and Johansen, B.S. (2013) 'An Introduction to Alternative Spaces', in E.F. Jens Dahl (ed.), *A Comparative Ethnography of Alternative Spaces.* New York: Palgrave Macmillan, 1–18.

Moore, S. (2003) 'Writers' retreats for academics: exploring and increasing the motivation to write', *Journal of Further and Higher Education,* 27(3): 333–342.

Murray, R., Thow, M., Moore, S. and Murphy, M. (2008) 'The writing consultation: developing academic writing practices', *Journal of Further and Higher Education,* 32(2): 119–128.

Pritchard, C. (2015) 'Mentoring in the writing cafe: Identity, belonging and ownership', *Journal of Learning Development in Higher Education.* Special edition. https://doi.org/10.47408/jldhe.v0i0.305

Temple, P. (2008) 'Learning spaces in higher education: an under-researched topic', *London Review of Education,* 6(3): 229–241.

11

THE VIEW FROM OVER HERE

What the Students Think about Learning Development

Tom Burns, Kevin Brazant, Emma Davenport, Nahid Huda, Sandra Sinfield, Jarelle Smith, with Aaron Kuskopf, Chandrika McDonald, Shelene Macintosh, Oliver Selic, Kirstie Tucker and Maura Burns Zaragoza

> *Overall, it's been very positive because, you know, they're that bit further along than you are in the academic journey and they've been where you are as well. So they kind of know what it is that you're going through and, kind of, I guess, know how to get the best out of you.*
>
> *(Creative Arts undergraduate student)*

Introduction

University can be both a wonderful and a confusing place for students (Burns and Sinfield, 2022), and Learning Development is there to work alongside them to help them decode, critique, and succeed in HE. The ethos of Learning Development (LD) is broadly practised by personal academic tutors, academic mentors, peer coaches, student union advisors, and heads of student experience. Whilst this plethora of support might be designed with the best of intentions, how is the time-poor student (Tones et al., 2009) meant to discover, value, and harness this support? And how do students perceive LD roles and systems in relation to their learning, within their discipline or with respect to higher education as a whole?

In this chapter, we consider LD from the student perspective, by speaking with students about their experiences of working with Learning Developers and asking them to reflect on the value of these interactions. We are just as interested in why students might not interact with these services as this will seed the opportunity to rethink current LD provision across the sector. Of course, we interviewed and co-authored this chapter with students who had

DOI: 10.4324/9781003433347-14

engaged, but they revealed the reasons they were hesitant in the first place, which throws light on this issue.

Method

To gain an insight into student experience of LD, we adopted a qualitative approach and engaged in opportunity sampling (Bell and Waters, 2018) – harnessing existing staff–student networks, inviting conversations with students who may have engaged across a range of LD offerings. In practice, we invited students at undergraduate and postgraduate level, across two universities (one Oxbridge and one widening participation (WP)) and from a range of disciplines including social sciences, the sciences, and the creative arts, to reflect upon their experiences with Learning Development. Key questions covered in the interviews included:

> How did your university welcome you, draw you in, and make you feel part of the academic community (and was this a successful strategy)?
> How did your university flag up that there was additional support available to you (and was that a successful strategy)?
> What is your experience as a student of working with Learning Developers?
> What are your and other students' perceptions of its value for your learning?
> Why do you and your peers engage – or not – with Learning Development?
> What do you value in Learning Development, and how would you remake Learning Development?
> What would you like Learning Developers to know about your student perspective?

We used the questions as prompts to initiate conversations, encouraging students to describe their engagement with Learning Developers and Learning Development within their daily student lives (Lyons and Coyle, 2007). To analyse the data, we took a thematic analysis approach (Lyons and Coyle, 2007; Braun and Clarke, 2022) and then explored with the students the descriptions given.

Thus, we worked with the students as partners in this research, inviting them to be both participants and co-authors (Bowstead, 2011), in an effort to break down institutional hierarchies and facilitate a transformative knowledge experience between ourselves and our students (Molinari, 2022). The students gave informed consent and had the right to withdraw from the project at any time and without reason.

The limitation of this study is the small sample spanning two institutions; therefore, the findings cannot be generalised to make a definitive claim.

What it does offer is an insight to students' experiences of LD. The collaborative nature of the exercise also presents one example of students as partners in research and writing as good practice when eliciting students' feedback on LD.

How Did Your University Welcome You?

> It was, I think, a really successful way of us having a lot of fun, being able to experiment a lot in terms of how we were interacting with the lectures, with the lab content, because we knew it didn't count for our assessments. Then, you know, later on in the degree when it came to choosing supervisors for various presentations or for things like my Masters project, you had just from that original four weeks a much better idea, I think, of the variety of research that was going on in Oxford than we would have had otherwise.
>
> (Sciences postgraduate student)

The ways in which students are welcomed into a range of academic communities are important, as they impact on cohort identity and retention (Leathwood and O'Connell, 2003; Arthur and Huda, 2023). Students are typically acutely aware of not knowing anyone on arrival at university and how this might affect them and their progress (Burns and Sinfield, 2022). We discovered diverse 'welcome' strategies that vary in terms of their perceived success. These strategies are also bound up in the contemporary socio-economic climate of HE, with its emphasis on academic continuation and progression.

The Oxbridge example was perhaps the most surprising for Learning Developers who work in WP institutions. Alongside dinners and quiz nights with personal and subject tutors within induction week, an active and integrative 'welcome' – the building of belonging, College and cohort identity, and the integration of academic development in the curriculum – was emphasised the moment a prospective student accepted a place at the University. Regardless of where they studied, however, all our participants positively identified with social approaches to welcome, including interactions with teaching staff, course-based social events, and being invited to get involved in learning support communities. These social approaches invited students to feel included within their subject, School, or College: they belonged (Arthur and Huda, 2023).

The Value of Working with Learning Developers

> They just knew what they were doing. And had the right answers and things that I wanted to hear, but I didn't know what I needed to hear before I spoke to them.
>
> (Creative Arts undergraduate student)

It was clear to all of our students that there was a range of support on offer. Students identified peers, the student union, academic mentors, Learning Developers, PhD students integrated into classes, and Writing Fellows as providing learning development. There was also a sense that this support was embodied – there was a person who could be contacted – thereby establishing a social relationship within their particular academic community.

The value of these interactions was threefold. One was the opportunity for a 'fresh pair of eyes' on their current academic capabilities; for example, essay writing guidance from Academic Mentors or Writing Fellows was seen as especially useful. Another was being invited to share academic experiences, abstract or literal, and the third was a chance to develop meta-cognition and make pedagogical connections in their own learning whilst in the very process of learning:

> It's almost like playing piano whilst you're learning piano. Everything else will improve, not just how you perform on the song, but actually how you make a garment because everything is connected.
>
> (Creative Arts undergraduate student)

At the same time, the students pointed out the challenges of navigating their new academic communities when they felt they had very little previous experience on the one hand, whilst on the other, they were being encouraged to be independent and self-reliant when it came to academic engagement. This contradiction meant that students were unsure about what support they were 'allowed' to access amongst all the developmental opportunities available to them. This then evoked concerns about belonging and academic entitlement.

Overall, their experiences were very positive, regardless of how they came to work with LD in the first place. For example, some students were referred to LD provision while other students were seamlessly offered support by more experienced peers within their teaching spaces. Students frequently mentioned the positive impact of interactions with their peers where everyone was able to practise specific academic skills together, including reading, drafting and editing assignments. Activities that foster positive relationships with peers were recommended, whether that be orientation programmes, group presentations, buddy schemes between different levels, or an emphasis on interaction within the teaching spaces.

(Dis)engaging with Learning Development

> The complexity of all these different aspects is what makes it sometimes challenging for people to come and say 'I need help' or 'I don't even know where I need help'... I'm only more recently starting to realise where there

may be gaps in my learning and understanding and how that is having an effect on me now. But then, how do I move past that? How do I fill in those gaps? Where do I find the time to fill in those gaps? How do I articulate that?

(Education undergraduate student)

Students perceived a 'gap' in their learning and acknowledged that if they were able to reflect upon why this might be, they would be in a better position to address their anxieties. However, the experience of not knowing felt lonely and scary. Students noted that it takes a certain level of confidence to be able to approach LD services. This confidence is informed by an ability to reflect on their learning needs in order to clearly articulate, to LD staff, what it is that they want.

Disengagement from LD seemed to be strongly associated with individual anxieties about academic proficiency, such as the quality of their written outputs, the level of knowledge and application concerning their subject area. Some students suggested that this 'general fear' might only be addressed by pastoral services, rather than those concerned with LD. Several students observed that the support for academic writing, for example, was not sufficient to overcome their procrastination and a heavy reliance on mitigation processes. Others suggested that their anxiety was also linked to negotiating ways of thinking where there are no definitive answers, whether this be in relation to assessments or even forms of support on offer.

One student mentioned how previous educational experience can have a bearing on the extent to which a new student might engage with Learning Development. For example, a school leaver may feel less autonomous than a mature student who has spent several years working before starting university. This will frame their attitude towards the academic support on offer and their ability to cross the threshold in order to access it. At the same time, they noted that students are not always certain of what they are allowed to have and this includes being able to enquire about it in the first place. These reflections do suggest that there may be more work to be done on how to create awareness around LD, that it offers a 'third space' where students can be 'themselves', their emerging academic selves, and develop confidence, self-awareness, and academic literacy (Gutiérrez, 2008) in order to feel entitled to LD and, arguably, develop a stronger sense of belonging within the university.

Sometimes You Just Need a Hug

When you think about all the things, there's the learning side and then there's just the personality fear side and the university gives a lot of resources, but it's like people need people to come and hug them and there's something there that's a little different.

(Education undergraduate student)

From a student's perspective, support should span a range, from academic needs to emotional wellbeing. For students, studying is bound in emotional responses, and perhaps this is what students need to see emphasised in university LD services: developmental work will improve self-efficacy and self-belief and thus wellbeing (Gutiérrez, 2008). The notion of compassion was acknowledged and attributed to individual members of staff, but there also seemed to be a desire for that compassion to be integrated seamlessly throughout the services provided: a compassionate pedagogy (Gilbert, 2017) – nuanced, reflexive, and humane in its response to complex needs (Abegglen et al., 2020).

Don't Mention the Pandemic

> I think they could have helped with that by encouraging talking/on screen cameras. I know there's been chat about actually, you know, inclusiveness or inclusivity about having the screens on. But I remember always thinking that was an issue and I would take the initiative and put my screen on and when I talked, I did a lot of talking.
>
> (Education undergraduate student)

Engagement and the extent to which this happens were often associated with the students' experience of technology, which makes sense given that these students arrived at university during a global pandemic where face-to-face contact was almost entirely replaced with online interaction. New students were faced with the challenges of navigating an unfamiliar environment and doing so through the use of remote technology, adding further stress in transitioning to the role of being a new student. Whilst efforts were made to create a sense of community online, the experiences were patchy for students.

Recommendations for Remaking Learning Development

> I think when we engage, it's an aspect of fun. Of a kind of real enjoyment of it. I think the parts which may be slightly more dry or maybe less interactive, are harder to engage with. When we're being included as being able to shape what that looks like for ourselves, I think that's much more engaging.
>
> (Creative Arts undergraduate student)

Reasons for engaging with Learning Development included the quality of the experience, peer engagement, building self-efficacy, and the impact it would have on their assessments. Students described how activities that were fun, which created opportunities for different perspectives or approaches, led to more engagement on their part.

Students felt that academic support in general was not only comprehensive but also available at any given time. One student described this as an atmosphere where 'you can always ask someone and you're never in anyone's way'. Their suggestions for a revised approach focused on clarity around what and when they could expect support.

They also suggested that more integrated, in-class sessions at specific times in the academic year would be an improvement, offering the opportunity to learn socially and build networks. It would also highlight that Learning Development is beneficial for all students, not just those who might have a specific issue or perceived 'gap'.

Students also wanted more involving, active, and interactive learning, where the emphasis in learning and assessment was on their exploration of and reflection on subject material rather than the tutor's judgement of the student's capabilities. Here the students' desires are in line with ALDinHE values: working alongside students to make sense of and get the most out of HE learning; partnership working and collaboration; critical self-reflection; and ongoing learning. However, an over-competitive, more individualistic classroom space can shut down that love of learning:

> Um [big big pause] I think sometimes the environment can be … a little bit competitive or it can make you feel like there's a pressure I guess to perform and so that can maybe make you a bit less willing to make mistakes or to try, try something a bit different or try a different way. In case that, you know, it goes wrong and then either you feel like I made a mistake or I don't want to answer a question again.
>
> (Sciences postgraduate student)

A key issue to accessing LD is time, and students have recommended more integrated LD. With the Oxbridge example, we saw this integration across the first half of the first term. Students were given time for a creative and engaging introduction to the University, to the spaces, places, and people with whom it is connected, who make the place so special and from where future research collaboration and collaborators might emerge:

> We got to talk to the heads of those stations, the principal investigators about their research and what they were doing and that then culminated at the end of this four week period in a mini project that we did.
>
> (Postgraduate sciences student)

The students appreciated this four-week playful space, where they were encouraged to develop friendships alongside their subject interests without the pressure of it being formally assessed, and where they got to experience the whole of what their university offered and had the time to explore, reflect, and grow.

Ironically, at WP universities this is typically not made available in the same way. WP students are acutely aware that they need time and space to engage with and reflect on their learning if they are to feel confident enough to thrive and to access the resources available to them. Typically, time poverty is their reality.

Conclusion

> Being connected to others in order to feel self-confident. Modelling the learning i.e. stages of writing practice, stages of research, is really appreciated, especially when done by the teachers.
>
> (Sciences postgraduate student)

From the various conversations that we had with our students, there is no doubt that they are under immense pressure to quickly achieve academic success in a range of social contexts. These include their course, their subject area, their campus, and their university. And all of this happens through their personhood, both historical and present. As a result, the academic experience is inherently overwhelming so it feels like there is never enough time or space to reach out for support. Students noted how important it was to know a Learning Developer by name and face, someone whom they could directly contact about their concerns or questions. Being able to identify a person, rather than a service, allowed them to overcome reservations and insecurities and access support more quickly.

Several barriers persist to accessing support in a widening participation institution. Whilst they believed that a student was responsible for developing their learning, not least managing their assessments in terms of organising their time and effort, students reported responsibilities outside of their university studies, termed 'time poverty', as a barrier to accessing support. Thus they valued LD integrated into the curriculum in various and creative ways, highlighting that this also facilitated peer-to-peer learning, a more active and interactive classroom, and a de-stigmatising of LD. While sometimes LD is only offered to those with 'real needs', the students in this study emphasised that LD should be open to all. To navigate use of LD, we would argue LD would greatly benefit from involving students as partners in the devising, delivery, and reflection on LD – as here in this chapter, where the student participants are also co-authors.

It is interesting that on the whole students did not seem to perceive wellbeing as emerging from engagement with Learning Development services – that is, the benefit of LD was cognitive and effective rather than emotional and affective. At the same time, it was clear overall that students conceptualised LD as perhaps more integral to the learning and teaching experience than we are in practice. It was assumed that we could influence the development of engaging and sustained welcome experiences, that we could promote active learning, dialogic teaching, and more creative and authentic assessments. Addressing this lies at the heart of LD philosophy and practice: we are there to work with and alongside students to make university more meaningful. Many times, it is LD that has to recognise student needs and argue for a compassionate and critical pedagogy, driven by our values, competences, aptitudes, and capacities. It is LD that is diverse, responsive, and flexible – and, yes, we do want to lobby for an LD-shaped university.

References

Abegglen, S., Burns, T., Maier, S. and Sinfield, S. (2020) 'Global university, local issues: Taking a creative and humane approach to learning and teaching', in: P. Blessinger, E. Sengupta, and M. Makhanya (eds), *Improving Classroom Engagement and International Development Programs: International Perspectives on Humanizing Higher Education.* Emerald Publishing Limited.

Arthur, R. and Huda, N. (2023) 'Coming in Together: Staff-student collaboration in a "Decolonizing" Induction Process', in: S. Abegglen, T. Burns and S. Sinfield (eds), *Collaboration in Higher Education: A New Ecology of Practice.* Bloomsbury Academic, 167–172.

Bell, J. and Waters, S. (2018) *Doing Your Research Project. A Guide for First Time Researchers.* 7th edn. Open University Press.

Braun, V. and Clarke, V. (2022) *Thematic Analysis.* Available at: https://www.thematicanalysis.net/ (Accessed: 1 May 2023).

Burns, T. and Sinfield, S. (2022) *Essential Study Skills: The Complete Guide to Success at University.* London: Sage.

Bowstead, H. (2011) 'Coming to Writing', *Journal of Learning Development in Higher Education,* 3. https://doi.org/10.47408/jldhe.v0i3.128

Gilbert, T. (2017). When Looking Is Allowed: What Compassionate Group Work Looks Like in a UK University. in: P. Gibbs (eds), *The Pedagogy of Compassion at the Heart of Higher Education.* Cham: Springer. https://doi.org/10.1007/978-3-319-57783-8_13

Gutiérrez, K. D. (2008) 'Developing a sociocritical literacy in the third space', *Reading Research Quarterly,* 43(2): 148–164.

Leathwood, C. and O'Connell, P. (2003) '"It's a struggle": the construction of the "new student" in higher education', *Journal of Education Policy,* 18(6): 597–615.

Lyons, E.E. and Coyle, A.E. (2007) *Analysing Qualitative Data in Psychology.* Sage Publications Ltd.

Molinari, J. (2022) *What Makes Writing Academic: Rethinking Theory for Practice.* Bloomsbury Academic.

Tones, F., Fraser, J., Elder, R. and White, K. (2009) 'Supporting mature-aged students from a socioeconomic background', *Higher Education,* 58(4): 505–529.

PART III

Reflecting in and on Learning Development

Cultivating Criticality

In Part III, we invite our readers to engage critically with the established ideas and epistemological assumptions in LD, and consider how Learning Developers can not only interrogate their own practice but also contribute to current discussions about the most pressing social and political issues. In the first of the five chapters in this part, Sunny Dhillon opens with a call for immanent critique of LD, its knowledge and practices. Such a critique allows LD to engage holistically and coherently with wider sector conversations around equality, diversity, and inclusion (EDI), as Anne-Marie Longford and Emma Kimberley argue in Chapter 13. Similarly, Ryan Arthur contends in Chapter 14 that LD as a field needs to engage more fully with issues around race, if it is to meaningfully enhance the learning experiences of students and recognise them as individuals. The necessity for the decolonisation of LD is addressed in Chapter 15. Georgia Koromila and Edward Powell present the case for LD's role in supporting students to embrace diverse ways of knowing and multiple forms of knowledge by first questioning our own choices and decisions in our practice. The part concludes by considering the crisis of the neoliberal university and LD's existence within it, with Gordon Asher summoning hope through the growth of a critical turn in LD.

DOI: 10.4324/9781003433347-15

12

CRITICAL SELF-REFLECTION IN LEARNING DEVELOPMENT

Sunny Dhillon

'*The problem with you, Sunny, is that you overthink things. What can you "do" with your theories? Can you please stop with the intellectual masturbation? Or at least do it in private and stop subjecting the rest of us to it?!*'

That's the stock response from loved ones and colleagues to my philosophical musings. Until the final year of my BA Spanish, I didn't know Groucho from Karl. Thereafter, enraptured by the diagnoses of Friedrich Nietzsche, and challenged by the works of Theodor Adorno and Max Horkheimer, I've been away with the Critical Theory fairies ever since.

Overview

I argue that Learning Developers may better enact the values articulated by the Association for Learning Development in Higher Education (ALDinHE, 2022) through engaging in immanent critique (Adorno, 1984) of their roles, of knowledge (re)production within higher education (HE), and of normative learning practices. This piece builds upon the principles of Critical Pedagogy (Freire et al., 2018), and, reading them through a Frankfurt School of Critical Theory lens, combines them with tenets of heutagogy (Hase and Kenyon, 2013). There is no 'how-to' approach articulated below. At this juncture (2023) in the historical development of this community of practice, the context deems that Learning Developers must negotiate the need to continuously articulate their worth (Biesta, 2015), whilst resisting falling foul of undertaking their roles in an instrumental manner. Instead, enacting an ALDinHE ethos means that Learning Developers could transmute fear, and critically reflect upon what they, as well as fellow staff and students, are often encultured to do in the name of effective practice and outcomes (Allen and Goddard, 2017).

DOI: 10.4324/9781003433347-16

Critical Theory

From the Ancient Greek *kritikos*, 'critical' means a skilled ability to judge (Allen and Goddard, 2017, p.139). In HE, countless texts, resources, and how-to guides abound, promising to provide checklists of how to do 'it' effectively; namely, in the service of high grades. I read 'critical' after the Frankfurt School thinkers Adorno and Horkheimer. Horkheimer differentiates 'critical' from 'traditional' theory, arguing that whilst the latter seeks to understand the workings of society in order to better serve its needs and interests, Critical Theory is 'dominated at every turn by a concern for reasonable conditions for life' (Horkheimer, 1975, p.199). This broad conception can be sharpened by Adorno's (2005) declaration that 'there is tenderness only in the coarsest demand: that no one shall go hungry any more' (p.156). So, to be critical in this Frankfurt School–inspired reading is not about a checklist approach or instrumental toolkit. Rather, it is about highlighting existing tensions and contradictions that prevent a life of dignity. Such criticality is, in my repeat experience, often subjected to the kind of disparaging remarks as noted in the epigraph. Those invested in mores often

> attack critical voices for having nothing positive to offer, which is to say, nothing which can realistically be rolled out. Critics are attacked for their self-righteous judgmentalism, for refusing to reduce their expectations to what can be practically achieved.
>
> (Allen and Goddard, 2017, p.151)

Critical Theory is not, however, mere abstract intellectualism. Materially grounded in seeking to cultivate conditions where 'no one shall go hungry anymore', it is a way of spotlighting 'hidden assumptions which underlie dominant social practices' (McArthur, 2016, p.973).

LD may be conceptualised as critically reflective practice in action. Giving over to a 'totally administered' (Adorno, 1973, p.141) culture through measurements and metrics would be to render LD merely instrumental. Writing in the context of post–World War II, when musing on the efficiency of the administered machine of the Third Reich, Adorno (2005a) argued that 'the only education that has any sense at all is an education toward critical self-reflection' (p.193). Put in a milder context, but certainly more ambitious manner, is that university education ought to focus upon producing 'reflective, responsible citizens free from political, military, bureaucratic or market demands in a modern industrial society' (Strohl, 2006, p.134, as cited in Barlow et al., 2011, p.48). The best-intentioned Learning Developers cannot 'produce' such individuals, for we ourselves cannot be free from such demands. To claim such a vantage point would be at best naïve, and at worst hubristic. Rather, the Learning Developer may, in

Adornian manner, engage in continual critical self-reflection and subject contingent concepts to rigorous scrutiny. This kind of critical self-reflection cannot be neatly rendered into a ten-point plan of instrumental, results-oriented, action.

Immanent Critique

The ostensible function of LD has, since its inception, been about demystifying HE practices for 'non-traditional' learners, and in turn, contributing to high satisfaction, retention, and completion rates. LD must continually recognise that its very existence is thus founded in a neoliberal project (Ball, 2021); it is an inextricable part of an ideology that so many Left-leaning colleagues rally against (for example, the messaging in University and College Union (UCU) materials). The role of a critical Learning Developer is, arguably, one of necessary immanent critique; we cannot claim a holier-than-thou Archimedean standpoint from where we are supposedly exempt from the critiques against the ills of the neoliberal university. Rather, our livelihoods, and potential resistances, are funded by a neoliberal project.

Whilst Learning Developers may model heuristic critical thinking models when engaging with literature, policies, and practices, it is more ontologically taxing (Barnett, 2011, p.43) to engage in critical self-reflection, as well as embolden students to be critical in the context of a culture of instrumental outcomes; for example, when narratives surrounding student success, as well as LD efficacy, involve metrics of grades, improvements, and intervention outcomes. As Biesta (2016) argues, what makes a '"good education" requires value judgments, and cannot be articulated through measurable outcomes, or "managerial forms of accountability"' (p.128). It is tricky, for example, to instrumentally measure the value of supporting a final year BA Education Studies student to write a dissertation that argues against entering the teaching profession (which yes, I unapologetically did, and yes, the student graduated with a grade that they were happy with).

Inspired by the mythical archetype of the Trickster (Bassil-Morozow, 2015), as opposed to the Hero, I see it as my role as a Learning Developer to encourage students to continually spotlight the contingent, over apparently necessary, working practices of HE. That is, none of this has to be the way it is, but in this particular context, these are the norms of engagement. They are not sacrosanct. They can be played with, stretched, and squeezed. Amidst a culture where HE staff are too often busy going nowhere on a 'treadmill of justification' (Education Support Partnership, 2018, p.12), too often falling foul of the pitfall of justifying existence, value, and likeability (often through doctored satisfaction surveys), this piece challenges Learning Developers to transmute fear-based practices into ones of generative immanent critique. Simply put, this means to recognise the contradictions and tensions within normative discourse and, instead of attempting to continually weave a positive story about 'value added', engage in a critical task of persistent self-reflection, including of one's own professional role.

ALDinHE Values

Practising LD in a critically self-reflective manner, it is important to subject the ALDinHE (2022) values to scrutiny. Whilst there is not the capacity to do so in a detailed manner here, below is a snippet of the approach I argue for.

1 Working in partnership with students and staff to make sense of HE – Genuinely transgressive partnerships of this kind, most notably championed by the late Mike Neary at Lincoln University through the 'student as producer' project (Neary, 2020), is to be encouraged, as is any sense-making exercise. Regarding the latter, note how 'sense' is not necessarily concomitant with 'solution'.

2 Respecting diverse learners through critical pedagogy and practice – This is to be encouraged, especially when critical pedagogy is employed along with heutagogy; that is, self-directed learning (see Hase and Kenyon, 2013, below). The recent update (June 2023) to this value marks a significant shift from the previous iteration, which argued for 'making HE inclusive through emancipatory practice'. Biesta (2015) argues against the notion of 'emancipatory practice', noting via its colonial connotations that it implies 'one who knows better and best and who can perform the act of demystification that is needed to expose the workings of power' (p.83). Returning to the point above concerning hubris, this value update changes the self-concept that Learning Developers would like to have; in effect, one that emphasises critical self-reflection over potentially opaque emancipation.

3 Advocating for effective Learning Development practice to promote student learning – 'Effective' is a contested concept. See above concerning the tension of disseminating what is neatly measurable.

4 Critical self-reflection, ongoing learning, and a commitment to professional development – I am, predictably, all in favour of item one. 'Professional development', however, contains tensions. Being a 'professional' can often be all too concomitant with acting as a 'functionary' (Hargreaves, 2000). In the interest of social justice, again, it may be appropriate to act in an unprofessional manner.

5 Commitment to a scholarly approach and research related to Learning Development – What is deemed 'scholarly' changes depending on discipline related, as well as sociopolitical, norms. Consider, for example, contemporary debates surrounding Eurocentric modes of knowledge exchange (Gopal, 2021) (such as this chapter and the volume as a whole!).

Understandably, some readers may now wish to return to the comments cited in the epigraph and skip to the next chapter! For those who continue, I will explore how Learning Developers may harness their positionality within institutions to enact critical self-reflection.

Marginality

As Linda Morrice (2009, as cited in Sinfield et al., 2011) argues, 'knowledge is not the value-free, decontextualized, neutral and apolitical construct it is thought to be' (p.54). Critical Pedagogy after Freire et al. (2018) advocates a 'problem-posing education', in which participants 'develop their power to perceive critically the way they exist in the world with which and in which they find themselves; they come to see the world not as a static reality, but as a reality in process, in transformation' (p.56). This perception involves recognising perpetual contingency over necessity. Being in an often marginalised 'third space' (Whitchurch, 2008), instead of continually trying to argue our way into existence via that consuming 'treadmill of justification', efforts may be better served in problem-posing provocation. So, embracing the relative marginality of LD within HE, rather than experiencing this as a lack to be rectified through laborious claims to exist, playing, and taking risks within a precarious field means having the ability to act with utopian curiosity, enacting the 'desire for a better way' (Levitas, 2011, p.198).

In concrete terms (lest there be yet another charge of intellectual masturbation), as Rebecca Bell argues (2011), 'Learning Developers have a very important central role to play not only in the creation and support of teaching resources, but also in challenging teaching and learning methods and perspectives' (p.153). Furthermore,

> working closely with academics, support staff and students, Learning Developers are privy to most sides of the learning process. Being in a unique position; they are often able to see the whole picture, mediating between the often-competing perspectives of students and staff.
>
> (Bell, 2011, p.144)

Acting as problem posers in quasi-intellectual exile, Learning Developers are well placed to model Adornian critical self-reflection. What they cannot do, however, is 'see the whole picture'; therein lie the risks of naivety and hubris, again. Instead, the Learning Developer may engage with content and context in a continually critically reflective manner.

Beyond Pedagogy

The value of a Freire-inspired Critical Pedagogy to LD is apparent through the above. Indeed, Freire and his successors, such as Peter McLaren and Henry

Giroux, are often cited in works in the field. However, one theory of education mostly conspicuous by its absence is heutagogy (Hase and Kenyon, 2013). Whilst Pedagogy is the teaching of others and Andragogy is the teaching of self-motivated adults (Knowles et al., 2020), Heutagogy builds upon the latter, and, foregrounding the learner, would advise that the Learning Developer facilitate self-directed and self-determined enquiry. This is not to argue against pedagogy, but to recognise its limits. Heutagogy helps to evade the limitations of a strictly pedagogical approach, which, owing to the predilections of the Learning Developer, will necessarily limit the possibilities and creative articulations of the learner.

So, linked to a heutagogical approach, Critical Pedagogy is not a formula about a repeatable formula, but instead, as McLaren (2000) articulates: 'a politically informed disposition and commitment to marginalized others in the service of justice and freedom' (McLaren, as cited in Trifonas, 2000, p.169). Similarly, heutagogy is about the learner going beyond the inevitable dogmas (however socially progressive) and limitations of the Learning Developer, who in a heutagogical approach would embody King's (1993) oft-quoted 'guide on the side'.

Critical Pedagogy is instructive in the development of thinkers invested in a concept of social justice and Critical Theory-informed 'reasonable conditions for life'. Whilst we may ostensibly be Vygotsky's 'better knowing others' (1978), we too, as argued throughout, are implicated in the very neoliberal tensions and contradictions that we often rail against. Thus, as critically self-reflective Learning Developers, we ought to encourage heutagogy (Abbeglen, Burns, and Sinfield, 2019). Still, whilst Abbeglen, Burns, and Sinfield (2019) refer to themselves as 'emancipatory educationists' (p.7), this piece argues to supplant such a self-concept with that of immanent critique in Adornian vein, as it more transparently recognises complicity and entanglement. The tensions in the discourse of emancipation are, as noted above, rooted in colonialism (Biesta, 2015, p.7). Though well-intentioned, emancipatory education becomes a manner of legitimising one's position (based upon measurable worth, etc.) and relies on 'something that is done to somebody and hence relies on a fundamental inequality between the emancipator and the one to be emancipated' (Biesta, 2015, p.71). Instead, what critical reflection grants the Learning Developer is an 'infinitesimal freedom' (Adorno, 2005b, p.6); a recognition of their complicity and positioning within a discourse that they seek to redress.

Discomfort over Fear

Allowing the fear of needing to justify one's worth and impact upon desirable student outcomes problematically implicates the processual nature of LD practice. Discussing teaching and education practices is often an emotionally loaded issue, exacerbated by the anxieties of practitioners (SEDA, 2014). In a community of practice like LD that consists of members from a variety of academic and professional backgrounds, the strength of having a multiplicity of perspectives is somewhat mitigated by many of us who feel that we have either accidentally landed into the community, or had the moniker thrust upon us. As such, Learning Developers may often shy away from engaging in critical self-reflection – it is too epistemologically and ontologically taxing. It then becomes simpler to practise 'helping' students, and demonstrate worth, invariably in metrics related to satisfaction, retention, and completion rates. In sum, the modus operandi becomes to act pedagogically and pastorally, and showcase the efficacy of input as much as possible to secure employment under precarious working conditions concomitant with the norms of neoliberalism. A summary to describe the ethos of the majority of colleagues I have worked with in the community would be along the certainly well-intentioned lines of 'I want students to do well, be well, and like me' (not necessarily in that order!). However, a problem with this ethos is that 'the dark irony of hegemony is that teachers take pride in acting on the very assumptions that work to enslave them' (Brookfield, 1995, p.17); namely, that efficacy ought to be measured by 'happy and healthy students who like me'. Rather, in our unequal and unjust society, holding a space for heutagogical, over pedagogical, discomfort (Amsler, 2011) is crucial to nurturing learners who can critically reflect and develop creative articulations of 'better' ways.

Conclusion

To be critical in LD is to continually foreground contingency and positionality, and undertake immanent critique of what we are doing, in the service of what, and in the interests of whom. Whilst this may appear a sobering take on the potentiality of LD, it actually is – sorry. Eschewing reifying and paradoxically limiting conceptions such as being emancipators, and thus, perhaps unwittingly, privileging ourselves and our practices owing to professional insecurities that remain concomitant with neoliberal governance, immanent critique means that nothing is sacred, including our professional identities (Eyre and Slawson, 2018). The tension remains, then, how to confidently articulate what LD is, how to be a Learning Developer, and engage in social justice pursuits such as championing the causes of historically marginalised demographics within HE, without undertaking some reification (McArthur, 2016, p.974). Perhaps there are, on balance, more positive aspects to having a hook on which to hang one's identity hat than not. Still, it is hoped that this chapter will foster an ethos of immanent critique when engaging with arguments put forth in subsequent contributions.

References

Abbeglen, S., Burns, T and Sinfield, S. (2019) 'It's Learning Development, Jim – but not as we know it: academic literacies in third space', *Journal of Learning Development in Higher Education*, 15: 1–19.

Adorno, T. W. (2005a) *Critical Models: Interventions and Catchwords*, trans. H. W. Pickford, New York: Columbia University Press.

Adorno, T. W. (2005b) *Minima Moralia: Reflections from Damaged Life*, trans. E. F. N. Jephcott, London: Verso.

Adorno, T. W. (1973) *Negative Dialectics*, trans. E. B. Ashton, New York: Routledge.

Adorno, T. W. (1984) 'The Essay as Form', trans. B. Hullot-Kentor and F. Will, *New German Critique*, 32(Spring/Summer): 151–171.

Allen, A. and Goddard, R. (2017) *Education and Philosophy: An Introduction*. Los Angeles: SAGE.

Amsler, S. (2011) 'From "therapeutic" to political education: The centrality of affective sensibility in critical pedagogy', *Critical Studies in Education*, 52(1): 47–63.

Association for Learning Development in Higher Education. (2022) *About ALDinHE*. Available at: https://aldinhe.ac.uk/about-aldinhe/ (Accessed: 30 October 2022).

Ball, S.J. (2021) *The Education Debate*. 4th edn. Bristol: Policy Press.

Barlow, A., Ackroyd, J. and Phillips, A. (2011) 'Is Learning Development "Part of the Problem"?', in P. Hartley, J. Hilsdon, C. Keenan, S. Sinfield and M. Verity (eds), *Learning Development in Higher Education*. London: Palgrave Macmillan.

Barnett, R. (2011) *Being a University*. Oxford: Routledge.

Bassil-Morozow, H. (2015) *The Trickster and the System: Identity and Agency in Contemporary Society*. London: Routledge.

Bell, R. (2011) 'Negotiating and Nurturing: Challenging Staff and Student Perspectives of Academic Writing', in P. Hartley, J. Hilsdon, C. Keenan, S. Sinfield and M. Verity (eds), *Learning Development in Higher Education*. London: Palgrave Macmillan

Biesta, G.J.J. (2015) *Beautiful Risk of Education*. Oxford: Routledge.

Biesta, G.J.J. (2016) *Good Education in an Age of Measurement: Ethics, Politics, Democracy*. Oxford: Routledge.

Brookfield, S. D. (1995) *Becoming a Critically Reflective Teacher*. San Francisco: Jossey-Bass.

Education Support Partnership. (2018) *Staff Wellbeing in Higher Education*. Available at: https://www.educationsupport.org.uk/media/fs0pzdo2/staff_wellbeing_he_research.pdf (Accessed: 12 November 2022).

Eyre, J. and Slawson, T. (2018) 'Dramatising Learning Development: towards an understanding without definition', *Journal of Learning Development in Higher Education*. https://doi.org/10.47408/jldhe.v0i0.472

Freire, P., Macedo, D. P., and Shor, I. (2018) *Pedagogy of the oppressed*, trans. M. B. Ramos. New York: Bloomsbury Academic.

Gopal, P. (2021) 'On Decolonisation and the University', *Textual Practice*, 35(6): 873–899.

Hargreaves, H. (2000) 'Four Ages of Professionalism and Professional Learning', *Teachers and Teaching*, 6(2): 151–182.

Hase, S. and Kenyon, C. (2013) *Self-Determined Learning: Heutagogy in Action*. London: Bloomsbury.

Horkheimer, M. (1975) *Critical Theory: Selected Essays*, trans. M. J. O'Connell and others. London: Bloomsbury.

King, A. (1993) 'From Sage on the Stage to Guide on the Side', *College Teaching*, 41(1): 30–35.

Knowles, M.S., Holton, E.F., Swanson, R.A., and Robinson, P.A. (2020) *The Adult Learner: The Definitive Classic in Adult Education and Human Resource Development*. Oxford: Routledge.

Levitas, R. (2011) *The Concept of Utopia*. Oxford: Peter Lang.

McArthur, J. (2016) 'Assessment for social justice: the role of assessment in achieving social justice', *Assessment and Evaluation in Higher Education*, 41(7): 967–981.

McLaren, P. (2000) 'Unthinking Whiteness: Rearticulating Diasporic Practice', in P. P. Trifonas (ed.), *Revolutionary Pedagogies: Cultural Politics, Instituting Education, and the Discourse of Theory*. London: Routledge.

Neary, M. (2020) *Student as Producer: How do Revolutionary Teachers Teach?* Winchester: Zero Books.

Sinfield, S., Holley, D., Burns, T., Hoskins, K., O'Neill, P. and Harrington, K. (2011) 'Raising the Student Voice: Learning Development as Socio-Political Practice', in P. Hartley, J. Hilsdon, C. Keenan, S. Sinfield and M. Verity (eds). *Learning Development in Higher Education*. London: Palgrave Macmillan.

Staff and Educational Development Association (SEDA). (2014) *Fear and Anxiety are the Enemies of Learning*. Available at: https://www.seda.ac.uk/resources/files/publications_174_25%20Fear%20and%20anxiety%20are%20the%20enemies%20of%20learning.pdf (Accessed: 12 November 2022).

Vygotsky, L.S. (1978) *Mind in Society: The Development of Higher Psychological Processes*. Massachusetts: Harvard University Press.

Whitchurch, C. (2008) 'Shifting identities and blurring boundaries: the emergence of Third Space professionals in UK higher education', *Higher Education Quarterly*, 62(4): 377–396.

13

PRACTICE VERSUS POLICY

Learning Development's Role in Supporting, Developing, and Challenging Equality, Diversity, and Inclusion in the Higher Education Sector

Anne-Marie Langford and Emma Kimberley

> *Our local hospital has a 'proud' zebra crossing. The floor markings are black and white but, on the signposts next to it, there are signs with the full rainbow flag including transgender and BAME colours. Passing that zebra crossing, we always wonder what is it really like to work and use that hospital as a person represented on that flag? What about the people with protected characteristics not represented by the flag? The crossing provides a starting point physically and metaphorically but makes us wonder where does the job begin and end? What does equality, diversity and inclusion mean for Learning Developers?*

Introduction

From highlighting power relations (Sinfield, Holley and Burns, 2009) to embracing pedagogies of discomfort (Dhillon, 2018), Learning Developers have interpreted and responded to key challenges around inclusion. Equality, diversity, and inclusion (EDI) addresses a broad spectrum of disadvantage in higher education (HE), advocating for interests based on ethnicity, class, disability, sexuality, gender, and religion, which could be seen as aligning with key Learning Development values. The HE sector as a whole has been criticised for gestural approaches and for focusing on policy statements rather than engaging with challenges faced by 'diverse' students (Tate and Bagguley, 2017, p.290). With its roots in initiatives such as the widening participation agenda (Samuels, 2013), the Learning Development sector has been associated with institutional expectations around supporting diverse students to assimilate (Hartley et al., 2011, p.22). However, in its own practice and theory, Learning Development has tended to move away from the deficit assumptions (Johnson, 2018) that often form part of this discourse, instead working towards more student-centred understandings through values such as development (Hill et al., 2010) and

DOI: 10.4324/9781003433347-17

emancipatory practice (ALDinHE, 2023). The field has used its unique position to work towards more holistic and student-centred conceptions of equity and inclusion.

To get a sense of how Learning Developers themselves currently conceptualise their work in terms of EDI policy, we circulated a survey on the LDHEN mailing list, using open-ended questions to prompt answers on how participants understand EDI, how they shape their practice in relation to it, and how they would like to develop. A thematic analysis was carried out on the results in relation to the literature. The survey received ethical approval from the University of Northampton. There were 19 respondents, with six coming from management or leadership roles, and two indicating specific responsibilities for EDI. The sample comes from a self-selecting population of active Learning Developers with a stated interest in the subject. In this chapter we use literature from the Learning Developers and HE community to contextualise their responses around several themes: EDI policy and Learning Development; moving from policy to practice; conversations and barriers; working with EDI on an institutional level; and future actions.

EDI Policy and Learning Development

Fossland and Habti (2022, p.1) suggest that equality, diversity, and inclusion is 'the most important social responsibility within higher education institutions today', partly because it represents the intersection of a range of changing experiences and perspectives. While there has been a 'proliferation of policy statements' in relation to EDI, the policies themselves have been criticised for being gestural and for failing to create real change (Tate and Bagguley, 2017). In the discourse around race, which has been an issue at the forefront of EDI discussions and policies, this superficial policy response has been identified as coming from two areas particularly: the tendency to focus on including diverse students in an unchanged system (Puwar, 2004, p.1), and the emphasis on measurable signifiers of inequality, such as award gaps, rather than deeper and less easily quantifiable issues such as belonging (Loke, 2018, p.387).

While respondents to the survey saw EDI as 'essential' and 'fundamental' to their role, some expressed frustration with the abstract approach and 'vague value statements' of EDI policies. One participant noted that the meaning of words and phrases used in policy to describe concepts around inclusivity are often 'undefined, and hugely subjective' and that '[a]s a result, a working definition gets decided ad hoc by whoever either (a) has the authority ... or (b) has the loudest voice'. Such ambiguity around definitions can lead to a wide variety of interpretations. Inclusion, for example, has been seen as a focus of marketing strategies (Dhillon, 2020) as well as a gestural and ineffective response to deeper inequalities in higher education (Pathak, 2021). Koutsouris et al. (2022, p.887), in their review of inclusion policies from UK elite universities, found similar discourses at work, emphasising neoliberal ideas of globalism, excellence, production, and performance as amongst the rationales for EDI policies. EDI is often seen as an act of legal compliance. This results in inclusion in policy documents becoming connected to human resources and being seen as managerialist and legalistic (Koutsouris et al., 2022). The implementation of EDI has become associated with neoliberal managerialism. This has impacted on policy's ability to encompass student-centred perspectives which means that processes for policy development sometimes leave the most vulnerable stakeholders 'voiceless and powerless' (Holley et al., 2011, p.200).

There is a tension inherent in recognising that EDI is mediated through institutional policies which aim to stimulate positive change, while, in one participant's words, 'realising that the academy and institution reproduces issues of inequality'. This tension also exists in the gap between the top-down approach to EDI that prioritises policy, contrasting with practitioners' focus on delivery. Contributions to the survey showed efforts to bridge that gap by translating 'typical EDI language' into concrete concepts that can be embedded into practice and making links 'between values and action'.

Moving from Policy to Practice

In contrast to the vague language of policy, the understandings of EDI revealed in the survey were more practice-based and student-focused. One participant noted that 'unless an EDI policy is being discussed specifically, most conversations are applied ones and focus on particular aspects'. When asked how Learning Developers understood EDI and how it applied to their role, they characterised it in terms of concrete actions. Ten of the nineteen respondents mentioned accessibility as key to inclusivity in teaching, and there were also multiple comments citing co-creation and collaboration, representative resources, and use of inclusive language as important factors. These actions are commonly related to student-centred practice. Although participants identified that the ALDinHE values 'focus more on inclusivity than diversity' and that a commitment towards diversity is not 'explicitly stated', many of the responses showed a strong movement beyond inclusion and towards placing a higher value on diversity. One respondent described trying not to 'cave to the need to work normatively' and to celebrate unconventional ways of working despite the 'normative pressures' coming from practices and expectations of students and academics. Survey participants identified using a wider range of practices and resources in response to learning about their students' needs and preferences as key to their focus on EDI. Much of the literature sees widening the mix of approaches to learning and teaching as a positive way to respond to the diversity of the student body (Wilkinson, 2018; Hill et al., 2010).

A strong theme in the community literature and the survey is an awareness of the intermediary role of Learning Developers in 'addressing systemic as well as individual issues of equality and inclusion'. Often, Learning Developers feel caught between dual imperatives: socialising students into the academy's existing conventions, while also empowering them to be aware of the sociopolitical context in which these operate. The survey reflects an anxiety about this position as 'part of the system that gatekeeps', and the risk of falling 'into familiar patterns which unintentionally exclude'. Lillis (2019, p.1) sees the ability to work 'within/across the transformative-normative' as not only a skill but a responsibility for those who work with students; this boundary is particularly porous in the work of Learning Developers as they negotiate between different sets of expectations.

Although most conversations focus on practice, the actions they describe often spring from ethical thinking. Learning Developers answering the survey showed a moral connection to EDI, recognising that '[a]s well as being a legal requirement it is also an ethical one'. In her analysis of the LDHEN Hive Mind, Stapleford (2019, p.15) finds social justice values to be at the core of Learning Developer identity: 'it is what informs Learning Development practice and provides a source of unity'.

Johnson (2018, p.17), in his survey of fourteen Learning Developers, also identified the perception of a common unifying purpose 'around delivering a morally-founded "service" to students'. This sense of shared purpose within the community is particularly expressed through recommendations in the Learning Development literature that Learning Developers should see themselves as 'cultural critics' within the university (Parkes, 2018). This might involve being aware of when pressures and demands from neoliberal HE around issues such as retention detract from core Learning Development values that centre on students (Parkes, 2018, p.6).

Dhillon (2018, p.9) argues that such an awareness might be developed through consistent attention to 'the affective quality of HE' and the uncomfortable social realities that it reveals. In addition, students can be empowered when staff resist the gestural closure provided by the wellbeing agenda within institutions as a response to EDI issues, and instead foreground openness and criticality. This approach suggests that listening to and understanding student perspectives around the contexts in which EDI policies exist might work as an antidote to responses that seek to tick boxes or where change is more visible than meaningful.

Conversations and Barriers

Learning Developers' commitment to EDI could be shaped by biases stemming from their own identity and characteristics. These may prevent or allow them to perceive the barriers that diverse students face. While Learning Development 'embraces diversity', one participant stated that 'it isn't a diverse profession'. The survey shows an awareness of the range of stakeholders involved in EDI conversations, and the 'invisible barriers' that these conversations can reveal. Many respondents saw the insights such conversations give into the lived experience of their diverse colleagues and students as fundamental to working against the vagueness and abstraction of policy. At the same time, respondents recognised that educating staff 'isn't the responsibility of diverse colleagues and students' and were aware of the risk of reinforcing 'othering' and the repetition of historical and social disadvantage that these conversations might entail. There was an emphasis throughout on decentring majority perspectives and making space for diverse voices. While some still spoke in terms of 'accommodating' or being inclusive, there is a sense that many practitioners are moving beyond this and making space for diverse views to change the practice. This is seen as something that can be practised actively by getting 'into the habit of shifting focus outside ourselves and our experience' to form an understanding of 'how issues affect different student communities based on their positionality, i.e., ethnicity, gender, disability, etc'.

Lack of time for the conversations and self-education needed was identified as a barrier to engaging with EDI. Many respondents expressed a desire for 'more time and space for learning and thinking about EDI'. Respondents also wanted more time to spend on the practicalities of accessibility such as checking captioning, and for reflection with students. One respondent explained that 'these issues often get lost in the madness of semester teaching'. Addressing inequalities often requires additional time and resources; policy consistently fails to explicitly recognise this. These responses might suggest that without the capacity to work towards deeper understandings, Learning Development staff are limited to responding reactively when issues come up, rather than being able to be proactive in changing conditions.

Working with EDI on an Institutional Level

As Pritchard (2022, p.4) points out, using Bourdieu's terms, Learning Developers are good at 'helping students understand and adapt to the game' by revealing the hidden rules of academic practices, but the more challenging task is changing the game at a strategic level. Learning Developers have specific expertise here because of their intermediary position, but advocacy is needed in order to develop the perception of who we are and what we can do. Buchanan (2015, p.2) states that if we are to be part of the debate, we 'must be able to converse about [our] role and contribution to the university's commitments, as laid out through government and wider recognised bodies such as the Higher Education Authority (HEA)'. This suggests that Learning Development needs a clearer understanding of how it fits into the broader policy landscape at all levels. This could assist Learning Developers to negotiate a path between the dual imperatives of neoliberal HE marketisation and its own values.

Koutsouris et al. (2022, p.880) argue that sometimes HE practitioners have limited awareness of the complexities around inclusion and how such principles might be translated into practice, which can also apply to Learning Developers' relationship to policy. If Learning Developers wish to contribute to the EDI discussion, they need to alter their perception of themselves and how they are perceived within their institutions by working to gain influence within areas of the university system to which they have not traditionally had access. Wingate (2019, p.5) similarly points out that academics need to do more than take an academic literacies approach with students to effect wide-ranging change at an institutional level, with collaboration with other university departments being key to this effort.

Johnson (2018, p.17) suggests that '[a] stronger and more coherent research voice for Learning Development may be vital in allowing that influence to be heard'. The Learning Development community is currently active in shaping and defining a professional culture from within (Stapleford, 2019, p.6; Johnson, 2018) and shaping Learning Development as a field through research (Syska and Buckley, 2022), but there is also an awareness that the profession could and should be more involved in wider institutional debates on issues such as EDI. Pritchard (2022) argues that instead of waiting to be invited to the table, Learning Developers can work on shaping institutional policies by actively defining their own roles in relation to them. Our survey results showed an awareness of this gap and a sense that developing more social currency within the institution to promote our unique role could help to bridge it. One respondent stated they were unsure of how to gain influence in their institution but felt that Learning Developers have a level of insight on student diversity that should be used to participate actively in discussions on EDI:

> [T]here are so many missed opportunities here. Learning Developers are a rich source of data, can feed into APPs, can contribute to policy development and implementations, and should really be pushing back against the deficit models that are so often dominant. Learning Development is poorly understood or not even known about in senior management.

Hilsdon et al. (2011, pp.255–8) voiced a hope that leaders in management would come to see Learning Developers as 'uniquely valuable institutional assets' who can 'feed vital insights back into the lifeblood of our institutions'. A few of the survey's participants were active in such roles, either involved in or leading on discussions around writing and applying EDI policy. This suggests that Learning Development can contribute to institutional EDI policies on a number of levels: by bringing a practical and student-focused approach in our practice; by using our role as insider/outsider critics of academic culture; and by bringing the unique 'ethos' (Sinfield et al., 2011, p.66) of Learning Development to the table to advocate for change on an institutional level.

Future Actions

While Learning Developers see EDI as fundamental to their role, our values and the wider literature indicate that the broad range of deeper understandings needed to embed it in practice come from attention to the feelings and experiences of a diverse range of staff and students. Learning Developers are uniquely well placed to take part in these conversations, but also need to play a role in sharing them upwards within their institutions. In this way we can support the grassroots institution-wide change that is fundamental to our values. Opening conversations about how students learn and the barriers they face, rather than aiming to predict needs and offer accommodations, and acting as intermediaries in institutional conversations, can help us work towards a sense of belonging for all students.

References

ALDinHE (2023) *About ALDinHE*. Available at: https://aldinhe.ac.uk/about-aldinhe/ (Accessed: 10 February 2023).

Buchanan, A. (2015) 'Anecdotal to actual: identifying users of learning development to inform future practice', *Journal of Learning Development in Higher Education*, 9. https://doi.org/10.47408/jldhe.v0i9.295

Dhillon, S. (2020) 'An immanent critique of decolonisation projects', *LD Theory*. Available at: https://ldtheory.wordpress.com/ (Accessed: 10 February 2023).

Dhillon, S. (2018) 'Whose wellbeing is it anyway?' *Journal of Learning Development in Higher Education*. https://doi.org/10.47408/jldhe.v0i0.460

Fossland, T. and Habti, D. (2022) 'University practices in an age of supercomplexity: Revisiting diversity, equality, and inclusion in higher education', *Journal of Praxis in Higher Education*, 4(2), 1–10. https://doi.org/10.47989/kpdc355

Hartley, P., Hilsdon, J., Keenan, C., Sinfield, S. and Verity, M. (2011) *Learning Development in Higher Education*. Basingstoke: Palgrave Macmillan.

Hill, P., Tinker, A. and Caterall, S. (2010) 'From deficiency to development: the evolution of academic skills provision at one UK university', *Journal of Learning Development in Higher Education*, 2. https://doi.org/10.47408/jldhe.v0i2.54

Johnson, I. (2018) 'Driving Learning Development professionalism forward from within', *Journal of Learning Development in Higher Education*, Special edition. https://doi.org/10.47408/jldhe.v0i0.470

Koutsouris, G., Stentiford, L. and Norwich, B. (2022) 'Critical exploration of inclusion policies of elite UK universitie', *British Education Research Journal*, 48: 878–895.

Lillis, T. (2019) "Academic Literacies': sustaining a critical space on writing in academia', *Journal of Learning Development in Higher Education*, 15. https://doi.org/10.47408/jldhe.v0i15.565

Loke, G. (2018) 'So what next? A policy response', in: J. Arday and H. Mirza (eds), *Dismantling Race in Higher Education: Racism, Whiteness and Decolonising the Academy*. London: Palgrave Macmillan.

Parkes, S. (2018) 'A learner developer perspective: critiquing dominant practices and cultures within university spaces', *Journal of Learning Development in Higher Education*, Special edition. https://doi.org/10.47408/jldhe.v0i0.464

Pathak, P. (2021) *Why It's Time to Retire Equality, Diversity and Inclusion*. Available at: https://wonkhe.com/blogs/why-its-time-to-retire-equality-diversity-and-inclusion/ (Accessed: 10 February 2023).

Puwar, N. (2004) *Space Invaders: Race, Gender and Bodies out of Place*. Oxford: Berg.

Pritchard, C. (2022) 'Learning Developers as their own cultural critics?' *Journal of Learning Development in Higher Education*, 25. https://doi.org/10.47408/jldhe.v0i0.464

Samuels, P. (2013) 'Promoting Learning Development as an Academic Discipline', *Journal of Learning Development in Higher Education*, 5. https://doi.org/10.47408/jldhe.v0i5.146

Sinfield, S., Holley, D., and Burns, T. (2009). 'A journey into silence: students, stakeholders and the impact of a strategic governmental policy document in the UK', *Social Responsibility Journal*, 5(4), 566–574. https://doi.org/10.1108/17471110910995401

Sinfield, S., Holley, D., Burns, T., Hoskins, K., O'Neill, P. and Harrington, K. (2011) 'Raising the student voice: Learning Development as socio-political practice', in: P. Hartley, J. Hilsdon, C. Keenan, S. Sinfield and M. Verity (eds), *Learning Development in Higher Education*. Basingstoke: Palgrave Macmillan.

Stapleford, K. (2019) 'The LDHEN hive mind: Learning development in UK higher education as a professional culture', *Journal of Learning Development in Higher Education*, 16. https://doi.org/10.47408/jldhe.v0i16.510

Syska, A. and Buckley, C. (2022) 'Writing as liberatory practice: Unlocking knowledge to locate an academic field', *Teaching in Higher Education*, 28(2): 439–454. https://doi.org/10.1080/13562517.2022.2114337

Tate, S.A. and Bagguley, P. (2017) 'Building the anti-racist university: Next steps', *Race Ethnicity and Education*, 20: 289–299.

Wilkinson, J. (2018) 'Engagement in higher education. Who's not engaging?' *Journal of Learning Development in Higher Education*, Special edition. https://doi.org/10.47408/jldhe.v0i0.474

Wingate, U. (2019) 'Achieving transformation through collaboration: the role of academic literacies', *Journal of Learning Development in Higher Education*, 15. https://doi.org/10.47408/jldhe.v0i15.566

14

CLOSING THE GAP

Learning Development and Race

Ryan Arthur

> *A student emailed me her proposed research project; as soon as I saw the details of her project, I knew that I would have to have an uncomfortable conversation with the student. A conversation that would pit my being against my profession. Her project sought to place racial discrimination as a public health crisis. Her project brilliantly spoke truth to power, but I was intimately aware of the race-averse department that would grade her project. So, I worked with the student to dilute her language to make it more palatable for the department. But, sometimes, I wonder: did I help or harm her?*

Introduction

Teaching academic skills is not neutral or universal; 'it's a discourse through which we inculcate and reinforce certain behaviours and values' (Webster, 2018b). These implicit values and behaviours we teach can create a positive learning environment or socialise students into what we believe is 'their place' (Webster, 2018b; Arthur, 2023). It is vital that we are mindful of our 'invisible lessons about gender, class, ability or race' (Webster, 2018b).

Higher Education and Race

Singh's article about the ethnic minority student experience in the autumn of 1990 was barely able to muster source material or any interest, to the extent that he conceded, 'This analysis may raise more questions than it provides answers' (p.345). During this same decade, it appears that US scholars were also contending with the same issues: 'Race remains undertheorized, unproblematized, and underinvestigated ... leaving us with no means to confront the racialized atmosphere of the university and no way to account for the impact

DOI: 10.4324/9781003433347-18

of the persistence of prejudice on writers and texts' (Prendergast, 1998, p.36; Gilyard, 1996). It was not until another Singh (2011) published his synthesis of research evidence on Black and minority ethnic (BME)[1] students' participation in higher education that we could distinguish a body of literature.

Learning Development and Race

The growth of literature from the 2010s was not mirrored in the scholarship of LD. Although the practice of LD addressing race has promising signs, scholarship has lagged behind. For example, the premier text on LD, *Learning Development in Higher Education* (Hartley et al., 2010), fails to engage with race explicitly. Though this text recognised that diversity has increased within the field of higher education, there was not more than a passing reference to a conference paper penned by Lillis (1999). Moreover, a routine search of the leading journal of LD (*JLDHE*) and journal repositories reveals LD's minimal engagement with race.

There are several possible reasons for the lack of literature. The first reason relates to the field itself; LD is a relatively young and developing field (Hartley et al., 2010). Race is one of the issues that LD theory and practice have failed to engage with fully. As the field of LD matures and expands, we will hopefully see more attempts to tackle issues around race. Also, as a young field of study, LD may not carry the same legitimacy as long-standing academic fields (Webster, 2018a). Thus, Learning Developers may opt to situate their research in these other fields, foregoing any particular reference to LD. A related reason could be that as LD developed, some may have decided to keep the scholarship of LD neutral; they consciously confined their focus to how students learn and how we can help students achieve their goals. They did not want to overly politicise or overburden their research with extraneous issues since there are other fields in which 'race talk' or other controversial issues can be considered. Although it is an understandable position, consciously avoiding race prevents one from appreciating the full picture of the learner; Lena Williams's (2000) account in *It's the Little Things* exemplifies this point. A white colleague mentioned at a diversity meeting that he does not see colour and only sees 'people as people'. Several attendees took offence at this comment: 'You don't see how offensive that sounds when you take away a vital part of a person's identity? ... take the same observation and replace the word color with gender or age and maybe you'll get the point'. Williams (2000, p.25) added, 'How unfortunate women might feel if men said they "don't see gender". How harmful it would be to elderly people if we "don't see age"'.

The second reason, the 'whiteness' of the LD field, may arguably explain the lack of literature. Although there is no data on the ethnic diversity of Learning Developers, it would be safe to assume black and brown Learning Developers constitute the minority, reflecting the wider HE sector; in 2020/2021, just 17% of academic staff were Black and Minority Ethnic (BME) (HESA, 2022). This is not to say that all white colleagues are indifferent to race and its relationship to learning; what is implied is that white colleagues are more likely to be 'privileged' with the option to engage or not to engage (Cabrera, Franklin and Watson, 2016). Also, they may not have access to the lived experiences of people of colour, so race may appear further down on their list of issues in HE, optional or unimportant (Cabrera, Franklin and Watson, 2016). Since universities reflect wider society, it would not be far-fetched to believe that the ideology of colour-blindness has seeped into LD practice and theory. Colour-blindness is a figurative way of claiming an inability or refusal to be conscious of race or its implications (Agostoa, Karanxhaa and Bellara, 2015; Hitchcock, 2001: Korgen, 2002). Colour-blindness is affronted by the acknowledgement of race, stresses individuality, emphasises our common humanity, and works towards achieving 'one people' status (Hitchcock, 2001; Korgen, 2002). Race is meaningless and should be treated as such. Not so for many of their black and brown counterparts who experienced its impact as students and continue to experience it as staff members (Arthur, 2022).

Third, rather than focusing on race explicitly, LD theory and practice lean towards umbrella issues under which race may fall, such as academic literacies, widening participation, new entrants, inclusion, diversity, equality, non-traditional students, access and participation, social deprivation, and inequalities (Arthur, 2022). Arday and Mirza (2019, p.322) observe that within the current sociopolitical context, it is 'unusual to name race, racism or racial injustice so explicitly. Such language is politely subsumed within palatable umbrella terms. Race or racism is seldom named or foregrounded'. Although these umbrella terms will undoubtedly relate to students of colour, they do not go to the heart of the matter. For example, while widening participation (WP) is necessary for tackling racial inequality in HE, it is insufficient by itself. It is problematic to recruit BME students while holding onto deficit models (Arday and Mirza, 2019).

Though the literature is sparse, there are promising signs if one looks diligently enough. Buchanan's pioneering study in 2015 sought to discover the diversity of students availing of LD, with regard to characteristics such as gender, ethnicity, disability, age, parental education, and module marks. Though ethnicity/race was not her explicit focus, her research indicated that students at De Montford University using LD services were more likely to be from a BME background compared to the university student profile and that the BME attainment gap between white ethnic background students reduced year on year. Loddick and Coulson (2020) looked at the impact of LD tutorials on student attainment. They gathered student assessment data (over 16,000 students and 175,000 assessments) for over three and a half years. Once again, even though race/ethnicity was not a focus, their study revealed students from a black ethnic background and aged 25 years or below also gained the most in terms of attainment compared to other ethnic groups and more mature students. Finally, Davison et al. (2022) reviewed the 'Skills for Success' (SfS) in an East Midlands university to support the transition into higher education for students from diverse backgrounds. SfS is a non-credit-bearing compulsory unit co-devised by students and a range of academic, clinical, and support staff to address the non-academic challenges underrepresented groups face as they adjust to university life. Preliminary data from SfS indicate that a focus on non-academic skill development during an extended transition period positively impacts the attainment of those from BME groups, mature students and those who report mental health conditions.

As of writing, the only study with an explicit focus on race is Arthur's 2023 article, which advocates a pedagogy of race consciousness (PRC) to enhance the critical thinking abilities of undergraduate students. The article called for Learning Developers to become conscious of their positionality to bring about change in the academy. There are also a few blog posts authored by Learning Developers; Steve Rooney (2020) discusses possible responses to the BME award gap in the University of Leicester staff blog; Helen Webster's *Rattus Scholasticus* blog contains several posts that touch on race and LD; and Sunny Dhillon explores the practical difficulties of tackling racial disparities in the academy. Kevin Brazant wrote an article for *Times Higher Education*, which advocated the creation of spaces for academic colleagues to think about race as part of pedagogy. Moreover, the Association for Learning Development in Higher Education (ALDinHE) and its sister associations have recently hosted conferences and workshops that explore the intersection between race and LD.

Although the above activity does not constitute a body of literature, it demonstrates the propensity of LD to confront race in the academy.

BAME Award Gap

All UK HEIs have to contend with the 'award gap' between the proportion of white British students receiving 'good' degree classifications compared to UK-domiciled students from minority ethnic groups (Webb et al., 2021). The few LD studies in this area inform us that black students walk through our doors more often than their white counterparts and that LD tutorials can help close the award gap (Buchanan, 2015; Loddick and Coulson, 2020; Davison et al., 2022). Learning Developers often have to engage with significant numbers of students of colour whom the academy has failed; it would be prudent of us to not replicate the same problematic institutional practices that led them to our doors (Huda, 2022; Arthur, 2023).

Closing the Gap

As a result of the unique position that LD holds, there is significant evidence of Learning Developers working to close the award gap. Table 14.1 documents the range of activities of Learning Developers seeking to close the award gap. The information in the table is derived from survey data and a literature review.

TABLE 14.1 LD Activity to address the BME Award Gap

University	Activity
Birkbeck College, University of London	**Enhancing Student Achievement Pilot Project** This project supports students by mentoring, coaching and critical friendship.
Birkbeck College, University of London	**Black Question Time: The Call of Success** Black Question Time is an online monthly interview series with inspirational public figures from the Black community.
De Montfort University (DMU)	**Review of support and engagement** At regular intervals, Learning Services review their support and engagement with selected programmes impacted by the award gap.
De Montfort University (DMU)	**Assessment checklist** As part of the Decolonising DMU toolkit, a non-remedial Assessment Checklist was developed to signpost students to crucial study skills resources.
London College of Communication, University of Arts London (LCC)	**Critical imagining** As part of a wider anti-racist approach, critical imaging utilises images and texts that represent marginalised communities.
London College of Fashion (LCF)	**Proactive Personalised Support** Academic Support lecturers perused internal grade data and developed a theory of change to identify students to contact.
London Metropolitan University (LMU)	**Education for Social Justice Framework (ESJF)** ESJF is essentially a two-pronged approach, staff-facing and student-facing; the University's Centre for Professional and Educational Development focused on staff training on issues around EDI literacy and Academic mentors (AMs) focus on supporting students to develop academic literacies.
London Metropolitan University (LMU)	**Disrupt the Discourse (DtD)** The DtD project aids lecturers to find creative ways to collaborate with students as part of learning and teaching. These resources included podcast interviews, articles, webinars, and live-streamed intimate conversations with leading academics, community partners, and activists.
London Metropolitan University (LMU)	**Academic Reading Circles** Establishment of Academic Reading Circles (ARCs) which consists of three component areas: common text shared with the whole group; defined roles taken up (in rotation) by each member; and discussion time spent on the readings.

Table 14.1 (Continued)

University	Activity
London South Bank University (LSBU)	**Inclusive Curriculum** LSBU introduced LD workshops at key progression stages of the BA (Hons) Social Work to support the transition between years.
University of Brighton	**The Inclusive Practice Partnership Scheme (IPPS)** IPPS is a five-year, funded student–staff partnership project that reviews module curricula in relation to the representation of racial, ethnic, and cultural identities to make recommendations to diversify or decolonise the curriculum.
University of Kent	**Academic Coaching for Excellence (ACE)** The ACE programme partners students with an ACE coach. The ACE coach functions as a supportive, non-judgemental, critical friend providing a degree of academic and professional support and guidance.
University of Lincoln	**Skills for Success (SfS)** SfS is a semester-long transition support unit incorporated into an existing, compulsory Study Skills module. SfS addresses the non-academic challenges of adjusting to university life.
University of Northampton	**Research on measurable impact on attainment** Undergraduate student profile and assessment data were taken from the university records system over a three-year period and linked to the LD tutorial database based on whether a student had a tutorial with Learning Development within 30 days of its hand-in date.

For more details, refer to ALDinHE (2023).

Closing the gap is not without its difficulties. Attempts to speak frankly about race are 'fraught with risk and challenge'. Leonardo and Porter (2010, p.140) state that by sharing your real perspectives on race, you might become a target of personal and academic threats. It would be inconsiderate for the author to urge fellow Learning Developers to discuss race without acknowledging that their wellbeing is at stake. Thus, the Developer, particularly the Developer of colour, must decide whether or not to place safety as their central consideration.

Recommendations

- Given the positive impact that LD tutorials have on the Award Gap, LD teams should strive to play an active role in crafting and implementing their universities' Access and Participation Plans (Buchanan, 2015; Loddick and Coulson, 2020; Davison et al., 2022).[2]

- As demonstrated by Table 14.1, approaches are wide and varied but often carried out in isolation. A collective effort in the form of a nationwide working group can enhance these approaches. This group can be a platform to exchange ideas and experience of tackling the award gap. By exploiting existing cross-institutional links between Learning Developers, there is the potential to develop a collective response to the award gap, which is unprecedented in the UK HE sector.
- Hosting award gap-themed conferences at universities to highlight our current activities and success stories. As 'third space professionals', such a spotlight can help Developers 'overcome ambiguities and maintain clear links between our individual tasks and institutional goals' (Smith et al., 2021, p.512).
- Learning Developers delivering academic skills or foundation modules is becoming increasingly commonplace. However, instead of focusing on academic skills, developers can enhance academic literacies by developing an 'anti-module' that interrogates the conventional modules and facilitates a greater expression of identity. For example, the conventional module 'caring for vulnerable adults' can be accompanied by an anti-module that provides a space for students to unpack the core tenets and hidden assumptions of caring for vulnerable adults and identify areas where students could benefit the field of caring for vulnerable adults.

Conclusion

At present, LD practice appears to be the home of a race-conscious LD, not necessarily in print. Nonetheless, with time, print will eventually compete with practice. Until that time, it is vital that Learning Developers seize the moment; the pressure on universities to close the award gap presents opportunities for developers to play more significant roles. Additionally, justifying LD activities with the language of the award gap offers us significant protection from the 'violence' of the academy by legitimising our passions. What is most important is that Developers should not be 'empty vessels'; they come to the academy with their rich lived experiences. Instead of casting these experiences aside before they enter the classroom, why not use them in their sessions to enhance the learning experiences of our students and also feel a sense of wholeness?

Notes

1 BME is used this article 'to refer to individuals from Black British, Black African, British Indian, Pakistani and Bangladeshi, Chinese and those from other non-White backgrounds' (Bhopal and Pitkin, 2020, p. 544). The author is aware of the limitations of the term; primarily, BME individuals are not a homogenous group. However, it is used because it is a 'useful designation in a field such as higher education in which White identities remain dominant', and it is now crucial for a literature search (Bhopal and Pitkin, 2020, p. 544).
2 Access and Participation Plans set out how UK higher education providers will improve equality of opportunity for underrepresented groups.

References

ALDinHE (2023) *LoveLD Magazine*, Issue 3. Available at: https://aldinhe.ac.uk/news/loveld-magazine (Accessed: 31 March 2023).

Abegglen, S., Burns, T. and Sinfield, S. (2019) 'It's Learning Development, Jim - but not as we know it: academic literacies in third-space', *Journal of Learning Development in Higher Education*, 15. https://doi.org/10.47408/jldhe.v0i15.500

Agosto, V., Karanxha, Z. and Bellara, A. (2015) 'Battling inertia in educational leadership: CRT praxis for race conscious dialogue', *Race Ethnicity and Education*, 18(6): 785–812. https://doi.org/10.1080/13613324.2014.885420

Arthur, R. (2023) '"Conscious" learning development: towards a pedagogy of race-consciousness', *Journal of Learning Development in Higher Education*, 26. https://doi.org/10.47408/jldhe.vi26.928

Arthur, R. (2022) 'I want to learn new things but still be myself: a decolonial approach to Education for Social Justice', *Investigations in University Teaching and Learning*, 13:1–7.

Brazant, K. (2021) 'Making space for academic colleagues to think about race as part of pedagogy', *Times Higher Education*. Available at: https://www.timeshighereducation.com/campus/making-space-academic-colleagues-think-about-race-part-pedagogy (Accessed: 31 March 2023)

Bhopal, K. and Pitkin, C. (2020) '"Same old story, just a different policy": race and policy making in higher education in the UK', *Race Ethnicity and Education*, 23(4): 530–547.

Cabrera, N., Franklin, J. and Watson, J. (2016) 'Whiteness in Higher Education: The Invisible Missing Link in Diversity and Racial Analyses', *ASHE Higher Education Report*, 42: 7–125. https://doi.org/10.1002/aehe.20116

Davison, E., Sanderson, R., Hobson, T. and Hopkins, J. (2022) 'Skills for Success? Supporting transition into higher education for students from diverse backgrounds', *Widening Participation and Lifelong Learning*, 24(1): 165–186.

Dhillon, S. (2020) 'Decolonisation isn't as simple as plenty of people suggest', *WONKHE*. Available at: https://wonkhe.com/blogs/decolonisation-isnt-as-simple-as-plenty-of-people-suggest/ (Accessed: 31 March 2023)

Ellsworth, E. (1989) 'Why doesn't this feel empowering? Working through the repressive myths of critical pedagogy', *Harvard Educational Review*, 59(3): 297–325. https://doi.org/10.17763/haer.59.3.058342114k266250

Gilyard, K. (1996) 'Higher Learning: Composition's 'racialized reflections'', *Watson Conference on Rhetoric and Composition*. Louisville, KY; New Hampshire: Boynton Cook.

Gutiérrez, K (2008) 'Developing a sociocritical literacy in the third space', *Reading Research Quarterly*, 43(2): 148–164. https://doi.org/10.1598/RRQ.43.2.3

Gutiérrez, K.D., Rymes, B. and Larson, J. (1995) 'Script, counterscript, and underlife in the classroom: James Brown versus *Brown v. Board of Education*', *Harvard Educational Review*, 65: 445–471.

Hartley, P., Hilsdon, J. Keenan, C., Sinfield, S. and Verity, M. (2010) *Learning Development in Higher Education*. New York: Palgrave Macmillan.

HESA (2022) 'Higher Education Staff Statistics: UK, 2020/21'. Available at https://www.hesa.ac.uk/news/01-02-2022/sb261-higher-education-staff-statistics (Accessed: 31 March 2023)

Huda, N. (2022) 'Towards the setting up and evaluation of academic reading circles: a critical commentary on academic reading practices in Higher Education institutions', *Investigations in University Teaching and Learning*, 13: 1–9.

Leonardo, Z. and Porter, R. (2010) 'Pedagogy of fear: Toward a Fanonian theory of 'safety' in race dialogue', *Race, Ethnicity and Education*, 13(2): 139–157.

Loddick, A. and Coulson, K. (2020) 'The impact of Learning Development tutorials on student attainment', *Journal of Learning Development in Higher Education*, 17. https://doi.org/10.47408/jldhe.vi17.558

London Metropolitan University. (2022) *ED7143 – Facilitating Student Learning (2022/23)*. Available at: https://intranet.londonmet.ac.uk/module-catalogue/record.cfm?mc=ED7143 (Accessed: 31 March 2023)

Korgen, K. (2002) *Crossing the Racial Divide: Close Friendships between Black and White Americans*. Connecticut: Prager.

Prendergast, C. (1998) 'Race: The absent presence in composition studies', *College Composition and Communication*, 50(1): 36–53.

Rooney, S. (2020) 'The BAME awarding gap: what we know, what we don't know, and how we might respond', *Leicester Learning Institute*. Available at: https://staffblogs.le.ac.uk/lli/2020/01/31/the-bame-awarding-gap-what-we-know-what-we-dont-know-and-how-we-might-respond/ (Accessed: 31 March 2023)

Smith, C., Holden, M., Yu, E. and Hanlon, P. (2021) '"So what do you do?": Third space professionals navigating a Canadian university context', *Journal of Higher Education Policy and Management*, 43(5): 505–519. https://doi.org/10.1080/1360080X.2021.1884513

Singh, G. (2011) 'Black and minority ethnic (BME) students' participation in higher education: improving retention and success', *AdvanceHE*. Available at: https://www.advance-he.ac.uk/knowledge-hub/black-and-minority-ethnic-bme-students-participation-higher-education-improving (Accessed: 31 March 2023)

Singh, R. (1990) 'Ethnic minority experience in higher education', *Higher Education Quarterly*, 44: 344–359. https://doi.org/10.1111/j.1468-2273.1990.tb01547.x

Webb, J., Arthur, R., McFarlane-Edmond, P., Burns, T. and Warren, D. (2022) 'An evaluation of the experiences of the hidden curriculum of Black and minority ethnic undergraduate health and social care students at a London university', *Journal of Further and Higher Education*, 46(3): 312–326. https://doi.org/10.1080/0309877X.2021.1915967

Webster, H. (2018a) 'National Teaching Fellowship'. Available at: https://rattusscholasticus.wordpress.com/2019/08/05/national-teaching-fellowship/ (Accessed: 31 March 2023)

Webster, H. (2018b) 'Learning Development and the hidden curriculum'. Available at: https://rattusscholasticus.wordpress.com/2018/02/19/learning-development-and-the-hidden-curriculum/ (Accessed: 31 March 2023)

Williams, L. (2000) *It's the Little Things: Everyday Interactions that Anger, Annoy and Divide the Races*. Florida: Harcourt.

15

DECOLONISATION IN LEARNING DEVELOPMENT

Georgia Koromila and Edward Powell

When asked to share my 'decolonising practice' in supporting international students, I was confronted with a sobering realisation: helping students excel within the established structures of a Western Higher Education institution felt more 'colonising' than not...

The overarching question becomes: (How) can we reconcile decolonising LD practice with the mandate of facilitating student success?

The concept of 'decolonising the curriculum' (DtC) has been gaining traction in higher education (HE) worldwide since 2015, following the Rhodes Must Fall protests at Rhodes University, South Africa, and the University of Oxford, UK. It is a complex idea whose meaning remains contested and evolving, and which intersects with other efforts to democratise HE. DtC calls for changes not just to curricula, but also to teaching practices, learning spaces, research processes, and institutional policies. As such, it is relevant to academic teaching staff, and also to many 'third space professionals' (Whitchurch, 2013), including Learning Developers. Given their comparatively close involvement in student learning, Learning Developers in particular ought to consider their potential contribution(s) towards DtC.

DtC proceeds from observations that HE is marked by the same racialised inequalities that pervade the sector's wider social contexts, and which are a legacy of European colonialism. Universities in Europe, North America, and Australasia dominate HE worldwide, with their – predominantly white – research staff having access to significantly greater resources and publication opportunities than those based in the Global South. As a result, the perspectives, experiences, and idioms of white Europeans and their settler descendants

DOI: 10.4324/9781003433347-19

are overrepresented in global knowledge production, to the extent that all others are disqualified as legitimate forms of knowledge. In many respects, therefore, the global dominance of Eurowestern thought has little to do with its epistemological merits but is instead a product of structural inequalities that have persisted beyond the dissolution of direct European colonial rule, a process that itself remains incomplete.

As a corrective, DtC demands that HE institutions (HEIs) place colonial histories at the centre of their curricula and challenge the simplistic distinction between Eurowestern rationalism and non-Eurowestern irrationalism, according to which only the former constitutes 'real' knowledge. This effort remains subject to debate and misrepresentation, predominantly in the STEM subjects, where the status of science itself is often regarded as being in question (see Roy, 2018). Advocates of DtC, though, maintain that DtC is not about 'abolishing science' or removing white voices from curricula. Instead, DtC calls for existing curricula to be expanded to include a more diverse array of voices, ideas, and perspectives, including those of thinkers from the Global South (Dennis, 2018). This expansion will then bring the university's colonial entanglements into sharper focus.

Notably, though, a curriculum or HEI may never be fully decolonised, because the historical relationship between colonialism and Western HE is potentially too deep to ever be undone. Universities helped rationalise colonialism (Bhambra, Dalia and Nişancıoğlu, 2018) and the neoliberal logic underpinning contemporary HE is incompatible with the aims of decolonisation (Adebisi, 2020; Dhillon, 2021). The end goal of DtC, therefore, might be better understood as a 'decolonising' rather than a 'decolonised' curriculum – that is, a curriculum in an ongoing process of decolonisation that will likely never be complete. Alternatively, a 'decolonial' curriculum might be a better way of articulating the goal of DtC. By this we mean a curriculum that 'decolonises', that contributes to wider efforts to overcome the ongoing legacies of European colonialism, by training students in ways that do not perpetuate those legacies. The question, then, becomes what a decolonial curriculum looks like, which, in turn, invites reflection on its implications for LD.

LD's Role in DtC

Scholarly accounts of curricular changes being made under the aegis of DtC indicate key skills students will need to succeed in a decolonial curriculum. Many of these skills are already familiar to Learning Developers. For example, if students are encouraged to work with non-academic partners, such as local community groups, the required skills will include groupwork and engaging non-academic audiences. Elsewhere, reflective practice takes a central role, as reported in Dache et al. (2021), where students are encouraged to explore their place within local and global networks of unevenly distributed power, and when facing cases of injustice and systemic oppression. Such exercises take students across disciplinary boundaries, notably into history, sociology, and anthropology; they will need support with learning to work between wide-ranging disciplines. Meanwhile, this process may challenge many students' deep-seated understandings of their subjects, of what defines knowledge, even of themselves as producers of knowledge. In addressing how unjust social circumstances influence knowledge production, DtC challenges what Dennis (2018, pp.192–3) calls 'the unmarked scholar', whose knowledge is untainted by their position within the ongoing history of colonial inequality. This challenge can be disorienting and traumatising, and can provoke resistance (Edwards and Shahjahan, 2021). Learning Developers can help ease this experience, given the centrality of doubt and discomfort to the process of critical analysis. A decolonial curriculum, though, might demand an extension of this aspect of critical analysis, a reminder that it applies to all ways of defining knowledge.

Perhaps the most challenging skillset for students to learn, therefore, will be the ability to recognise diverse ways of defining and expressing knowledge. Many of the pedagogical innovations described in the DtC scholarship introduce ways of claiming and expressing knowledge that are demonstrably different to Eurowestern conventions (see Pete, 2018; Cicek et al., 2021; Dache et al., 2021; Pratt and Gladue, 2022). Encountering these non-Eurowestern forms of knowledge will require students to remain open-minded, curious, and self-reflexive, and to be ready and willing to reconsider some of the most fundamental precepts of Eurowestern epistemology, including the possibility of knowing for sure. If Learning Developers are to support students with revising these precepts, then they must also be willing to do so themselves.

Learning Developers must consider, therefore, the case for decolonising LD itself. Sibanda (2021) describes current LD support – what he calls 'Academic Literacies', following Lea and Street (1998) – an 'apprenticeship to Western rhetorical norms'. Bohlmann (2022, p.1) echoes this critique when asking whether Learning Developers can be decolonisers if their 'role is to develop academic literacies by training students to conform to dominant reading and writing conventions' and 'to support students to succeed in the curriculum as it is'. These are pertinent questions, but the LD role they both describe is closer to what Lea and Street (1998, p.159) call 'academic socialisation' rather than 'academic literacies'. Lea and Street define the former as a process of 'induct[ing] students into a new "culture", that of the academy … whose norms and practices have simply to be learnt to provide access to the whole institution'. This approach figures academic writing as 'a transparent medium of representation' that students just need to learn. In contrast, academic literacies figures academic writing as laden with values that are often at odds with students' own values, identities, and experiences, which become difficult to convey in academic writing. Academic literacies, therefore, aims to help students develop a writing style that is both academic and able to express those values, identities, and experiences. Alongside improving students' sense of belonging at university, this approach promises to broaden the scope of acceptable academic writing in terms of both content and style. Understood this way, academic literacies appears in fact to have much in common with DtC.

Another useful framework can be found in Perry's (2020, p.307) 'pluriversal literacies', a concept that questions the primacy of writing found in the academic literacies approach and, instead, encompasses 'a much broader understanding of relational human experience'. This concept seems to align with a decolonial curriculum that emphasises the multifaceted ways humans produce and communicate knowledge, and assigns value to wide-ranging skills and competencies. Accepting such a premise would broaden the scope of LD, to include helping students appreciate, use, and develop the full range of explicit and/or implicit knowledge and skills they possess. In practice, this approach could manifest as flipping perceived weaknesses into strengths. For example, international students may mention that 'English is not my first language', implying a disadvantage in writing; however, knowing more than one language can alternatively be viewed as having access to unique insights from a linguistic intersection. Similarly, finding 'academic writing' unsettling can mean that one is best situated to critique it; or mature students expressing desire to 'relearn how to be a student' can, instead, build on their rich experience. In a similar vein, Yosso (2005) argues that students from marginalised communities carry valuable cultural capital that enables them to enrich and/or challenge established perspectives in academia. It is, therefore, important that Learning Developers encourage students to draw from their unique backgrounds, to contextualise literacy as practice and reframe their own contribution to knowledge. Opportunities to do so seem likely to increase, as DtC agendas gain traction.

Decolonising LD?

The extent to which Learning Developers have progressed towards a 'literacies' approach, as opposed to mere 'socialisation', is open to question. For one thing, this push must overcome institutional hurdles, such as the institutional marginality of Learning Developers (Sibanda, 2021). What influence we have on agendas in our institutions must be fought for and gained. Currently, there seems to be very little demand from academic colleagues for Learning Developers to help with decolonial design, possibly due to misconceptions about our role and potential contributions to the DtC agenda. To increase our recognition and reach, we can start building individual collaborative relationships incrementally. Another path is to showcase LD in institutional committees as a scholarly field that can add pedagogical value. If disciplinary silos are serving to reinforce traditional conventions, and interdisciplinarity can be a step towards challenging these, then Learning Developers have a unique vantage point to act as translators for students and academic practitioners alike, and thus enable the cross-pollination of ideas among disciplines at the institutional level.

Another barrier arises from the institutional and student expectations regarding the purpose and role of LD. Indeed, revealing the 'hidden curriculum' is a long-standing premise of how LD can enhance the chances of success for students from marginalised backgrounds, by clarifying the structures, rules, and expectations for students entering academia. Although this practice enhances sense of belonging, retention, and progression, it can equally work to normalise the status quo, thereby directly conflicting with decolonial goals. From a similar standpoint, Bohlmann (2022, p.2) asks: 'If our role is to support students to succeed in the curriculum as it is, can we really be part of the DtC movement?' This question illustrates the contradiction LDs must contend with, echoed in the distinction between the 'socialisation' and the 'literacies' approach (Lea and Street, 1998). As pragmatic needs and institutional requirements inevitably condition our practice, we must examine to what extent the academic literacies approach can underpin Learning Developers' practices, as opposed to academic socialisation. We can use this tension and associated sense of dissonance as a tool for metacognitive analysis of our own praxis. Such reflexive questioning is required for any true progress in the DtC path. Other conditions include personal reflexivity, awareness of context(s), and student buy in.

How can we, then, envision our practice changing through the decolonial lens? Bohlmann (2022, p.4) identifies two preliminary steps for Learning Developers:

> The first key area is knowing ourselves: decolonising starts with reflecting on our role as practitioners within a colonial higher education system. Where do we stand? And can we help our students find their own position within, or in relation to, this value system? The second key area is getting to know our students: decolonising means acknowledging our students as individuals and actively including them through rapport and community building activities.

In line with this suggestion, Learning Developers should look inwards and question our assumptions and how these manifest in our practice. Awareness of our biases and privileges as individuals and as a professional community is a condition for acknowledging our positionality and bringing this recognition into our interactions with students. The role of LD bears great potential for rapport building, particularly as it is distanced from the role of assessor and its associated imbalanced power dynamic. Exposing our positionality in our tutorial interactions may create the space for students to (re-)contextualise the tutor–student relationship; allow them to question authority; encourage them to explore their own cultural capital; and identify more explicitly their agency. The potential of small-group tutorials for decolonisation is discussed by Hassan (2022) in the context of South African HE as a way to support students from disadvantaged backgrounds to develop their sense of belonging and achieve academic success. These tutorials are described as 'a decolonised space where students are made to feel accepted and treated in a humanistic manner' (Hassan, 2022, p.81). Such 'decolonised spaces' might involve small practical measures like learning students' names and discussing their individual challenges, while also nurturing an inclusive learning environment (Bohlmann, 2022; see also Lee et al., 2017). Such measures can increase students' sense of belonging at university and, by extension, their sense of empowerment and ability to offer unique contributions towards the DtC goals.

One area with potential for decolonial practice in LD is that of academic integrity, where we can already see concrete evidence of work that challenges Eurowestern epistemological assumptions. Magyar's (2012) study with a group of international students in the UK showed that the concept of academic integrity has much deeper links to cultural values and epistemological traditions than has been usually assumed when offering referencing tutorials. The author distinguishes between referencing, that is, the mechanics, and attribution, that is, the principles, of academic integrity. By approaching the 'avoiding plagiarism' theme from an attribution standpoint, therefore, we can make the concept of academic integrity easier to understand for students of diverse cultural backgrounds. Taken further, broadening academic integrity and embedding it in values rather than practical rules is exemplified in the Indigenous Academic Integrity approach introduced at the University of Calgary (Pratt and Gladue, 2022): a conceptualisation of academic integrity founded on indigenous paradigms, based on the values of relationality, reciprocity, and respect, which takes academic discourse and knowledge attribution beyond the Eurowestern ideas of 'ownership' and 'rights'. In addition to following this example to enrich our approach of academic integrity, could we theorise other academic skills through similar indigenous paradigms?

Another area of debate is the use of English as primary language for instruction and writing in HEIs where English is not the native language of many students. The primacy of English has been viewed as a pervasive colonial remnant that perpetuates Eurowestern hegemonic structures (see summaries in Kubota, 2022; Parmegiani, 2022). The embedded inequities in use of English have implications Learning Developers should consider. For instance, Hassan (2022) argues that use of native language(s) in tutorials benefitted black students as it enhanced their sense of belonging. Parmegiani (2022) advocates for linguistic diversity in the classroom: introducing the mother tongue in instruction and writing was shown to succeed in both decentring English and helping students appropriate English as a tool for academic success and socioeconomic mobility. As use of language is central in LD practice, there are alternatives we could be exploring. For example, should we encourage students to use source materials in languages other than English? Is there a benefit from exercising writing in more than one language? Taken further, similar questions can apply to the primacy of academic English. From an academic literacies perspective, students should be supported in challenging conventions and experimentation, but how much might that conflict with pragmatic needs?

More broadly, Learning Developers can contribute to the DtC goals by examining (and changing) our implicit 'othering' structures, behaviours, and choices that may reinforce colonial ideals. These can be found everywhere: for example, in the configuration of our spaces; the names of our buildings; the role models we promote; the classifications of academic skills in our webpages; the examples we use to illustrate concepts; our technologies; the ways we acknowledge, measure, and reflect upon impact; and our agendas in teaching and research. All of it contributes to the establishment and reproduction of norms around what matters. We posit here that there are always ways to challenge this 'everyday colonial' practice, starting from simple things like diversifying our examples or asking students to think of some that speak to their experiences; setting up spaces that offer opportunities for multiple types of social interaction; co-producing our learning objectives in taught sessions; or being flexible with time and availability in online, face-to-face, or hybrid environments. Questioning the underpinnings and implications of our choices can only take place through reflexivity in our routine practice.

As a final note, DtC presents a framework for revisiting our professional structures and LD identity. The roots of our discipline in widening participation and deficit models of socialisation and inclusivity have set out goals that, although challenged, remain influential. If we want to set out new goals that align with decolonising visions, then what might these look like at the strategic level? One important step would be to acknowledge the whiteness of the demographic composition of our profession and ask who is currently motivated to become a Learning Developer. Do we foster diversity in recruitment? And how can we make diversity efforts meaningful (as opposed to tokenistic representation)? There is an argument to be made for internationalisation and connections outside the Anglosphere, as well as the potential for incorporating indigenous voices, as a meaningful step for expanding LD's relevance, although it is up for debate whether that would mean we have 'decolonised' LD. Another area we should examine is our research agendas. What themes are we promoting and funding? What do we publish in our journals? Where else do Learning Developers publish, and what audiences do we reach? (How) do we include student voices in our work? Considering our role in the decolonisation context offers potential for an agenda with global scope that can enrich the voices of the LD community.

References

Adebisi, F. (2020) *Decolonisation Is Not About Ticking a Box: It Must Disrupt*. Available at: https://criticallegalthinking.com/2020/03/12/decolonisation-is-not-about-ticking-a-box/ (Accessed: 31 March 2023)

Bhambra, G.K., Dalia, G. and Nişancıoğlu, K. (2018) 'Introduction: Decolonising the University?', in G.K. Bhambra, G. Dalia and K. Nişancıoğlu (eds), *Decolonising the University*. London: Pluto Press, 1–15.

Bohlmann, J. (2022) 'Decolonising Learning Development through reflective and relational practice', *Journal of Learning Development in Higher Education*, 24. https://doi.org/10.47408/jldhe.vi24.913

Cicek, J.S., Steele, A., Gauthier, S., Mante, A.A., Wolf, P., Robinson, M. and Mattucci, S. (2021) 'Indigenizing Engineering education in Canada: critically considered', *Teaching in Higher Education*, 26(7–8): 1038–1059. https://doi.org/10.1080/13562517.2021.1935847

Dache, A., Blue, J., Bovell, D., Miguest, D., Osifeso, S. and Tucux, F. (2021) 'A *Calle* decolonial hack: Afro-Latin theorizing of Philadelphia's spaces of learning and resistance', *Teaching in Higher Education*, 26(7–8): 1077–1097. https://doi.org/10.1080/13562517.2021.1940927

Dennis, C.A. (2018) 'Decolonising Education: A Pedagogic Intervention', in: G.K. Bhambra, G. Dalia and K Nişancıoğlu (eds), *Decolonising the University*. London: Pluto Press, 190–207.

Dhillon, S. (2021) 'An Immanent Critique of Decolonization Discourse', *Philosophical Inquiry in Education*, 28(3): 251–258. https://doi.org/10.7202/1085079ar

Edwards, K.T. and Shahjahan, R.A. (2021) 'Navigating student resistance towards decolonizing curriculum and pedagogy (DCP): a temporal proposal', *Teaching in Higher Education*, 26(7–8): 1122–1129. https://doi.org/10.1080/13562517.2021.1928063

Hassan, S.L. (2022) 'Reducing the Colonial Footprint through Tutorials: A South African perspective on the decolonisation of education', *South African Journal of Higher Education*, 36(5): 77–97. https://dx.doi.org/10.20853/36-5-4325

Kubota, R. (2022) 'Decolonizing second language writing: Possibilities and challenges', *Journal of Second Language Writing*, 58: 1–11. https://doi.org/10.1016/j.jslw.2022.100946

Lee, A., Felten, P., Poch, R.K., Solheim, C. and O'Brien, M.K. (2017) *Teaching Interculturally: A Framework for Integrating Disciplinary Knowledge and Intercultural Development*. Sterling: Stylus Publishing, LLC.

Lea, M.R. and Street, B.V. (1998) 'Student writing in higher education: An academic literacies approach', *Studies in Higher Education*, 23(2): 157–172. https://doi.org/10.1080/03075079812331380364

Magyar, A. (2012) 'Plagiarism and attribution: an academic literacies approach?', *Journal of Learning Development in Higher Education*, 4. https://doi.org/10.47408/jldhe.v0i4.141

Parmegiani, A. (2022) 'Using the Mother Tongue as a Resource: Building on a Common Ground with "English Only" Ideologies', *Literacy in Composition Studies*, 10(1): 25–45. Available at: https://licsjournal.org/index.php/LiCS/article/view/1232 (Accessed: 31 March 2023).

Perry, M. (2020) 'Pluriversal literacies: Affect and relationality in vulnerable times', *Reading Research Quarterly*, 56(2): 293–309. Available at: https://ila.onlinelibrary.wiley.com/doi/10.1002/rrq.312 (Accessed: 31 March 2023).

Pete, S. (2018) 'Meschachakanis, a Coyote Narrative: Decolonising Higher Education', in: G.K. Bhambra, G. Dalia and K Nişancıoğlu (eds), *Decolonising the University*. London: Pluto Press, 171–189.

Pratt, Y.P. and Gladue, K. (2022) 'Re-Defining Academic Integrity: Embracing Indigenous Truths', in S.E. Eaton and J.C. Hughes (eds), *Academic Integrity in Canada: An Enduring and Essential Challenge*. Cham: Springer, 103–123.

Roy, R.D. (2018) *Decolonise Science – Time to End Another Imperial Era*. Available at: https://theconversation.com/decolonise-science-time-to-end-another-imperial-era-89189#:~:text=The%20path%20to%20decolonisation,of%20science%20can%20be%20helpful (Accessed: 31 March 2023).

Sibanda, B. (2021) *Non-Violent Pedagogical Perspectives in Decolonising Academic Literacy*. Available at: https://www.saaalp.com/post/non-violent-pedagogical-perspectives-in-decolonising-academic-literacy (Accessed: 31 March 2023).

Whitchurch, C. (2013) *The Rise of Third Space Professionals: Paradoxes and Dilemmas*. London: Routledge.

Yosso, T.J. (2005) 'Whose culture has capital? A critical race theory discussion of community cultural wealth', *Race Ethnicity and Education*, 8(1): 69–91. https://doi.org/10.1080/1361332052000341006

16

LEARNING DEVELOPMENT IN, AGAINST, AND BEYOND THE NEOLIBERAL UNIVERSITY

Critical Learning Development and Critical Academic Literacies

Gordon Asher

> **Gordon Asher:** *Where do we find hope in increasingly dark times – in Hall's 'hopeless university'?*
>
> **Antonia Darder:** *To say there is no hope in the university is to say there is no hope anywhere. Instead, we need to recognize that radical hope must be rooted in our actual material conditions, it must be embodied through an ethos of possibility and unfinishedness, which signals that, indeed, a different reality is possible – that we can construct together, by way of the shared political vision that we bring to our collective labour. So powerful is radical hope, that hegemonic structures and relationships within institutions (such as higher education) function to systematically impede its expression – conserving the deadening, hegemonic, culture of the contemporary university.*
>
> *(Excerpt from an email conversation between GA and AD)*

Our contemporary conjuncture is one of convergent and cascading crises – including existential threats of eco-environmental catastrophe and ever-increasing dangers of nuclear conflict (Chomsky, 2020) – as we stand on the precipice of another global economic crash (Robinson, 2022). Relatedly, we are witnessing vicious assaults on what levels of democracy and human rights protections exist across the globe, and the rise of the far-right – tending to fascism in many countries.

The root causes are accelerated processes of capitalism's prevailing form, neoliberalism; the relentless repurposing or subsumption of all of social life in the name of profit (Hall, 2021). Consequently, these crises are combining viciously to further destroy living conditions and standards, manifesting as an overarching crisis of social reproduction (Federici, 2021) in which the struggle to merely survive is increasingly the predominant horizon for many.

DOI: 10.4324/9781003433347-20

Immanently, the contemporary university is in crisis (Bacevic, 2017); the direct impact of decades of neoliberal restructuring, further compounded by government and management responses to COVID-19 (Fleming, 2021). The immiserating consequences for both staff and students in 2023 prompted the most significant industrial action across UK higher education in recent decades, as well as deeper consideration of alternatives – both emerging from long-standing grassroots struggles within and over the university.

This chapter explores how Learning Development (LD) and Learning Developers might locate it/themselves within the increasingly neoliberal university. Its focus draws in on the emergence of a critical Learning Development movement (CLDM) and a conception of critical academic literacies (CAL), as seeking to respond to our crisis-ridden contemporary conjuncture through the development of resistances and the creation of alternatives that foreground education as a social and public good working towards eco-social justice.

The Neoliberal University

Across UK higher education (HE), staff and students are experiencing the pernicious and profoundly debilitating consequences of iterative processes of neoliberal restructuring permeating the public university, driven by conjoined processes of corporatisation, privatisation and outsourcing; marketisation, consumerisation and competition; commercialisation, commodification and financialisation, delivered through the imposition of the human capital model of 'new managerialism' (neoliberalism's 'mode of governance' (Lynch, 2014)). 'The University is being explicitly restructured for the production, circulation and accumulation of value, materialised in the form of rents and surpluses on operating activities' (Hall, 2020, p.830), reflected in the predominance of neoliberal narrativising, which serves to shut down criticality, creativity, social agency and imagination, and, thus, alternatives.

Under neoliberalism, universities are competing businesses with CEOs, corporate strategies and branding, business plans and partnerships, cost-benefit analyses, and key performance indicators. Degree programmes are investment opportunities for students as indebted consumers; staff are service providers and research entrepreneurs. The growth of income and revenue streams is prioritised over teaching and learning, and profit and 'stakeholder' interests over public benefit.

Central to the deepening crisis of HE is its fundamental incapacity to respond meaningfully to societal and global crises, given its enduring role in contributing to their formation and exacerbation (Hall, 2021). This applies equally to its abject refusal to understand or address its own crisis (ibid.), for which familiar responses of yet further neoliberalisation are prescribed – reflecting 'disaster capitalism' in HE contexts. A paradigmatic example is the utilisation, by government and senior management, of the pandemic shock of COVID-19 as 'justification' to permanently embed desired changes – exploiting short time frames that evade consultation and staff/student contestation, thereby closing down critical alternatives (Asher, 2021). Thus, universities are not mere victims of local and global pressures; rather, they are deeply complicit in neoliberalising not just HE and those who labour within it, but wider society. Understanding universities as increasingly integral to linking and shaping neoliberalism's evolving configurations at both national and global level (Ball, 2021) helps to explain these incapabilities of the HE system.

While there is continuity as to the university's systemic role in (re)producing what and whom the dominant powers in society have sought (Chomsky, 2004), there is also continuity in understanding the university as a social and public good and as a long-contested terrain of struggle, generating liberatory possibilities and transformative potentialities.

Learning Development in the Neoliberal University

Learning Development, while still a nascent academic field, is already a site of contestation (Webster, 2022); unsurprisingly so, given that its critical roots and the academic literacies model at its heart sit in deep tension with HE's neoliberalising processes. The concepts of Learning Development and thus Learning Developers foreground a deeply pedagogical and dialogical, developmental ethos of 'working with and for' (Webster, 2019). The centring of academic literacies is important for what it critiques and rejects: dominant deficit/banking and socialisation models of learning and teaching, where uncontextualised, generic skills are learnt through transmission and reception or assimilation/acculturation; and for the critical alternative which it embodies – learning and teaching as 'concerned with meaning-making, identity, power and authority' (Lea and Street, 2006, p.369).

Academic literacies foregrounds the social, cultural, and contextualised nature of academic learning, with literacies understood as 'social practices that are shaped by ideologies and institutional power relations' (Wingate, 2019, p.2). Thus, learners and educators are recognised as social actors at situational and cultural levels, and the university as a site of power-laden practices and relations, of contested meaning-making. These constitutive factors speak to LD's values of empowerment and emancipation, to a critically rooted field with concerns for personal and collective transformation and eco-social justice at its heart (Asher, 2022). As such, it stands in opposition to neoliberal and neocolonial practices within the institution, and for a conceptualisation of education as for the public and social good. Neocolonial – foregrounding the ongoing (not just historical) role of the university in empire and (neo)colonialism, as intimately tied to capitalism's development, and thus the coloniality deeply inscribed in its culture, practices, and relations (Emejulu, 2017).

During the early years of LD's existence, it was not conspicuous on management's radar and evolved principally on its own terms, initially appearing to escape some of the worst ravages of neoliberalising processes; no longer, however. As it has become more prominent, it is increasingly contested, its tensions exacerbated by the intensification of the neoliberal turn in HE, manifesting as pressures both on and within the field. LD is being increasingly de-professionalised, de-skilled, and outsourced – diluted as to focus and ethos, theory and scholarship, values, and criticality (Webster, 2022). There is a perpetual restructuring and recomposition, in 'the reconfiguring of LD as "professional services", low-skilled support and administration rather than teaching or academic' (ibid.). This evidences a concerning trajectory, with LD increasingly confined to hierarchical advice-and-guidance managerialist methods of 'delivery', as unreflexive skills and information provision – a palpable (re)turn to a deficit model, with HE's pandemic responses intensifying such pressures (Asher, 2021).

Perhaps most worryingly, due to its reach and reception across the university, LD is being co-opted, instrumentalised by senior management to deliver students and staff to the short-term economistic imperatives of corporate strategies and implementation plans focused on influencing rankings/league table positioning. As per Hilsdon's observation: 'I have … begun seeing LD (or at least the managerial interpretations of its functions) in terms of the project, described by Foucault, of "governmentality" – the exercise of control over people by the state under neoliberalism, whereby people control themselves through their language and practices' (2018). Thus, often under misleading rhetoric of 'development', 'literacies', and 'student-centredness', the neoliberal model of education is steadily but ruthlessly imposed across institutions. So mediated, it makes awareness of and resistances to such processes less likely than if this were more explicitly imposed.

Critical Learning Development and Critical Academic Literacies

Immanent to the tensions and contradictions of its contestation, we are in a struggle over the future of LD. The coalescence of the factors and tendencies discussed above, as conflicting with LD's emancipatory foundational ethos and pedagogy, is of mounting concern to those who embody such values, who fear that LD is being subsumed within HE's neoliberalising processes, reflected in the emergence of a critical Learning Development movement (CLDM). Its focus is on resisting such pressures, re-emphasising LD's critical roots (academic literacies in particular) to develop a more explicitly critical foundation for the field, connecting with wider HE and societal struggles, to ensure its potentialities are utilised to evolve emancipatory alternatives (Asher, 2022).

Freire (1992) advocates starting from the concrete situations of communities, entailing the need to collectively engage in iterative processes of being and becoming critically academically literate (Asher, 2017). Doing so enables us to 'read' the LD field and the university – its affective social relations and situatedness within neoliberal configurations – so as to best position and orientate ourselves with respect to ongoing struggles. For doing so, I have proposed a conceptualisation of Critical Academic Literacies (CAL) (Asher, 2019, 2022). CAL's reinvigoration of LD's critical roots, so as to develop a more explicitly critical political practice and through doing so extend our understandings of the potential scope of academic literacies, is intended to inform the nascent CLDM as focused on being able to live and work sustainably within the university, successfully navigate its ever-changing terrain, while simultaneously understanding and developing struggles over its present and future forms (ibid.).

CAL emerged through placing LD's academic literacies model, in concert with its pedagogical ethos of working 'with and for', into productive dialogue with wider critical educational theory and practice; with long-established traditions of critical pedagogy (Darder et al., 2017), popular education (Crowther et al., 2005), radical adult education's critical literacies (Crowther et al., 2012) and the emergent fields of critical university studies (Morrish, 2018) and abolition university studies (Boggs et al., 2019) (see Figure 16.1).

The prefix 'critical' foregrounds a more explicit framing and orientation of academic literacies within a political project focused on radical democracy and eco-social justice, a world beyond capitalism and the nation state system (Dinerstein et al., 2020). This formulation also provides wider scope and thus potential influence, encompassing all student and staff communicative processes and practices, relations, and cultures. A focus on staff-staff as well as student–staff inter-relations, serving to situate academic literacies in wider educational contexts and attendant power relations, is important for

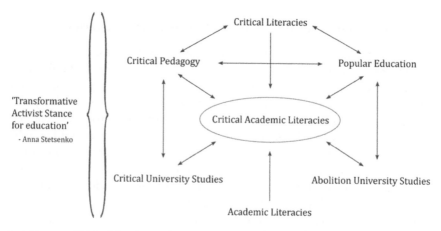

FIGURE 16.1   Critical Academic Literacies – Theoretical Influences and Relationships

comprehending and contributing to HE struggles; reflecting calls from within the emergent CLDM, as to 'the need for a shift from the practices of individual students to the broader institutional and socio-political landscape' (Lea, 2016, p.97) and 'the need to critique the overall enterprise and context of higher education itself' (Hilsdon, 2018, p.52).

Being and Becoming Critical

The emergent CLDM holds significant potential for contributing to nested struggles, most evidently within and over LD itself. With LD's potential to be identified as an increasingly important node within HE's neoliberalising processes, such contestations then speak to the wider struggle over the crisis-torn university.

CAL, as focused on being and becoming critically academically literate, draws on interdependent implorations to 'teach the university' (Williams, 2012): that we learn and teach about what the university was, is, will likely be, and could alternatively become. This signals a 'teaching' of the institution, as a critical pedagogical process of its (and our) transformation – that 'we need to act on the political imperative of ... remaking the critical and the university' (Petrina and Ross, 2014, p.63). We do so critically across and beyond the university.

Thus, critical LD focuses on staff and students working collectively and democratically to problematise our contemporary contexts while prefiguratively orienting our work and struggles towards more hopeful horizons, with three objectives in mind. Firstly, to demystify the turbulent exigencies of managerialism and the hidden curriculum, in order to successfully navigate the neoliberal university's increasingly difficult terrain, while attending to the collective self-care necessary in its immiserating contexts. Secondly, to resist its deep neoliberalisation processes. Thirdly, to connect and evolve emancipatory alternatives for the future of HE. These pro-active and prefigurative objectives commit to building and embodying alternatives in the present for the future, rather than reactive resistances to constantly changing pressures and processes. Not to roll back previous processes of neoliberalisation as focused on a largely mythical liberal university of the past, but for a hopeful, transformative future, beyond contemporary neoliberal, neocolonial, pandemic realities.

The combination of CAL and CLDM, as critical pedagogical approach and movement with reach across the sector, seeks to nurture and connect critically oriented staff and students, often isolated and alienated at both institutional and sector level, and critical educational traditions and fields, breaking down the insularities of a competitive neoliberal system and linking to the manifold struggles within and beyond the university. This entails the political engagement necessary for building the kind of critical educational movement, including critically oriented unions, so urgently needed – working within and connecting the 'cracks' in the neoliberal university, for the purposes of emancipatory teaching and learning.

The project before us is a deeply pedagogical one:

[b]oth domination and our struggles against it, for alternative futures and hopes of a just world, are inherently pedagogical in nature … by constraining or enabling ways of living and being, thinking and knowing, working and relating, they literally teach us.

(Amsler, 2015, p.4)

Resistances, Alternatives, and Hope

There is constructive affinity between the approach advocated here and that of those who, drawing on Holloway's (2016) thought, frame and orient their responses to the crisis of the university as 'working in, against, and beyond the neoliberal university' (e.g., Asher, 2015, 2022; Cowden et al., 2013; Ridley, 2017; Uniconflicts, 2015; Undercommoning, 2016):

- 'Working' – with both staff and students understood as 'academic labour';
- 'In' – inevitably within the neoliberal university, to navigate and intervene in it;
- 'Against' – to resist its ongoing neoliberalisations and oppressions;
- 'Beyond' – to nurture, evolve, and co-create transformative alternatives to it.

As such, a CLDM is a developing node within a wider critical HE movement, understood as working in, against, and beyond the neoliberal and neocolonial university of our contemporary conjuncture – a positionality that insists on connecting HE struggles to wider struggles for a world beyond the intersectional oppressions of capitalist identitarian categorisations (Gunn and Wilding, 2021) and institutions (Holloway, 2022). As focused on thinking and practising academia otherwise. This involves recognition that the university necessitates radical equity in all dimensions, inclusive of just relations with non-human species, and a pluriversity of radically democratic and dialogical, diverse, and decolonising epistemologies and ontologies. Pivotal are issues of knowledge democracy and cognitive or epistemological justice that challenge dominant world constructs. It is the 'moving beyond' that speaks to critical hope. Hope, as Freire (2004, p.2) argues, is 'an ontological need' as

without hope there is no possibility for resistance, dissent, and struggle. Agency is the condition of struggle, and hope is the condition of agency. Hope expands the space of the possible and becomes a way of recognizing and naming the incomplete nature of the present.

(Giroux, 2021, p.96)

Appreciating Dinerstein's (2021) exposition of 'hope as a category of praxis' emphasises the affective and embodied nature of critical hope as located in and between us, as a constituent aspect of our being and becoming with each other and in the world, in order to transform both it and ourselves in the process. Thus hope, as informing and emerging through struggle, is a pedagogical issue; it is 'a question of learning hope' (Bloch, 1995, p.1). Hence the urgency of a CLDM, that can speak to critically prefigurative praxis in contexts of what may seem an increasingly 'hopeless university' (Hall, 2021); to the countering of neoliberalism's (hegemonic) pedagogies of oppression and domination with (transformative) pedagogies of freedom and emancipation, and through doing so nurture and develop critical, pedagogical, hope.

References

Amsler, S, (2015) *The Education of Radical Democracy.* UK: Routledge.

Asher, G. (2015) 'Working In, Against, and Beyond the Neoliberal University', *SCUTREA* 2015, University of Leeds.

Asher, G. (2017) 'The Porous University: Opening up the university; being and becoming critically academically literate?' *Porous University Symposium*, UHI, 8 May.

Asher, G. (2019) 'Exploring possibilities for the "critical" in Learning Development practice and theory; critical academic literacies?' *ALDinHE Conference 2019*, University of Exeter, 16 April.

Asher, G. (2021) 'The pandemic neoliberal university – contemporary realities, crises and likely trajectories of UK higher education and learning development', *ALDinHE Conference 2021*, Online, 8 April.

Asher, G. (2022) 'Working In, Against, and Beyond the Neoliberal University: Critical Academic Literacies as a Critical Pedagogical Response to the Crisis of the University', in: G. Asher, S. Cowden, S. Housee and A. Maisuria (eds), *Critical Pedagogy and Emancipation: A Festschrift in Memory of Joyce Canaan.* Oxford: Peter Lang.

Bacevic, J. (2017) 'Why is it more difficult to imagine the end of universities than the end of capitalism, or: is the crisis of the university in fact a crisis of imagination?', *Jana Bacevic*, 17 October.

Ball, S. J. (2021) *The Education Debate*, 4th edn. UK: Bristol University Press.

Bloch, E. (1995) *The Principle of Hope.* Cambridge, US: MIT Press.

Boggs, A., Meyerhoff, E., Mitchell, N. and Schwartz-Weisten, Z. (2019) 'Abolitionist university studies: an invitation', *Abolition Journal*, 28 August.

Chomsky, N. (2004) *Chomsky on MisEducation.* Maryland: Rowman and Littlefield Publishers.

Chomsky, N. (2020) 'The fate of humanity hangs in the balance', *ROAR*, 18 September.

Cowden, S. and Singh, G., with Amsler, S., Canaan, J. and Motta, S. (2013) *Acts of Knowing: Critical Pedagogy In, Against, and Beyond the University.* London: Bloomsbury.

Crowther, J. Galloway, V. and Martin, I. (2005) *Popular Education: Engaging the Academy – International Perspectives.* Leicester: NIACE.

Crowther. J., Tett, L, and Hamilton, M. (2012) *More Powerful Literacies.* Leicester: NIACE.

Darder, A., Torres, R. and Baltodano, M. (eds) (2017) *Critical Pedagogy Reader*, 3rd edn. New York: Routledge.

Federici, S. (2021) *Patriarchy of the Wage: Notes on Marx, Gender, and Feminism.* New York: PM Press.

Dinerstein, A.C. (2021) 'Decolonising critique: reconnecting critical theory with radical praxis', *CURA Annual Lecture*, 14 April.

Dinerstein, A.C., Vela, A.G., Gonzalez, E. and Holloway, J. (eds) (2020) *Open Marxism 4: Against a Closing World*. London: Pluto Press.

Emejulu, A. (2017) 'Another university is possible', *Verso*, 12 January.

Freire, P. (1992) *Pedagogy of Hope: Reliving Pedagogy of the Oppressed*. London: Bloomsbury.

Freire, P. (2004) *Pedagogy of Indignation*. Boulder: Paradigm Publishers

Fleming, P. (2021) *Dark Academia: How Universities Die*. London: Pluto Press.

Giroux, H. (2021) *Race, Politics and Pandemic Pedagogy: Education in a Time of Crisis*. London: Bloomsbury.

Gunn, R. and Wilding, A. (2021) *Revolutionary Recognition*. London: Bloomsbury.

Hall, R. (2020) 'The hopeless university: intellectual work at the end of the end of history', *Postdigital Science Education*, 2: 830–848.

Hall, R. (2021) *The Hopeless University: Intellectual Work at the End of the End of History*. London: MayFly Books.

Hilsdon, J. (2018) 'The significance of the field of practice "Learning Development" in UK higher education', PhD Thesis, University of Plymouth.

Holloway, J. (2016) *In, Against, and Beyond Capitalism: The San Francisco Lectures*. UK: PM Press/Kairos.

Holloway, J. (2022) *Hope in Hopeless Times*. London: Pluto Press.

Lea, M. (2016) 'Academic literacies: looking back in order to look forward', *Critical Studies in Teaching and Learning*, 4(2): 88–101.

Lea, M.R. and Street, B.V. (2006) 'The "academic literacies" model: theory and applications', *Theory into Practice* 45(4): 368–377.

Lynch, K. (2014) '"New managerialism" in education: the organisational form of neoliberalism', *Open Democracy*, 16 September.

Morrish, L. (2018) 'Can critical university studies survive the toxic university?' *Academic Irregularities*, 8 June.

Petrina, S. and Ross, E.W. (2014) 'Critical university studies: workplace, milestones, crossroads, respect, truth', *Workplace: A Journal for Academic Labour*, 23.

Ridley, D. (2017) 'Institutionalising critical pedagogy: Lessons from against and beyond the neo-liberal university', *Power and Education*, 9(1): 65–68.

Robinson. W. I. (2022) *Can Global Capitalism Endure?* Atlanta: Clarity Press.

Undercommoning (2016) 'Undercommoning: Revolution Within, Against and Beyond the University', *Undercommoning*.

UniConflicts (2015) 'UNICONFLICTS in spaces of crisis: Critical approaches in, against and beyond the University', *UNICONFLICTS Conference*.

Webster, H. (2019) 'Emancipatory practice: the defining LD value?', *Rattus Scholasticus*, 4 February.

Webster, H. (2022) 'Supporting the Development, Recognition and Impact of Third Space Professionals', in: E. McIntosh and D. Nutt (eds), *The Impact of the Integrated Practitioner in Higher Education Studies*. London: Routledge.

Williams, J.J. (2012) 'Deconstructing academe: the birth of critical university studies', *Chronicle of Higher Education*, 19 February.

Wingate, U. (2019) 'Achieving transformation through collaboration: the role of academic literacies', *Journal of Learning Development in Higher Education*, Special Edition, 15.

PART IV

Knowledge Making

Learning Developers as Researchers

The fourth part acknowledges the importance of broadening out the conversations that demarcate the field over four chapters that encourage Learning Developers to engage with the theory and pedagogy on which their work is based, to challenge assumptions through research, and then to write, publish, and share their ideas and practices to create a body of knowledge. Silvina Bishopp-Martin and Ian Johnson advocate for the ongoing expansion of the theoretical base of the field through the sharing of knowledge and practice, and use Chapter 17 to present an LD Scholarship Manifesto. This, in turn, is supported by a critical appraisal of the research methodologies at the Learning Developer's disposal in Chapter 18. For Lee Fallin, authentic LD ontology and epistemology are firmly grounded in the emancipatory and participatory values of the field. In Chapter 19, Alicja Syska and Carina Buckley focus specifically on the central role of writing and the nature of the expectations that surround it, with the goal of recognising and working with those expectations. Finally, the same authors conclude the part in Chapter 20 with a primer for those wishing to publish in LD, whether they are experienced writers or not.

DOI: 10.4324/9781003433347-21

17

RESEARCH AND SCHOLARSHIP IN LEARNING DEVELOPMENT

Silvina Bishopp-Martin and Ian Johnson

> *We write because we want to practise what we preach, because we choose to be part of a community that wants to keep these conversations alive, because we are committed to this field, because we are academics and because despite all the odds, we feel we have things to say. We write because we don't want our thoughts to remain hidden; we want those thoughts to be heard.*

Introduction

The chapter begins by situating Learning Development (LD) as a hybrid profession (Whitchurch, 2013) which cuts across traditional HE functions: *teaching*, *research*, and *service* (Macfarlane, 2011). Like other hybrid roles, Learning Developers' involvement in scholarship is somewhat limited due to a prevalent lack of contractual need to engage in research (Syska and Buckley, 2022). However, it has been highlighted that it is paramount for Learning Developers to engage with the pedagogical and theoretical underpinnings of their work to be able to articulate and disseminate LD's values and principles beyond their own institutional practice (Samuels, 2013; Johnson, 2018).

This chapter aims to present distinctive features of the scholarship of LD and will advocate for a need to engage with scholarly developments in the field, in order to continue to grow its knowledge base, create a more coherent collective identity and memory, and increase LD's institutional visibility. The chapter also intends to encourage both novice and experienced Learning Developers to commit to the field's development, join the mission to theorise LD, and help this field firmly establish itself as a key element of teaching and learning in HE.

DOI: 10.4324/9781003433347-22

Scholarship in Third Space

The HE sector has gone through significant changes in the past 40 years, including the creation of new universities (Hilsdon, 2018); the marketisation and internationalisation of universities (Jones-Devitt, 2022); the introduction of widening participation policies (Stapleford, 2019); a decline in public funding (Loddick and Coulson, 2020); and government policies seeking an increase in the graduate workforce (Dickinson, Fowler and Griffiths, 2022). These changes have altered relationships between education stakeholders, resulting in HE functioning like a marketplace in which institutions compete to encourage student-customers to purchase attractive products.

This transformation has inevitably affected what it means to be a part of the academic workforce (Whitchurch, 2019), shifting the traditional understanding of academic practice as teaching, research, and service. This, together with the expansion of professional activity in universities, has led to the 'unbundling' of the traditional academic role (Macfarlane, 2011, p.59) and the emergence of new roles and identities.

Blended professionals (Whitchurch, 2013) or *integrated practitioners* (McIntosh and Nutt, 2022) tend to perform one of those traditional functions, and operate across professional and academic boundaries, in a hybrid space known as *third space* (Whitchurch, 2013). As third space professionals, Learning Developers are aware their work is clearly understood by the LD community, other hybrid workers, and the students we work alongside (Johnson, 2018; Webster, 2022). Yet institutionally, third space roles are still poorly understood and recognised (Akerman, 2020), which can be observed in diverse LD job titles, LD team locations, contract types, opportunities for career progression, and scholarship options.

Clearly, the complexities involved in articulating our role and achieving institutional recognition have led to LD scholarship outputs involving self-explanation and self-justification, rather than aiming at growing 'a coherent body of knowledge' (Syska and Buckley, 2022, p.4). This trend may be driven by low levels of confidence (Webster, 2022) and self-doubt (Syska and Buckley, 2022), generating feelings linked to imposter syndrome (Akerman, 2020). Feelings of self-doubt and lack of research infrastructure could make it quite difficult for Learning Developers to get involved in scholarship, resulting in LD continuing to be not sufficiently theorised and not 'satisfactorily written into existence' (Syska and Buckley, 2022, p.2).

For Learning Developers, involvement in scholarship is often limited and down to the individual, due to lack of contractual need to engage in research (Bickle et al., 2021; Syska and Buckley, 2022). This lack of contractual need to publish, however, does not necessarily close off opportunities for Learning Developers to be involved in scholarship; in fact, it may present a space to develop scholarship creatively. There is, in fact, evidence of an emergent wave of LD scholarship outputs stressing the importance of becoming scholarly active (Johnson, 2018; Parkes, 2018; Stapleford, 2019; Bickle et al., 2021; Syska and Buckley, 2022), which could enhance our visibility, knowledge base, and ability to confidently partake in academic debates.

Where institutional spaces do not allow Learning Developers to engage with scholarship, third space professionals tend to establish opportunities for research beyond their own institutions (Whitchurch, 2019). For instance, these professionals have been known for establishing communities of practice devoted to scholarship (Veles and Carter, 2016; Green et al., 2020; Lucas et al., 2021). Bickle et al.'s (2021) study exemplifies this process; by establishing their own research community of practice outside their relative institutions, the authors created a space where they could engage with research, thus reclaiming scholarship within their professional identities through the very act of writing it. It seems, therefore, that the voluntary creation of spaces for scholarship is a response to the imperative to theorise LD. We thus argue that our scholarship could become a vehicle to shape and maintain our professional identity, which can contribute to developing a more coherent collective memory. Enhancing our professional identity can, in turn, have an impact on LD institutional recognition, beyond those colleagues who are already operating in hybrid, third spaces.

LD Scholarship Manifesto

Responding to the call to write LD to existence, we will now present an *LD Scholarship Manifesto* – collaboratively developed with the community – which will outline what it is that our scholarship entails and values. To ensure the manifesto could capture various Learning Developers' views, an online survey was circulated via the LDHEN mailing list in January 2023. Thirty participants anonymously completed the survey and offered their definition of *the scholarship of LD*, rated ten key tenets according to their perceived importance, and provided qualitative comments regarding their ratings. The data were analysed and used to shape the *principles and definition*, *key features*, and *what LD scholarship entails* sections below.

Principles and Definition

Grounded in ALDinHE's values (2023), LD scholarship is:

- Critical: seeks to engage with complex aspects of learning and teaching in a diverse and constantly evolving HE landscape.
- Inclusive: aims to offer a voice to those often less heard in educational settings and is deeply concerned with social change and transformation, and a fairer, more inclusive HE.
- Collaborative: welcomes collaboration with a range of HE professionals, valuing interdisciplinary, multidisciplinary, and cross-institutional research.

Based on these principles, LD scholarship could be defined as an ongoing form of academic conversation about this professional field. This conversation allows LD to exist, establish boundaries, and solidify and advance its aims, identity, and knowledge base. Scholarship, hence, constitutes the *vehicle* which allows those invested in LD to have continual community discussions, sharing and exchanging resources, experiences, challenges, reflections, thoughts, and developments in this field. This scholarship is informed by and informs the teaching practice of LD, and fosters an environment for LD to grow its theory and practices.

The Ten Key Features of LD Scholarship

The LD scholarship features (Table 17.1) are ranked according to their importance – survey participants' level of agreement with the statements. A Likert

TABLE 17.1 The ten key features of LD scholarship

	LD scholarship:
1	is underpinned by a commitment to developing ourselves as educators, to disseminating best practices to others invested in HE learning, and to growing the knowledge base of the field itself. A key purpose of such developments is to guide students through their HE learning experience to ensure they are able to not only participate but also thrive.
2	is itself endemic to ALDinHE's values, and a crucial component of practising according to other values including critical self-reflection, and an ongoing commitment to learning and professional development.
3	is committed to the sharing of LD work, practices, and theoretical traditions in both local and external forums, in order to continue to enhance LD's professional identity and place in the academy.
4	values diverse scholarly outputs, including more creative and less formal forms and formats of knowledge exchange. This means that LD scholarship is not prescriptive; it has a generous, expansive conception of what counts as legitimate scholarly activity.
5	is broad and welcoming, driven by accounts of practice as much as by traditional theory-driven scholarship.
6	is deemed essential to the effective performance of LD as a praxis. If LD work with students and other HE professionals involves exploring research and academic literacy, then that praxis can only be truly enacted if LD professionals are themselves immersed in those processes.
7	recognises a distinct professional field, with practice- and theory-based traditions, drawing connections between new scholarship and that knowledge base.
8	encourages inclusion of diverse voices, including other HE professionals and the students the LD community serves.
9	often sides with those in marginal positions in HE, as it strives to promote inclusive practice and a fairer HE.
10	is critical, often radical, in line with its academic literacies foundations – it refuses to uncritically accept the norms of the HE system, and instead seeks to challenge and innovate.

scale from 1 (strongly disagree) to 5 (strongly agree) was used to rate the features. The average level of agreement with the statements ranged from 4.70 to 3.77. Features 3 and 4, and 5 and 6, have the same ratings.

The priority-based rankings from the practitioner-respondents (Table 17.1) illustrate that the LD community values its scholarship as a means of developing ourselves, our students, and the wider conversation about what LD represents and does within HE. Practitioners agree that being scholarly active is endemic to delivering a theoretically informed praxis in accordance with ALDinHE's values and those we tend to bring to our professional identities. All in all, these viewpoints favour a generous conception of LD scholarship. We take these insights forward into the next sections, as we propose what LD scholarship can entail, and where Learning Developers can get involved.

What LD Scholarship Entails

LD scholarship encompasses diverse scholarly outlets linked to learning and teaching in HE, a space we inhabit alongside students and other colleagues. Specifically, LD scholarship revolves around students' development of academic literacies, which allows them to navigate HE expectations, including the exploration and production of academic texts (in a broad sense); the development of higher-order cognitive skills such as critical thinking and argumentation; and the ability to develop a stance, based on evidence gathered through exposure to academic texts.

LD scholarship may explore:

- the Learning Developer's role, our remit, responsibilities, values, and philosophy, as well as improving and scrutinising our own practices;
- issues of professional identity, status, and role in HE;
- the foundations of LD practices – our commitment to supporting learners to thrive and develop in HE;
- pedagogical approaches to demystifying HE practices and enhancing students' academic abilities, to ensure they get the most out of HE;
- *how* to teach (and challenge) academic conventions, often taken for granted;
- institutional approaches to enhancing students' development of their academic literacies;
- working with staff and students to create a culture that allows people to grow as individuals and as part of an organisation;
- ways in which we may collaborate with staff to create an LD-influenced HE;
- understanding how HE works, including how LD interacts with other professionals and its impact on student learning;
- effective teaching, learning and assessment practices;
- barriers to learning and ways in which they could be overcome.

Engagement

Since the LD scholarship involves not just *engaging* with developments in our field but also *actively carrying out research*, this section will highlight opportunities to begin or continue your LD scholarship journey.

ALDinHE offers a range of options to involve yourself in scholarly activity. Formal opportunities for dissemination include submitting an article to the *Journal of Learning Development in Higher Education*. Several issues are published annually, including special issues and conference proceedings. Research funding for individual or team projects is also available. Once completed, you will be able to disseminate your findings to the wider LD community. If you are new to publishing articles or submitting research proposals, you can request a mentor, who can share their expertise and help you develop your confidence.

Another way in which you could contribute to our diverse scholarship is by presenting at ALDinHE's conference. Here, you could contribute online or face-to-face and deliver longer or shorter papers, lightning talks, mini-keynotes, or a poster. The conference offers an opportunity to network, find out what Learning Developers in other institutions are doing, and connect with like-minded individuals interested in cross-institutional collaboration.

ALDinHE has various working groups as well, including research and scholarship. There are often opportunities to join this group and be part of its key core strands: research funding, development, and scholarship. Joining working groups usually involves monthly online meetings and working with colleagues from several institutions to deliver on those core strands. This work offers opportunity for cross-institutional projects and contributing to LD scholarship beyond your own institution.

Those affiliated with ALDinHE can also create communities of practice, and there is currently one devoted to research. Joining such a community is likely to involve online meetings, opportunities to disseminate your research and make connections with practitioners interested in collaborative endeavours. There are digital ways in which you may want to share your research activity as well, including LD@3 – a live presentation of LD-related activities – and writing a #Take5 Blog. Detailed information on all these ALDinHE opportunities can be found in the *Research and Scholarship* section of the website (ALDinHE, 2023).

As much as the above opportunities provide encouragement about the scholarship activities *within* ALDinHE, it is also important that the LD field strives to achieve the reach of its messaging *beyond* our community's boundaries. Verity and Trowler (2011) and Samuels (2013) cautioned against the tendency for LD scholarship to look and talk inwards, when better progress for the field might be anticipated if its activity is consistently communicated to external stakeholders. To that end, there have been notable examples of publications about LD in journals including *Teaching in Higher Education* (Syska and Buckley, 2022) and *Journal of University Teaching and Learning Practice* (Bickle *et al.*, 2021; Webster, 2023), as well as in edited collections on third space professionals (Webster, 2022) and student support services (Coulson, Loddick and Rice, 2021). In addition, project funding bodies such as the *Society for Research into Higher Education* and the *Society for Educational Studies* have also funded projects concerning LD practice. LD scholars, especially those more established in the field, are thus encouraged to turn outwards to these external opportunities alongside continuing the vital ongoing developmental conversation within their own field.

Conclusion

This chapter set out to narrow down the elements which would allow us to present a definition of LD scholarship and its defining features. Based on the views gathered from the survey, scholarship has been defined as a vehicle which allows those invested in LD to become part of and initiate an ongoing academic conversation in which the community is able to discuss, share, and exchange resources, thoughts, and developments in this field. By engaging with these conversations, LD is able to exist, establish boundaries, and solidify and advance its aims, identity, and knowledge base.

The analysis of the survey data also established that LD scholarship is endemic to the ALDinHE values, and therefore aims to explore the complexities of teaching and learning in a diverse and evolving HE environment; fulfil its emancipatory mission by siding with those in marginal positions and working towards a fairer, more inclusive HE; and encourage collaborative, multidisciplinary, and cross-institutional scholarly endeavours. Furthermore, the chapter presented defining principles and features of the scholarship of LD, including a commitment to developing ourselves and others, the importance of sharing best practices and theoretical developments to enhance the field, and a generous and expansive understanding of what counts as a research output.

Our question asking the survey respondents to elaborate on their ratings surfaced two key debates. Firstly, respondents debated whether LD scholarship should open itself up to the wider base of scholarship within HE teaching and learning holistically. Despite some support, the more popular position was that LD's scholarship must fight for its place as a distinct professional field, and that too much blurring of boundaries could dilute the LD voice necessary towards meeting that goal. The need was emphasised, however, to encourage more diverse voices in the scholarship canon to move it away from a white Anglo-centric bias, which accords well with ALDinHE's emancipatory missions.

Secondly, several respondents highlighted concerns that the scholarship manifesto was aspirational rather than reflecting the realities of their day-to-day work, in which perceptions of low levels of power, place in the academy or working conditions often militate against greater scholarly engagement. As real as these concerns might be, they could indicate shades of the imposter syndrome (Akerman, 2020) which tends to afflict Learning Developers, and could continue to do so unless and until our scholarship creates improvement of the conditions; it is arguably a chicken and egg situation of sorts.

Hence, the manifesto hereby presented might, to some extent, sound aspirational, yet we argue that there is a need to be aspirational. The rationale for continuing to write LD into existence might not be obvious on day one of a Learning Developer's role but this chapter is intended as the type of introduction to the gentle routes into LD scholarship that, with hindsight, may have encouraged both of us, at the outset of our LD careers. If we can be part of this process, anyone can do it, and should do it. Without scholarship, we will continue to define ourselves by who we are and what we do, rather than by what we stand for and what sort of change we want to be a part of.

References

Akerman, K. (2020) 'Invisible imposter: identity in institutions', *Perspective, Policy and Practice in Higher Education*, 24(4): 126–130.

ALDinHE (2023) *Research and scholarship*. Available at: https://aldinhe.ac.uk/research/ (Accessed: 31 March 2023).

Bickle, E., Bishopp-Martin, S., Canton, U., Chin, P., Johnson, I., Kantcheva, R., Nodder, J., Rafferty, V., Sum, K. and Welton, K. (2021) 'Emerging from the third space chrysalis: experiences in a non-hierarchical, collaborative research community of practice', *Journal of University Teaching and Learning Practice*, 18(7): 135–158.

Coulson, K., Loddick, A. and Rice, P. (2021) 'Exploring the Impact of Learning Development on Student Engagement, Experience, and Learning', in: H. Huijser, M. Kek and F. Pedro (eds) *Student Support Services. University Development and Administration*. Singapore: Springer.

Dickinson, J., Fowler, A. and Griffiths, T. (2022) 'Pracademics? Exploring transitions and professional identities in higher education', *Studies in Higher Education*, 47(2): 290–304.

Green, C.A., Eady, M., McCarthy, M., Akenson, A., Supple, B., McKeon, J. and Cronin, J.G.R. (2020) 'Beyond the conference: Singing our SSONG', *Teaching and Learning Inquiry*, 8(1): 42–60.

Hilsdon, J. (2018) *The significance of the field of practice 'Learning Development' in UK higher education*. Doctoral Thesis. University of Plymouth. Available at: https://pearl.plymouth.ac.uk/handle/10026.1/10604 (Accessed: 10 May 2021).

Johnson, I. (2018) 'Driving Learning Development professionalism forward from within', *Journal of Learning Development in Higher Education*, 14: 1–29. Available at: https://doi.org/10.47408/jldhe.v0i0.470

Jones-Devitt, S. (2022) 'The viral landscapes of third space working', in: E. McIntosh and D. Nutt (eds) *The Impact of the Integrated Practitioner in Higher Education*. Abingdon: Routledge.

Loddick, A. and Coulson, K. (2020) 'The impact of Learning Development tutorials on student attainment', *Journal of Learning Development in Higher Education*, 17: 1–24. Available at: https://doi.org/10.47408/jldhe.vi17.558

Lucas, P., Wilkinson, H., Rae, S., Dean, B., Eady, M., Capocchiano, H., Trede, F. and Yuen, L. (2021) 'Knowing me, Knowing you: Humanitas in work-integrated learning during adversity', *Journal of University Teaching and Learning Practice*, 18(7): 159–176.

Macfarlane, B. (2011) 'The morphing of academic practice: Unbundling and the rise of the para-academic', *Higher Education Quarterly*, 65(1): 59–73.

McIntosh, E. and Nutt, D. (2022) 'Introduction', in: E. McIntosh and D. Nutt (eds), *The Impact of the Integrated Practitioner in Higher Education*. Abingdon: Routledge.

Parkes, S. (2018) 'A learner developer perspective: critiquing dominant practices and cultures within university spaces', *Journal of Learning Development in Higher Education*, Special edition. Available at: https://doi.org/10.47408/jldhe.v0i0.464

Samuels, P. (2013) 'Promoting Learning Development as an academic discipline', *Journal of Learning Development in Higher Education*, 5: 1–22. Available at: https://doi.org/10.47408/jldhe.v0i5.146

Stapleford, K. (2019) 'The LDHEN hive mind: Learning Development in UK higher education as a professional culture', *Journal of Learning Development in Higher Education*, 16: 1–23. Available at: https://doi.org/10.47408/jldhe.v0i16.510

Syska, A. and Buckley, C. (2022) 'Writing as liberatory practice: unlocking knowledge to locate an academic field', *Teaching in Higher Education*, 28(2): 439–454.

Veles, N. and Carter, M. (2016) 'Imagining a future: changing the landscape for third space professionals in Australian higher education institutions', *Journal of Higher Education Policy and Management*, 38(5): 519–533.

Verity, M. and Trowler, P. (2011) 'Looking back and into the future', in P. Hartley, J. Hilsdon, C. Keenan, S. Sinfield and M. Verity (eds.) *Learning Development in Higher Education*, Basingstoke: Palgrave MacMillan, pp.241–252.

Webster, H. (2022) 'Supporting the development, recognition, and impact of third space professionals', in E. McIntosh and D. Nutt (eds) *The Impact of the Integrated Practitioner in Higher Education*. Abingdon: Routledge.

Webster, H. (2023) 'The five Ps of LD: Using formulation in Learning Development work for a student centred approach to "study skills"', *Journal of University Teaching & Learning Practice*, 20(4). Available at: https://doi.org/10.53761/1.20.4.07

Whitchurch, C. (2013) *Reconstructing Identities in Higher Education: The Rise of 'Third Space' Professionals*. Abingdon: Routledge.

Whitchurch, C. (2019) 'From a diversifying workforce to the rise of the itinerant academic', *Higher Education*, 77(4): 679–694.

18

METHODOLOGIES FOR RESEARCH IN LEARNING DEVELOPMENT

Lee Fallin

I suspect this is a common query we have all seen: 'Why do we have to engage with stupid philosophy to do research?' It might even be something we've felt ourselves...

Though research methodology may seem like a dreaded necessity for many Learning Developers, we should always remember that it is the unsung hero of effective research, paving the way for impactful new strategies and ground-breaking new approaches. It is also an opportunity for Learning Development to define itself by taking a distinctive approach to the production of new knowledge.

Introduction

Methodologies explain and justify the theoretical approach to research and the practical collection and analysis methods used. As each discipline takes distinctive approaches to research, it is within methodology that Learning Development (LD) research has the power to distinguish itself from the broader field of education studies. Methodology is essential in research practice. Without a robust methodological approach, there is the risk that LD research will only evaluate practice, missing the opportunity to generate new knowledge and generalise it for the benefit of others. Saunders et al. (2019) liken the research process to the peeling layers of an onion, systematically working through the outer layers until reaching the middle (see Figure 18.1). This chapter will peel away these layers of the research onion from a Learning Development perspective.

DOI: 10.4324/9781003433347-23

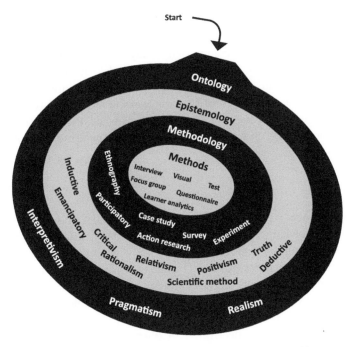

FIGURE 18.1 The research onion (Based on: Saunders et al., 2019)

Ontology

Ontology establishes the nature of reality and what can (or cannot) be known. While multiple nuanced approaches to ontology exist (Guba et al., 2017), there are three useful starting points for Learning Developers: realism, pragmatism, and interpretivism. Realists argue that there is an objective and definable world out there – finding the truth is possible. Their research tends to focus on quantitative (number-based) methods such as surveys, experiments, and big data, often using statistics to prove differences, correlations, or to predict. Realists focus on objective and reproducible research, so it can easily be applied in similar contexts. In contrast, interpretivists recognise that the world is a cacophony of different people, perspectives, and opinions. Their research embraces this diversity and explores thoughts, feelings, and actions through the use of qualitative methods. Qualitative methods focus on using unstructured data (words, images, audio/video) and include methods like observation, interviews, focus groups, and visual methods. Interpretivism has no universal truth, but the value is placed on depth and detail. Finally, pragmatism acknowledges the importance of realism and interpretivism and borrows from both philosophies as needed for a given research project. Pragmatists tend to focus on mixed methods, using a mixture of qualitative and quantitative approaches.

It may seem that interpretivist studies done in partnership with students should be the signature research approach for LD, but there are broader considerations. Interpretative approaches may better embrace the values of LD and work to produce a more student-centred form of knowledge creation. However, LD must also acknowledge that the hard numbers and statistics of realist research are one of the best ways to demonstrate significance and impact. For this reason, LD research must be inclusive of multiple research philosophies, and we should strive to produce research within both domains.

Epistemology

Epistemology needs to be carefully considered for LD research because it defines how knowledge can be created, produced, or discovered (Schubotz, 2020), essentially framing how researchers know what they know. This establishes the power dynamics of research, defining who has (or does not have) control in the research process. Epistemology defines to what extent the world is objective and can be (scientifically) understood, or subjective and (socially) constructed. This is not a binary choice, and there is much depth and nuance across the epistemological spectrum. As Cohen et al. (2018) suggest, communities of practice influence epistemology; I argue that participatory, emancipatory, and practitioner epistemologies should form the base of authentic research in Learning Development:

- *Participatory epistemologies* emphasise co-creation and co-delivery of research (Schubotz, 2020). Instead of having 'participants' who just take part in a study, they are framed as co-researchers and become an active part of the research process. At its fullest extent, participatory research invites co-researchers to define the scope of the project, design the method, conduct the research, support the analysis, and take part in the write-up.
- *Emancipatory epistemologies* place focus on giving voice to disadvantaged, oppressed, and exploited groups (Bagnall and Hodge, 2022). Such epistemological approaches have traditionally produced feminist, queer, and non-white perspectives on the world, challenging established (but biased) ways of knowing. In LD research, this approach may be turned to any disadvantaged group.
- *Practitioner epistemologies*, I propose, focus on developing professional knowledge. As Learning Development emerges as a distinct profession, there is a need for authentic, practitioner-led research. Learning Developers should produce such research and may draw upon autoethnographic and reflective practices (Kinsella, 2010).

Positionality

It is useful for LD research to consider positionality alongside epistemology. Positionality can be defined as 'the position [researchers] adopt about a research task and its social and political context' (Holmes, 2020, p.1). Positionality requires researchers to be self-aware of their own background and biography, and how it can influence the research process. For example, I write as a white, male, western, gay academic, the first in his family to go to university. Such experiences shape how I see the world – my institution, my practice, my students, and my colleagues. In research, positionality is the vehicle to account for the insights and biases the researcher brings to the research. It is also important to consider the 'position' of LD within any given institution as this can vary considerably across the sector.

Methodological Designs

The methodology is the strategy for inquiry – the process of seeking new knowledge (Guba et al., 2017). For this section, I provide an overview of approaches that align well with the values of Learning Development, and the 'insider researcher' status of most practitioners that are investigating their own practice, institution, or unit.

Case Studies

Case studies are the detailed examination of an individual unit (Flyvbjerg, 2011) – a specific intervention or university. They provide great depth, and, through their focus, can help identify causes of outcomes (Flyvbjerg, 2011). I argue that while a single case study cannot show how widespread a phenomenon is, the publication of multiple case studies across LD will provide broader insight into the profession. Case studies are a popular approach for LD researchers. One recent example includes McIntyre and O'Neill (2022), who share their approach to supporting student transition via a tailored online course. Their case study focuses on one course, providing detail of their intervention, with use of a survey to demonstrate student feedback on their development.

Ethnographic Approaches

Ethnography is a methodology that is often associated with LD (Sizer, 2019), and involves 'direct and sustained contact with human agents' (O'Reilly, 2009, p.3). The focus of ethnography is to help understand the everyday experience, something that is well applied to the university context. Ethnography is usually based on rich, written accounts, the application of theory, and the researcher's own reflexivity (O'Reilly, 2009), with methods including observation and interview. While the sustained aspect of ethnography can make it a challenging approach for Learning Developers, there is value in considering how ethnographic studies engage with social meanings, values, and structures (Madison, 2020). For this reason, ethnography is often adapted in application for LD research. Sizer (2019) cites ethnography as part of the root of their 'textography' approach, which investigates contexts, texts, and practices. Another example comes from Woods et al. (2019), who argue that their User Experience (UX) research is an applied form of ethnography. Closely related to ethnography is the field of autoethnography, the study of the self (Hughes and Pennington, 2017). Learning Developers successfully use this to explore their practice, a core aspect of practitioner-led epistemologies. Johnson et al. (2022) demonstrate the potential for collaborative writing and analysis to form a collaborative autoethnography, which, I argue, could help further the advancement of Learning Development.

Action Research

Action research is a rigorous methodology that intertwines theoretical and practical knowledge, engaging with people to draw on many ways of knowing with an end goal of positive change (Reason and Bradbury, 2008; McAteer, 2013). As such, action research can be seen as cyclic, allowing researchers to identify problems, develop and implement solutions, then evaluate outcomes. If necessary, this cycle can be repeated over and over, stopping when the problem is fully resolved. Action research is a popular approach in LD, as it aligns to practice and focuses on developing improvements. A recent example includes Hancock (2019), who uses action research to introduce a flipped-classroom approach. The author notes how action research allowed her to both make and analyse change in her teaching, amalgamating research and practice.

Participatory Research

While discussed as an epistemology, participatory research has methodological implications for deeply participatory research. In Learning Development, such approaches would involve participants throughout the research cycle. This would involve their direct input throughout the research cycle, including the identification of the issue to be investigated, the methods to investigate it, and the analysis of data collected. As such, a participatory methodology would be driven not just by Learning Developers, but those we work with (most often students). While some examples of LD research engage students (or others we interact with) in the research cycle, I believe there is much more potential to develop this. If LD is to be truly emancipatory and participatory, LD research should reflect this. One excellent example of this comes from Fromm et al. (2021), who reflect upon a participatory action research project involving students in two research cycles, presenting their findings in the students' words. This published article is co-written with five students, demonstrating a highly participatory, student-centred approach.

Surveys and Experiments

Survey methodology focuses on the systematic gathering of information from a sample of a larger population (Joye et al., 2016), and is often associated with questionnaires. Experimental designs involve an experimental group exposed to a treatment or intervention, which is then compared to a control group not exposed to the experimental treatment or intervention (Vaus, 2006). These approaches tend to be more quantitative and rely on statistical analysis situated towards a more realist ontology of research. While this may seem problematic when considering my argument for participatory, emancipatory, and practitioner-led approaches to LD research, it is possible to use these methodologies if prioritising students and adhering to core LD values. An example of this approach in practice comes from Loddick and Coulson's (2020) work on the impact of tutorials on student attainment. This research compares students who have attended LD tutorials (experimental group) with that of the university population (control group). This is not a true experimental design, but represents an approach that maintains the core values of LD. It aims to use statistical inference to ascertain impact, but does not actively 'experiment' on students or use them as 'subjects'. The authors are clear on the problems of this approach – the students are self-selecting (as opposed to random), and there are multiple other variables that are not controlled.

Mixed, Merge, and Multiple Methods

Mixed, merge, and multiple-method designs aim to weave together qualitative and quantitative approaches to overcome the weaknesses of each design in isolation. These approaches are one of the most popular for LD research, allowing the use of two or more research methods. *Mixed methods* explicitly use at least one quantitative and one qualitative method to either triangulate findings or provide both breadth and depth. *Merge methods* aim to fully merge epistemology and methodology, breaking away from the focus of two methods towards full integration. Finally, *multi-methods* embrace more than one method to provide a breadth of data. These do not need to be an explicit mix of qualitative and quantitative.

Research Methods

To measure the diversity of research methods in LD, I analysed the research article publications from the *Journal of Learning Development in Higher*

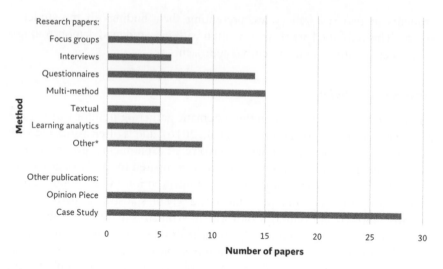

* Conceptual papers (3), case studies (3), autoethnography (3)

FIGURE 18.2 Research methods used in *JLDHE* research papers 2018–2022

Education (*JLDHE*) for 2018–2022. As you can see in Figure 18.2, a wide range of methods are used in LD research, and the rest of the chapter will focus on these approaches in practice.

Focus Groups and Workshops

Focus groups are based on facilitated activities (usually discussion-based) among a selected group of people to produce group – as opposed to individualised – meanings (Acocella and Cataldi, 2021). Focus groups are often facilitated as a group conversation but can involve the use of activities that use artefacts like LEGO, flipcharts, and photography to develop tangible outputs (Fallin, 2020). These visual and creative techniques can often make the session more manageable to 'capture' for the purposes of analysis. In Learning Development, focus groups may be pitched as 'workshops', and could be combined with teaching – with appropriate ethical clearance and consent.

Interviews

Interviews are a diverse instrument and are generally based on one-to-one conversations between a researcher and a participant (Billups, 2021). They allow Learning Developers to undertake an in-depth exploration of reasons, feelings, and language with students or other participants. Interviews can be conversational, semi-structured, or completely structured and questionnaire-like, giving researchers a choice of varying levels of flexibility. Interviews are always discussion-based but can use prompts and other objects for elicitation. Most researchers audio-record their interviews and transcribe them for analysis.

Questionnaires

Questionnaires are used to gather consistent information from a (potentially) large number of participants using a series of questions (Coleman, 2019). For Learning Developers, questionnaires allow the rapid collection of research or evaluation data. Questionnaires can be administered online, via pen and paper or via oral administration, giving more flexibility over how they can be administered – without the requirement for a researcher to be present. Questionnaires can use closed (quantitative), open (qualitative), or mixed approaches to collecting data.

Multi-method

Multi-method studies were the most prevalent approach, most often a combination of interviews with either questionnaires or focus groups, with an aim of triangulating data.

Textual

Textual-based approaches are a broad and diverse range of methods (Ledolter and VanderVelde, 2022). Approaches can involve the analysis of language or content of any form of document or written work. Texts for analysis can include emails, textbooks, web content, or even student summative assignments and VLE comments. Textual-based approaches can allow Learning Developers to engage with existing texts (ethics permitting) for new analytical approaches. There is much potential for Learning Developers to use this approach to engage with student work, helping to identify areas for future LD focus. Textual approaches also afford the opportunity to engage with linguistic analysis, allowing a deep analysis of student writing to identify functions of grammar, language, and structure.

Learning Analytics

Learning analytics allow the use of existing University data to provide new insights. This can be information from student records that covers demographics and student assessment details, or can cover detailed interaction reports from VLEs. There are interesting ethical questions around the application of big data and learning analytics, but there is also a call for universities to better use the data they have to support students. Learning analytics tend to be overly positive and insensitive to cultural factors (Rogers et al., 2016); therefore, caution is needed if LD is to enter this space.

Reflective and Reflexive Methods

Reflective and reflexive approaches to data collection usually sit within autoethnography, the study of the self (Hughes and Pennington, 2017). For Learning Developers, these approaches afford a practitioner-centred approach to data collection, using the thoughts, feelings, and reflections of the practitioners to produce new data. There are structured approaches to this, such as the use of a calendar or diary to record thoughts over time (Muncey, 2010). Alternatively, reflective frameworks like Brookfield's (2017) Four Lenses afford a structured approach to reflection. This approach to research requires strong links to theory and practice, and there is also opportunity to triangulate reflective data with that of other instruments (such as interviews or focus groups).

Conclusion

As Learning Development continues to write itself into existence, research is one of the significant opportunities to further establish what makes LD distinctive. This chapter demonstrated how participatory, emancipatory, and practitioner-led approaches can inform an authentic LD ontology, epistemology, and theory in the application of research methods.

I encourage readers to engage with the *JLDHE* for further examples of methodologies in practice. As you will see in Chapter 20, there are many routes into publishing in Learning Development, and you will find reading *JLDHE* a useful way to develop your own research style within the profession.

References

Acocella, I. and Cataldi, S. (2021) *Using Focus Groups: Theory, Methodology, Practice.* London: SAGE Publications.

Bagnall, R.G. and Hodge, S. (2022) 'Emancipatory epistemology and ethics in lifelong learning', in: R.G. Bagnall and S. Hodge (eds), *Epistemologies and Ethics in Adult Education and Lifelong Learning.* Cham: Springer, 161–189.

Billups, F.D. (2021) *Qualitative Data Collection Tools: Design, Development, and Applications.* Thousand Oaks: SAGE Publications.

Brookfield, S. (2017) *Becoming a Critically Reflective Teacher*, 2nd edn. San Francisco: Jossey-Bass.

Cohen, L., Manion, L. and Morrison, K. (2018) *Research Methods in Education*, 8th edn. Abingdon: Routledge.

Coleman, R. (2019) *Designing Experiments for the Social Sciences: How to Plan, Create, and Execute Research Using Experiments.* Thousand Oaks: SAGE Publications.

Fallin, L. (2020) *Reading the Academic Library: An Exploration of the Conceived, Perceived and Lived Spaces of the Brynmor Jones Library at the University of Hull.* Doctor of Education Thesis. University of Hull. Available at: https://hydra.hull.ac.uk/resources/hull:18417 (Accessed: 20 January 2021).

Flyvbjerg, B. (2011) 'Case study', in: N.K. Denzin and Y.S. Lincoln (eds), *The SAGE Handbook of Qualitative Research*. Thousand Oaks: SAGE Publications, 301–316.

Fromm, A., Adigun-Lawal, B., Akinmoju, S., Onyenucheya, N., Otchere, F. and Udeh, V. (2021) 'MSc student voices about learning together in an online academic conversation club: a collaborative student project', *Journal of Learning Development in Higher Education*, 22, 1–7.

Guba, E.G., Lincoln, Y.S. and Lynham, S.A. (2017) 'Paradigmatic controversies, contradictions, and emerging confluences', in N.K. Denzin and Y.S. Lincoln (eds), *The SAGE Handbook of Qualitative Research*, 5th edn. California: SAGE Publications, 108–150.

Hancock, J.C. (2019) '"It can't be found in books": how a flipped-classroom approach using online videos can engage postgraduate students in dissertation writing', *Journal of Learning Development in Higher Education*, 16, 1–27.

Holmes, A.G.D. (2020) 'Researcher positionality – A consideration of its influence and place in qualitative research – A new researcher guide', *Shanlax International Journal of Education*, 8(4), 1–10.

Hughes, S.A. and Pennington, J.L. (2017) *Autoethnography: Process, Product, and Possibility for Critical Social Research*. Thousand Oaks: SAGE Publications.

Johnson, I., Welton, K., Sum, K., Rafferty, V., Kantcheva, R., Nodder, J., Chin, P., Canton, U., Bishopp-Martin, S. and Bickle, E. (2022) 'Collaborative writing communities for Learning Development research and practice', *Journal of Learning Development in Higher Education*, 25, 1–7.

Joye, D., Wolf, C., Smith, T.W. and Fu, Y.-C. (eds) (2016) *The SAGE Handbook of Survey Methodology*. London: SAGE Publications.

Kinsella, E.A. (2010) 'Professional knowledge and the epistemology of reflective practice', *Nursing Philosophy*, 11(1): 3–14.

Ledolter, J. and VanderVelde, L.S. (2022) *Analyzing Textual Information: From Words to Meanings Through Numbers*. Thousand Oaks: SAGE Publications.

Loddick, A. and Coulson, K. (2020) 'The impact of Learning Development tutorials on student attainment', *Journal of Learning Development in Higher Education*, 17, 1–24.

Madison, D.S. (2020) *Critical Ethnography: Method, Ethics, and Performance*, 3rd edn. Thousand Oaks: SAGE Publications.

McAteer, M. (2013) *Action Research in Education*. London: SAGE Publications.

McIntyre, K. and O'Neill, J. (2022) 'The process of adapting an online induction course to support distinct student cohorts', *Journal of Learning Development in Higher Education*, 24, 1–28.

Muncey, T. (2010) *Creating Autoethnographies*. London: SAGE Publications.

O'Reilly, K. (2009) *Key Concepts in Ethnography*. London: SAGE Publications.

Reason, P. and Bradbury, H. (eds) (2008) *The SAGE Handbook of Action Research*, 2nd edn. Thousand Oaks: SAGE Publications.

Rogers, T., Dawson, S. and Gaevi, D. (2016) 'Learning analytics and the imperative for theory-driven research', in C. Haythornthwaite, R. Andrews, J. Fransman and E. Meyers (eds), *The SAGE Handbook of E-Learning Research*, 2nd edn. London: SAGE Publications, 232–250.

Saunders, M.N.K., Lewis, P. and Thornhill, A. (2019) *Research Methods for Business Students*. Pearson Education.

Schubotz, D. (2020) *Participatory Research: Why and How to Involve People in Research*. London: SAGE Publications.

Sizer, J. (2019) 'Textography as a needs analysis and research tool for English for Academic Purposes and Learning Development practitioners', *Journal of Learning Development in Higher Education*, 15, 1–21

Vaus, D. (2006) 'Experiment', in: V. Jupp (ed.), *The SAGE Dictionary of Social Research Methods*. London: SAGE Publications, 106–108.

Woods, L., Dockery, R. and Sharman, A. (2019) 'Using UX research techniques to explore how Computing undergraduates understand and use library and student guidance services', *Journal of Learning Development in Higher Education*, 16, 1–23.

19

LEARNING DEVELOPERS AS WRITERS

The Four Tendencies Framework to Get Writing

Alicja Syska and Carina Buckley

> *How do you get a Learning Developer to start writing for publication?*
> *Strivers are already writing as you speak; Pragmatists want to know why they should do it; give Actualisers a deadline and they will get it done; and if Freelancers tell you to go and write it yourself just wait until they think it was their idea in the first place.*

Picture this: a world in which writing is easy, disconnected from emotion, and allocated sufficient time and resources for it to flourish. A world in which we know exactly what we want to say and how we want to say it; a world in which we understand how we work, what blocks to writing we experience, and how to overcome them. That world would unlock our writing potential and make producing words a sheer pleasure.

Instead, in our imperfect reality writing is hard. More than that, writing may seem impossible at times. Even decades of experience do not protect anyone from struggling with writing, feeling hostile to or fearful of it, and considering it one of the most demanding, arduous, and frustrating aspects of their work in academia. We did not have to raid the thesaurus for words commonly appearing in both formal and informal conversations around writing: uncertainty, setbacks, criticism, rejection, failure, hesitation, disappointment, guilt, shame, anxiety, nervousness, embarrassment, risk, fear, even torture. Writing is a bumpy process filled with uncomfortable emotions, blocks and disruptions, twists and turns, and delays and breakdowns. It can be harrowing, intimidating, tiring, lengthy, unruly, emotionally taxing, and even threatening to our identity. Of course, those who love writing will readily counter this list with words implying joy, including excitement, liberation, the experience of creative

DOI: 10.4324/9781003433347-24

jolts, and a sense of accomplishment; all powerful aspects of writing. Nonetheless, acknowledging the difficulties around writing can be a crucial first step (Dunlap, 2007) before even attempting to connect with the writer in us.

The aim of this chapter is not to persuade our readers that these difficulties are figments of their imaginations and that all they need to do is 'get over it' and 'just write'. It is also not to offer advice on writing productivity or even to encourage anyone to write more; we have done it elsewhere (Syska and Buckley, 2022). What we want to do is inspire Learning Developers to examine their own writing circumstances so they can uncover their particular mechanisms that produce blocks and barriers, and – equipped with this self-knowledge – design individual strategies for managing them in order to derive more satisfaction from writing. In this spirit, we propose a framework for thinking about the ways we respond to outer and inner expectations around writing. The four profiles we created are based on Gretchen Rubin's (2017) Four Tendencies, which explain how and why we act, and when applied to writing may help us understand ourselves better as writers and use this foundation to build our own writing habits and processes. To help our readers identify their own tendency, we designed a quiz and created profiles filled with ideas that adapt their circumstances to better suit their writing disposition, invigorate their writing process, and gain confidence as writers in Learning Development (LD).

Writing as an Expectation

Due to the peculiarities of practising in third space (Whitchurch, 2008), which is not bound by the same 'publish or perish' ethos of traditional academia, the expectations around writing for Learning Developers can be either internal or external, neither, or both. Those for whom it is neither might not even be interested in reading this chapter. Those for whom writing is purely an internal expectation might be reading out of sheer curiosity. But those colleagues who feel pressured to write or who accept institutional or disciplinary expectations as their own will actively seek new ways of interpreting and managing their circumstances.

We acknowledge that many Learning Developers find themselves unprepared for the realities of writing for publication, and often unable to overcome the barriers that confront them. Over a series of workshops, surveys, and conversations around writing with colleagues in and associated with LD, we discovered a range of reasons why people write, as well as – more significantly – why they don't. However, strategies that work for one do not necessarily suit another. Even though Learning Developers know what is involved in academic writing and are skilled at guiding their students through its mysteries, they often seem to struggle to apply the advice given to students to their own writing process.

Part of the difficulty lies in the emotional aspect of writing. Emotions, far from being a private affair, mediate the relationship between the individual and the collective (Ahmed, 2014); so, too, does writing. The social nature of emotions ties them to the 'construction of knowledge' (Leathwood and Hey, 2009, p.432); so, too, with writing. With academia so strongly positioned as rational, masculine, and therefore desirable, and emotions as the more undesirable and irrational feminine attributes (Ahmed, 2014), the discomfort that comes from the uncertainty and ambiguity of writing too easily dominates the process and renders it undesirable. In fact, a previous negative emotional response to writing is often enough to act as an insurmountable block even to thinking about starting something new. Thus, supporting writing effectively requires deepening our understanding not just of our needs and proclivities, but of the underlying mechanisms that drive and – too often – inhibit them. For this reason, in this chapter we focus on the emotional and behavioural, rather than cognitive, aspects of writing, in the hope of finding a way of releasing writing from the often deep-seated and unnamed sense of disaffection.

The Four Writing Tendencies Framework

We have previously (Syska and Buckley, 2022) described writing as a form of liberatory practice, in the freedom it can offer the LD practitioner from self-explanation, self-justification, and self-doubt, as well as being a way to shift the focus from the self to the community. Rubin's Four Tendencies framework complements this shift in the possibilities it offers for actionable self-knowledge, focussed on our reactions – whether positive or negative – to internal and external expectations. By applying her framework to writing, we have a tool to understand why we respond to the call to write in the ways that we do and how we can support our colleagues and our students in achieving their own writing goals.

Rubin's devising of the Four Tendencies was prompted by her observation that the advice on habit formation she had given in her previous books was met with conflicting reader testimonials regarding its applicability. As respondents seemed to resonate with different recommendations, she began looking for more profound distinctions and behavioural patterns that shape our responses to the expectations others have of us and those we have of ourselves. This led her to developing a model that divides behaviours into four tendencies: Upholders (constituting 19% of Rubin's respondents), Questioners (24%), Obligers (41%), and Rebels (17%). These categories represent all four combinations of meeting or not meeting inner and outer expectations, with Upholders having little trouble meeting both, Questioners tending to respond to inner but resisting outer expectations, Obligers being happy to meet outer but struggling with inner expectations, and Rebels resisting both. Rubin notes that while the tendencies may overlap and mix and to some extent we may identify with each of the four, everyone has a *core* tendency that drives their decisions. Understanding not only one's own but also other people's core tendency may help us identify strategies that will allow us not only to meet our goals but also to work effectively together.

What we found appealing about Rubin's framework is that it allowed us to understand our own relationship with writing while also gaining an insight into why some colleagues we talked to are successful in writing for publication while others seem to struggle. In applying her model to the context of writing, we adapted the names of the four profiles so they would resonate more closely with the expectations linked specifically with the act of writing. As a result, we created the following four writing tendencies: Striver (Rubin's Upholder), Pragmatist (Questioner), Actualiser (Obliger), and Freelancer (Rebel). As our opening anecdote illustrates,

> *Strivers* respond well to both inner and outer expectations around writing;
> *Pragmatists* tend to question outer expectations but have few problems meeting their own writing goals;
> *Actualisers* prioritise the expectations and demands of others, often sacrificing their own writing needs; and
> *Freelancers* tend to do things in their own way, avoiding creating demands around their writing while also resisting those imposed by others.

Finding Yourself in the Four Writing Tendencies Framework

The eternal human quest for identity and the need to classify the ultimately unclassifiable self make personality quizzes not only popular and enjoyable but also productive in the context of research (e.g., Hu and Pu, 2009). Although not without controversy (see Paul, 2010), if approached with a bit of distance, personality quizzes can be a playful tool for self-knowledge. In that spirit of playfulness, we invite you to take the quiz below to identify your core tendency when it comes to writing (the scoring table will indicate your dominant tendency, Table 19.1). The four scenarios were designed to resemble real life situations and choices involved in the professional roles associated with Learning Development. Although you may find yourself torn between possible responses, choose the one that aligns most closely with your likely reaction.[1]

Quiz

Q1 At your annual performance review, your manager has included publishing a journal article as one of your objectives. How do you feel about that?

a. You would rather not do something just for the sake of doing it
b. Having a clear goal and resources should help you to achieve this by the next review meeting, especially if other team members want to work together towards it

c. You have already outlined the paper in your head by the end of your meeting

d. You could publish something, but why does it have to be a journal article?

Q2 An opportunity arises to contribute to a special issue of a journal, on a topic of which you have some experience. What is your response?

a. It triggers an idea for a blog post you could write on this subject instead

b. You are already working on something in this area and will publish it, but you might consider the outlet later

c. You forward the information to a colleague and ask if they're interested in writing with you

d. You note the deadline on your calendar and start thinking of your angle.

Q3 Your conference presentation went really well, and several attendees approached you afterwards to encourage you to write it up for publication. What do you think about that?

a. It's a natural progression; you'd be really pleased to follow up with publication

b. Writing feels a bit constraining; what about a digital poster or a podcast?

c. It's reassuring; if people want to read it, you'll be happy to deliver

d. It's something to consider; what would be the benefit of it, though?

Q4 You've been working with a group of students for a while and both you and the subject lecturer noticed some positive and interesting outcomes from your interventions that would be worth sharing through publication. What's the next step for you?

a. You might write it up, especially if the subject lecturer you've been working with expects it or wants to do it with you

b. What you're doing works, why does it have to be written about?

c. You investigate possible journals and design a survey to collect some data

b. You consider running a workshop or developing a resource pack for colleagues, to try for themselves.

TABLE 19.1 Scoring table

Q/A	a	b	c	d	your score
1	Freelancer	Actualiser	Striver	Pragmatist	
2	Freelancer	Pragmatist	Actualiser	Striver	
3	Striver	Freelancer	Actualiser	Pragmatist	
4	Actualiser	Pragmatist	Striver	Freelancer	

It is not expected that all four answers will produce identical results, but it is very likely that the dominant score will represent your tendency. If you find yourself with four different outcomes, however, we would recommend that you take Rubin's (n.d.) original quiz, which is more wide-reaching and may provide a clearer verdict. Nonetheless, you might still be able to identify yourself in one of the following profiles:

Striver

The sobriquet may sound a bit intense, but what it encompasses is a set of attitudes and inclinations that make you an effective writer. You are for the most part an autonomous writer, as your internal expectations provide enough motivation for you to get started and then to deliver. As such, you may become impatient with those who get stuck and, because of that, you may avoid collaborations (unless you pair well with another Striver or Actualiser). You are just as likely to write for yourself as you are for an externally-imposed goal in your specific context; setting clear personal goals is likely to be very effective for you as you will usually hold yourself to account for meeting those goals.

Effective strategies: scheduling writing (Silvia, 2007), the 15-minutes-a-day method (Bolker, 1998); outlining (Murray, 2020).

Traps to mitigate: getting too rigid in your planning and caught up in projects; not questioning what you put your time into; impatience around other people's struggles with writing.

Pragmatist

Because you tend to meet your inner expectations but question the validity of external demands, you won't commit to a writing project unless you understand its rationale and value to you. You might therefore challenge what you see as arbitrary expectations and only execute the projects important to you or which seem reasonable. You may benefit from taking the time to explore the reasons why writing for publication is important to you and how it aligns with your personal and professional goals. Once you have decided to write, then generally you're as likely as the Strivers to follow through and produce that writing.

Effective strategies: identify your best time of day for writing and protect it (Murray, 2020); keep your writing goals clear and use task-oriented approaches (Lamott, 1995); freewrite (Elbow, 1998) to unlock your ideas; set up a 'ventilation file' (Jensen, 2017) to record your doubts and questions about the writing project.

Traps to mitigate: questioning everything; lack of clarity on what you commit to; unprotected deadlines; need to always know more.

Actualiser

As the moniker suggests, you have no trouble actualising the expectations of others; your own, however, you may sacrifice if you feel they inconvenience others. You are generally good at keeping to deadlines, reliable and responsible in your commitments, and you tend to put others first. However, this is often at the expense of your own inner expectations, and you might find it difficult to motivate yourself to begin or complete a writing project alone. To overcome this, you are likely to benefit from transforming writing into a social activity; otherwise, there is a risk that eventually your frustrations will overwhelm you.

Effective strategies: write collaboratively (Bickle et al., 2021); set milestone deadlines to keep you motivated; set up a form of external accountability such as writing alongside or for someone, e.g., a mentor or editor; consider calls for contributions to edited volumes.

Traps to mitigate: saying yes to everyone; overwhelming guilt for not meeting a deadline; neglecting the importance of *self*-actualisation.

Freelancer

You are a maverick producer who resists both inner and outer expectations. The more someone wants you to write, the less you will be interested in writing. You like feeling that the writing project was your idea and that you have full creative control over it. You respond best to autonomy and the freedom to create your own expectations. As such, you might need to find ways to approach writing that align with your own style, interests, goals, and passions.

Effective strategies: ensure instant access to your writing document (e.g., as a bookmarked online doc or shortcut on your desktop) so you can dip in and out of it when you feel inspired; when you don't know what to write, 'follow your lilt' (Jensen, 2017, p.79); use creative tools such as metaphors (Boyd, 2022).

Traps to mitigate: resistance to deadlines; not recognising the difference between procrastination and stuckness (Boyd, 2023); difficulty in following strict timelines.

What Now, That You Have This Self-Knowledge?

While by no means a scientific tool, the value of the Four Tendencies is that it has allowed us to understand not only our own proclivities and preferences when it comes to writing but also how best to talk to our colleagues and students about it. As a Striver/Upholder and an Actualiser/Obliger, the two of us work well with schedules and deadlines, and tend to benefit greatly from writing in each other's (virtual) company. Because we found our ways into writing, we were initially less understanding of time poverty – a factor so ubiquitous in academia that it can be taken as a given – repeatedly provided as a sole reason for *not* writing. The Four Tendencies, however, allowed us to see better that - time constraints aside - for some, writing journeys are made easier by either increasing external accountability or strengthening rationale, or even by finding more flexible ways of working. Such insights have helped us adapt our approaches when teaching or mentoring, and created opportunities for fruitful conversations around writing.

And yet, what we can say with high certainty is that none of these tendencies guarantee success or predict failure when it comes to writing. Understanding our writing tendency gives us a way to work with our inclinations by identifying the best strategies that will help us achieve our goals. Strivers are self-motivated and will commit to their own expectations for their writing; Actualisers make reliable collaborative partners, while Pragmatists are certain in what they want to write and why. Freelancers write because they have freely chosen to write, which immediately reduces the pressure. On the other hand, each of the tendencies has its weaknesses that might hinder successful writing. If Strivers become too rigid then they may miss opportunities to build fruitful writing partnerships or struggle when unable to deliver as planned. Actualisers must learn to *self*-actualise and connect their inner desires to write to external factors. Pragmatists need to know when the research and reading process needs to stop so the writing can begin. And Freelancers may succumb to resistance (Pressfield, 2002) in the face of a deadline, and end up not writing anything at all. Every member of each of the four writing tendencies has the potential to write successfully, if they are able to manage their responses to internal and external expectations effectively.

This self-knowledge is the beginning rather than the end of the journey into writing. You get to decide what you do with it and how you use it to make your own writing happen.

Note

1 The quiz will produce the most accurate result if you focus on your own tendency when responding to the internal and external expectations around writing rather than considering specific institutional and interpretive (Boyd, 2023) barriers to writing, including time poverty.

References

Ahmed, S. (2014) *The cultural politics of emotion.* 2nd edn. Edinburgh: Edinburgh University Press.

Bickle, E., Bishopp-Martin, S., Canton, U., Chin, P., Johnson, I., Kantcheva, R., Nodder, J., Rafferty, V., Sum, K. and Welton, K. (2021) 'Emerging from the third space chrysalis: Experiences in a non-hierarchical, collaborative research community of practice', *Journal of University Learning and Teaching Practice*, 18(7): 135–158. https://doi.org/10.53761/1.18.7.09

Bolker, J. (1998) *Writing Your Dissertation in Fifteen Minutes a Day: A Guide to Starting, Revising, and Finishing Your Doctoral Thesis.* Holt Paperbacks.

Boyd, M.R. (2023) *Becoming the Writer You Already Are.* SAGE.

Clapton, J. (2010) 'Library and information science practitioners writing for publication: motivations, barriers and supports', *Library and Information Research,* 34(106): 7–21.

Dunlap, L. (2007) *Undoing the Silence.* Oakland: New Village Press.

Elbow, P. (1998) *Writing without Teachers.* 2nd edn. Oxford: Oxford University Press.

Hu, R. and Pu, P. (2009) 'A comparative user study on rating vs. personality quiz based preference elicitation methods', *Proceedings of the 14th International Conference on Intelligent user Interfaces.* New York, 367–372. https://doi.org/10.1145/1502650.1502702

Jensen, J. (2017) *Write No Matter What.* University of Chicago Press.

Lamott, A. (1995) *Bird by Bird: Some Instructions on Writing and Life.* Anchor Books.

Leathwood, C. and Hey, V. (2009) 'Gender/ed discourses and emotional subtexts: theorising emotion in UK higher education', *Teaching in Higher Education,* 14(4): 429–440.

Murray, R. (2020) *Writing for Academic Journals.* 4th edn. London: Open University Press, McGraw-Hill Education.

Paul, A.M. (2010) *The Cult of Personality Testing: How Personality Tests are Leading us to Miseducate Our Children, Mismanage Our Companies, and Misunderstand Ourselves.* New York: Simon and Schuster.

Pressfield, S. (2002) *The War of Art: Break Through the Blocks and Win Your Inner Creative Battles.* Black Irish Entertainment LLC.

Rubin, G. (2017) *The Four Tendencies: The Indispensable Personality Profiles that Reveal How to Make Your Life Better (and Other People's Lives Better, Too).* London: Two Roads.

Rubin, G. (n.d.) *The Four Tendencies Quiz.* Available at: https://gretchenrubin.com/quiz/the-four-tendencies-quiz/ (Accessed: 15 January 2023).

Silvia, P.J. (2007) *How to Write a Lot: A Practical Guide to Productive Academic Writing.* American Psychological Association.

Syska, A. and Buckley, C. (2022) 'Writing as liberatory practice: unlocking knowledge to locate an academic field', *Teaching in Higher Education,* 28(2): 439–454. https://doi.org/10.1080/13562517.2022.2114337

20

PUBLISHING IN LEARNING DEVELOPMENT

A Primer for New(ish) Authors

Alicja Syska and Carina Buckley

> *What use is my research if no one knows about it? I can't imagine doing my job without research, the boredom of repeating things without digging deeper and yes, it's nice to be recognised for what you're good at.*
> *AAAAAAAAAAAAAAAARRRRRGGGGHHHHHHH Torture!*
> *(Learning Developers responding to what publishing means to them)*

Introduction

Learning Development (LD) as a field of practice represents an impressive range of expertise related to how students learn and how this learning is facilitated. Yet most of this knowledge is shared through informal channels and does not get published. As demonstrated by Clapton (2010, p.8) in the context of library professionals, there remains a clear '[s]eparation between practitioner writing and academic writing'. Reasons for this vary (Syska and Buckley, 2022), but the perception that publishing is a daunting and painful process that requires specific knowledge, ability, and position adds to the mystique of it.

In its simplest and most perfect form, publishing creates a space for connecting with other people's ideas. It allows us to shape our thoughts, practices, and experimentations into something that might matter to others, especially if we move beyond the immediate context of our writing and use theoretical frameworks and discourses recognisable to other authors. The permanence of the written word forces us to hunt our assumptions (Brookfield, 2013); the length of time it requires to come into being allows us to rethink our ideas and clarify our arguments; and the academic publishing process expects us to submit ourselves to the judgement of others. All of these considerations – audience,

DOI: 10.4324/9781003433347-25

permanence, time, and the review process – give rise to a range of vulnerabilities that create certain perceived barriers to publishing.

The goal of this chapter is to demystify publishing and show that it is within everyone's reach. We hope that illuminating the reasons for publishing, the importance of identifying the audience we want to publish for, and the rules and mechanisms that govern the publishing world will encourage our readers to break through whatever barriers they experience in relation to writing for publication and to feel inspired to put their ideas out there.

Identifying Your Audience

The first question every author – whether experienced or first time – needs to ask themselves is who they are writing for and who might be interested in reading their work. 'Choosing a journal is in reality choosing a reader, a reader who is a member of a specific discourse community' (Thomson and Kamler, 2013, p.36); this may be as detailed as thinking about the potential readers' interests, jobs, and levels of experience, or as general as considering the appeal of the paper and its main purpose in terms of influencing other people's thinking and practice. Your most likely audience will be either other Learning Developers or practitioners interested in teaching and learning. Will they be familiar with your specialism and LD as a field? If not, how much context might your argument require? Can you make productive links with what they might have read in the same journal before? Journal editors often appreciate clearly establishing such connections. It is most effective to have your target readers in mind when beginning writing, so you can adapt the tone and have a better sense of how much context and conceptual framing is necessary for the given audience.

Your ultimate readers are not your only audience, however; you must also consider the editors who will be first assessing the suitability of your work to their publication. When choosing a journal, the best way of identifying the audience and understanding the needs of editors is by familiarising yourself with the guidelines for authors. If your work does not align with the priorities of the journal, it will be rejected no matter how brilliant it is. In fact, unsuitability of a submission is the most commonly cited reason for rejection (Springer, 2023; Ali, 2010); our own experience as editors confirms this. Making your work compelling for a particular outlet may become especially tricky if you are submitting to a discipline-specific journal, which might see pedagogy in a different light.

In contrast to quality refereed journals, which provide detailed information about their scope and readership, other publishing outlets are governed by different rules. If you are considering contributing a chapter to an edited collection, your audience will be easier to establish as it will have been defined by the book editors. Similar rules will apply to blog spaces and professional magazines. On the other hand, when writing a book, the publisher you approach will request that you specify your potential readers and reach in your book proposal. Regardless of the outlet, in order to be heard, you need to know your audience.

Preparing for Submission

Turning ideas into writing and making it public may feel intimidating, so we encourage you to take account of what you have already written before: what kind of writing was it? What strengths do you have as a writer? What do you need to develop further? Such self-introspection will allow you to see what you can build on when writing for publication.

Every Learning Developer has a unique way of practising LD and, therefore, something to contribute to the wider conversation. How you choose to do this is up to you. If a formal research article seems too constraining or you feel like you have done it all before, consider other 'writing genres' (Healey et al. (2020) identify 11 genres, including theoretical or conceptual articles, reflective essays, literature reviews, opinion pieces, empirical research articles, or case studies) or forums (such as blogs, conference proceedings, magazines, and social media). They can provide larger audiences and more opportunities for creativity released from the usual constraints of academic writing. Gale's (2023) advocacy of 'rebellious practices' could serve as an inspiration for such writing, with Bowstead reminding us that 'the spaces [for alternative writing] are there, you've just got to find them' (Buckley and Syska, 2023). Regardless of what and where you publish, the same principle holds: writing is a form of thinking, and good writing is indicative of good thinking. To write is to share knowledge and practice. To publish is to read, to draft, to respond to feedback, to edit, and to contribute to the larger conversation.

Editors will pay close attention to the clarity of your paper, so do your utmost to ensure it is ready to be seen. Check and critically assess the strength of your argument, the timeliness of your message, the relevance of your literature, the appropriateness of your methods, the quality of your analysis, the correctness of your references, and the clarity of your writing. Ask colleagues for a second opinion, as they might identify issues invisible to you. If the value of your work to other practitioners comes across to your colleagues, your piece is ready to be assessed by others. If your colleagues are confused or understand your aims differently to what you intended, the piece might require more work before being seen by editors.

Understanding How Journals Work

Your meticulously polished piece may feel like the end of an arduous writing journey, but it is only the beginning. Submitting it for consideration will take time as journals are slow and their requirements vary. You will need a full understanding of publication requirements and parameters such as the word limit, preferred referencing style, formatting, attachments, and expected sections (the usual ones include keywords, abstract, introduction, literature review, methodology, discussion, conclusion, and reference list). There is a formula to journal writing, which each outlet readily provides in author guidelines and which will help you focus when outlining and writing. You will also have to set up an account on the publisher's platform, write a cover letter to the editor (this usually mentions ethics and assures that the manuscript is not under consideration elsewhere), and even suggest names of potential reviewers. All this will take more time than you expect, so be prepared for the additional effort.

When publishing for the first time, submitting to a top-tier journal can be intimidating; these are vital only if you are pressured to be included in your institutional Research Evaluation Framework (REF in the UK) or similar publication output assessment. A quick search through Scopus or Web of Science will reveal hundreds of journals relevant to learning and teaching, with their ranking and impact factor. Considering that the higher the competition the greater the chance of rejection, choosing a less prominent outlet may make your first publishing experience a happier one, although aiming high occasionally produces surprising results. Professional journals which target practice-based studies (Murray, 2020) or institutional journals which have a more limited audience (Healey et al., 2020) might offer compelling alternative publishing avenues. In addition, responding to calls for chapters or special collections may alleviate any trepidation in selecting the right outlet and submitting independently. Whichever strategy you take, once you gain confidence and build your profile, these choices will become easier and more 'gates' are likely to open.

Table 20.1 introduces a few journals relevant to LD. The alphabetically ranked outlets represent a range, from highly esteemed publications to lesser-known ones; their inclusion is based simply on having published work by practitioners from the LD community. The selection may help with initial considerations regarding where to publish and broaden your options when deciding on the appropriate audience.

If it feels too easy to publish your paper, however, check for the red flags of an 'illegitimate publishing entity' (Shamseer and Moher, 2017), also known as predatory journals. If you are promised a quick turnaround time to publication, particularly in exchange for a small sum of money, then this is unlikely to be a legitimate or respected outlet. Do not be tempted. Not only will your work be lost, your credibility will suffer too. In order to protect yourself against it, follow Shamseer and Moher's (2017) guide to recognising pseudo-journals.

TABLE 20.1 Selection of journals for LD publishing

Peer-reviewed journal	Publisher data	Focus
Innovations in Education and Teaching International (IETI)	Published by Taylor & Francis (T&F) for the Staff and Educational Development Association (SEDA); 2.027 impact factor, 21% acceptance rate.	Innovation and educational change.
Innovative Practice in Higher Education (IPHE)	Open access; published by Staffordshire University.	Student experience; a range of creative formats, including posters and 'student voices' reflective accounts.
International Journal for Academic Development (IJAD)	Published by T&F for the International Consortium for Educational Development (ICED); 2.453 impact factor, 22% acceptance rate.	Research and practice; international reach and basis.
Journal of Learning Development in Higher Education (JLDHE)	Open access; published by the Association for Learning Development in Higher Education (ALDinHE); acceptance rate 61%.	Scholarship of LD and academic literacies; welcoming to new scholars; a range of formats.
Journal of University Teaching and Learning Practice (JUTLP)	Open access; published by the University of Wollongong, Australia; impact factor 1.012.	Research-led with a practitioner focus; innovative practice, curriculum design and leadership.
Research in Learning Technology (RLT)	Open access; published by the Association for Learning Technology.	Learning environments, digital pedagogy, and flexible learning; research- and critical practice-based.
Student Engagement in Higher Education Journal (SEHEJ)	Open access; published by the Researching, Advancing & Inspiring Student Engagement (RAISE) Network.	Student engagement from a disciplinary and multidisciplinary perspective; a range of formats and a 'developmental route' for new writers.
Studies in Higher Education (SHE)	Published by T&F for the Society for Research in Higher Education (SRHE); impact factor 4.017, 5% acceptance rate.	Top-ranking learning and teaching journal.

TABLE 20.1 (Continued)

Peer-reviewed journal	Publisher data	Focus
Teaching & Learning Inquiry (TLI)	Open access; published by the International Society for the Scholarship of Teaching and Learning (ISSOTL).	Research, theory, and commentary on the scholarship of teaching and learning (SoTL) in higher education; a range of formats.
Teaching in Higher Education (TiHE)	Published by T&F; 2.75 impact factor, 19% acceptance rate.	Critically examines the teaching and research nexus in HE; experimental 'Points of Departure'.

Receiving Feedback

If you have identified your target journal well and prepared your manuscript diligently, it will likely pass the editorial checks and be sent for peer review. However, a desk rejection is not a sign of failure. Silvia (2007, p.101) compares rejections to a 'sales tax on publications: The more papers you publish the more rejections you will receive'. Carry your rejections with pride – only those who do not submit at all will not get rejected. Rejections are an opportunity to refine your thinking and clarify your methodology and processes, so use them to create a message that will resonate with the journal's audience.

If sent for review, and assuming you are not the one-in-a-million writer who has their article accepted 'as is', you will receive revisions. These can fall into one of two categories: minor and major. Minor revisions, as the name suggests, will involve surface-level modifications to the text, such as queries around references (including number and currency), procedures (clarity of methodology), structure (flow and coherence), and the focus (distractions and detail). Depending on the journal, you might be offered between one and three months to make these changes as they should be reasonably straightforward to accomplish.

Major revisions are another matter. Your first response might be emotional: this person has not understood what you were trying to do. Or perhaps, I'm a terrible writer. The latter is unlikely, as you have made it this far. But the former is not unreasonable, and the feedback will be directed towards seeking that understanding. Major revisions involve deeper thinking and take more time. There might be issues with your theoretical framework, how you have collected or interpreted your data, or the conclusions you have drawn. You will be encouraged to think harder, reformulate your ideas, and edit ruthlessly. This will take longer than you anticipate, so keep an eye on the deadline given. You will need to submit a thoughtful commentary alongside your revised paper to outline how you have met the reviewers' recommendations (Black et al., 1998).

In the process of publishing a journal article, the reviewers – particularly the infamous 'reviewer 2' – are too frequently painted as the enemy trying to bring your paper down (Peterson, 2020). It is worth noting: you *do not* have to follow the reviewers' recommendations. You can ignore them, preserve your paper as it is and find somewhere else to publish. However, chances are you will go through a similar experience again. After the initial resistance, anger even, towards what might seem like being forced to change your ideas, it is usually prudent to make the revisions or negotiate the aspects of the paper you want to retain. As Annesley (2011) advises, among the reviewers' suggestions there will be 'requests you simply cannot meet', but there will primarily be valuable feedback you need time to process and address, remembering the mantra that all good writing is in *rewriting* (Zinsser, 2016). Whichever route you take, bear in mind that it is better to publish in a lower-ranking journal than to let it sit in your proverbial drawer. Even if it is not always easy, in our experience revisions usually make for stronger papers and 'should be high priority project goals' (Silvia, 2007, p.95).

A note about time. Many journals state their response times on their websites; some do not. Regardless, processing times vary widely, from one day or week to as long as six months to the first decision time. This means that a few rejections may extend your publication process considerably, depending on the speed of communication (remember: journals are slow!), the extent of revisions, and your availability to make them. These are important factors when planning your submission timeline.

After Publication

Eventually your resubmitted paper will be accepted, the reviewers and editor satisfied, and you receive the precious notification that your article has been published. This is another important stage of your paper's journey, so do not stop now. You have written it, but now people have to read it and reward your effort. With so much competing literature available, this is unlikely to happen by accident, so you should promote your publication. Some effective methods include adding the reference with its DOI to your email signature, sharing the link on social media (with appropriate hashtags), writing a blog post to highlight the key findings, or posting a summary with the URL on LinkedIn (Emerald Publishing, 2023). Register for an ORCID iD to connect with your professional profile and set up a Google Scholar account so you can receive alerts for when your work is cited.

You might feel uncomfortable or even annoyed about doing this; we urge you to do it anyway. The purpose of publication is to join the conversation, but if no one knows your work is there, you are not being heard. To have life, your paper must be read; to be read, it must be shared. Have confidence in your contribution and champion it!

Conclusion

There are so many ways to write for publication and so many reasons to do it that the only excuse that practitioners who do not publish regularly fall back on is the lack of time (Clapton, 2010). This, we cannot do anything about. What we hope, however, is that this brief primer to publishing in LD will make our readers feel that it is not only within their reach but also a worthwhile pursuit, no matter how experienced you are at writing. We hope to have shown that whatever your interest, writing style or professional goal, there is an outlet and a format to make sharing your ideas possible.

Nevertheless, writing for publication is rarely easy. While we are all responsible for our own time management and writing processes, it is not an unreasonable expectation that institutional leaders provide the support, resources, and professional development opportunities to help Learning Developers achieve a level of excellence in scholarship that will generate a sense of accomplishment, enable professional progression, and advance the field of LD. We thus encourage *managers* to actively advocate for writing in their teams; create opportunities for developing research projects; offer feedback for writing ideas; help teams secure time for writing; acknowledge their accomplishments through a dedicated forum; act as a writing mentor; and publish to set an example and model publication goals. *Teams* can reinforce these initiatives through collaborative projects; sharing experiences with writing in team discussions and mentoring each other; acting as a sounding board for colleagues' writing; and creating writing groups or communities of practice. Finally, on a more *individual* level, we can all start to prioritise publishing as part of our own professional development; make publishing an objective in our annual review; explore our writing tendencies (see Chapter 19); find collaborators; join writing groups; and respond to calls for contributions. Any of these small actions will be the first critical step in creating a culture of writing for publication that will transform your professional environment and personal satisfaction from writing.

References

Ali, J. (2010) 'Manuscript rejection: causes and remedies', *Journal of Young Pharmacists*, 2(1): 3–6. https://doi.org/10.4103/0975-1483.62205

Annesley, T. M. (2011) 'Top 10 tips for responding to reviewer and editor comments', *Clinical Chemistry*, 57(4): 551–554.

Black, D., Brown, S., Day, A., and Race, P. (1998) *500 Tips for Getting Published: A Guide for Educations, Researchers and Professionals*. London: Kogan Page.

Brookfield, S. (2013) *Teaching for Critical Thinking*. The Jossey-Bass Higher and Adult Education Series.

Buckley, C. and Syska, A. (2023) 'Episode 8: Helen Bowstead: the joy of writing', *The Learning Development Project Podcast* [Podcast]. 23 February. Available at: https://aldinhe.ac.uk/networking/the-ld-project-podcast/ (Accessed: 23 February 2023).

Clapton, J. (2010) 'Library and information science practitioners writing for publication: motivations, barriers and supports', *Library and Information Research*, 34(106): 7–21.

Emerald Publishing (2023) *How to Promote Your Work*. Available at: https://www.emeraldgrouppublishing.com/our-services/author-services/promote-your-work (Accessed: 24 February 2023).

Gale, K. (2023) *Writing and Immanence: Concept Making and the Reorientation of Thought in Pedagogy and Inquiry*. Milton: Routledge.

Healey, M., Matthews, K.E. and Cook-Sather, A. (2020) *Writing about Learning and Teaching in Higher Education: Creating and Contributing to Scholarly Conversations Across a Range of Genres*. Elon, NC: Elon University Center for Engaged Learning. https://doi.org/10.36284/celelon.oa3

Murray, R. (2020) *Writing for Academic Journals*. 4th edn. London: Open University Press, McGraw-Hill Education.

Peterson, D.A. (2020) 'Dear reviewer 2: Go f'yourself', *Social Science Quarterly*, 101(4), 1648–1652.

Shamseer, L. and Moher, D. (2017) 'Thirteen ways to spot a "predatory journal" (and why we shouldn't call them that)', *Times Higher Education*, 27. Available at: https://www.timeshighereducation.com/blog/thirteen-ways-to-spot-a-predatory-journal-and-why-we-shouldnt-call-them-that (Accessed: 24 February 2023).

Silvia, P.J. (2007) *How to Write a Lot: A Practical Guide to Productive Academic Writing*. American Psychological Association.

Springer (2023) *Common Reasons for Rejection*. Available at: https://www.springer.com/gp/authors-editors/authorandreviewertutorials/submitting-to-a-journal-and-peer-review/what-is-open-access/10285582 (Accessed: 24 February 2023).

Syska, A. and Buckley, C. (2022) 'Writing as liberatory practice: unlocking knowledge to locate an academic field', *Teaching in Higher Education*, 28(2): 439–454. https://doi.org/10.1080/13562517.2022.2114337

Thomson, P. and Kamler, B. (2013) *Writing for Peer Reviewed Journals: Strategies for Getting Published*. Abingdon: Routledge.

Zinsser, W. (2016) *On Writing Well: The Classic Guide to Writing Nonfiction*. New York: Harper Perennial.

PART V

Becoming Established in Learning Development

The Potential in and for LD

The book completes the journey through LD by exploring what it means to develop the field itself and ourselves as practitioners within it. Sonia Hood begins in the first of the six chapters by drawing on her long experience as a Learning Developer to consider how the role can effectively challenge and influence institutional approaches to learning and teaching. In Chapter 22, Kate Coulson flags the importance of measuring our impact in order to lend credence and support to our goals for change, noting that 'impact' can take a range of definitions, depending on the context. Recognition of professional development is addressed in Chapters 23 and 24. First, Carina Buckley encourages Learning Developers to see leadership as an attainable goal, based on collaboration and influence mediated by networks of socially situated relationships. Then, Steve Briggs outlines the options for professional forms of recognition open to Learning Developers and the value of seizing these opportunities. In Chapter 25, Helen Webster maps LD's position within the wider higher education sector, highlighting LD's distinct perspective on the student experience as adding a richness to learning and teaching conversations. Ed Bickle, Steph Allen, and Marian Meyer conclude the part by questioning what LD's future might be or what we hope it could be: whether we fight off an AI-dominated dystopia or achieve the seamless integration of LD into the curriculum that marks a possible Utopia.

DOI: 10.4324/9781003433347-26

21

SUCCEEDING AT LEARNING DEVELOPMENT

Sonia Hood

A few years ago, if you asked me to deliver a 'skills session', no matter the notice period or perceived efficacy, I would gratefully accept. Now I have the confidence to challenge a session's benefit to students, to be certain in Learning Development values and to say 'no' when appropriate. Being committed to our values, recognising the expertise we bring and developing effective relationships has led to a greater understanding and appreciation for what we do. In turn, this has led to more effective embedded teaching requests. And hence the paradox: saying 'no' (when appropriate) has led to me saying 'yes' more. An important lesson, and one I wish I had learned years ago.

Introduction

Carving out a career in Learning Development (LD) is possible but only if we are confident in the knowledge, perspectives, and expertise we bring. Central to this is the unique insight that we, as Learning Developers, offer. Through our interactions with students, we obtain honest accounts as to how students are approaching study, the support they need, and challenges they face. We are, perhaps, not seen as part of their academic team, not responsible for marking their work and act as a bridge between the student body and academics. But our role is often misunderstood and our expertise undervalued. This *third space* (Whitchurch, 2008) in which many of us operate has its challenges, but there is much we can do to make the most of the opportunities it affords us. This chapter focuses on how we, as Learning Developers, can develop our roles and remain committed to our core values (ALDinHE, 2023). It reflects on my experience of being a Learning Developer for over 15 years and shares approaches that I have taken to navigate this third space. It begins by highlighting the unique perspective we offer and the strategies we can use to demonstrate

DOI: 10.4324/9781003433347-27

our expertise and relevance to our academic colleagues. It argues that we should make full use of university structures, working groups, and funding opportunities to promote our values. It raises the need for us to demonstrate and defend our professional expertise. Finally, it discusses the importance of enhancing and promoting our own professional development. Navigating this third space can be challenging, but by being nimble, tailoring our approaches, evidencing our expertise, and using informal and formal structures, we have an opportunity to develop our role into one with influence and recognition.

Our Unique Perspective

It was back in 2008 that Celia Whitchurch explored what she believed was the blurring of structural and institutional boundaries within our HEIs and conceptualised 'third space', at the interface between the academic and professional activity (Whitchurch, 2008). Since then, work has focused on what this means for those of us working in this space, with the addition of terms such as blended professionals, integrated practitioners, dual professionals, or pracademics (McIntosh and Nutt, 2022). As Learning Developers, many of us can recognise ourselves within these descriptions. Existing outside the traditional structures of academic or professional services can have its issues, but with the right approach we can harness the opportunities that this positioning affords us. It requires us to be cognisant of the strategic objectives of those we work with, to speak their language and build effective relationships with a wide range of colleagues. It sounds like challenging work, but it is rewarding, not only for our own development and sense of achievement but also for the students we all aim to support.

At the heart of what we do is the student, and being outside of academic structures allows us to have a unique insight. Such insight is valuable to the university: our currency that we must learn to sell. If we are to effectively support students, we need them to be honest with us. The lack of any repercussions to this honesty can allow for more fruitful discussions. As Learning Developers, we occupy a distinct professional space, as Johnson (2018) puts it, to demystify and mediate, acting as a bridge between students and the wider university. Such work requires us to use a complex skillset (Webster, 2022) and offers us a valuable and unique insight. We often get to know what lectures they find challenging, what assignment briefs they struggle to decipher, and the real study practices they employ. All of this helps us to create effective resources to support our students. In our institution, we write blog posts that react to current issues and speak to students' concerns in a language that they would use. But also, this insight allows us to have fruitful discussions with our academic colleagues, feeding back the honest accounts of their students and helping to improve student outcomes with clearer assignment briefs and expectations. We must learn to harness this knowledge, not only to support our students but demonstrate our relevance and 'usefulness' to our academic colleagues.

Harnessing the Power of Third Space

There is much to be gained by working with other third space professionals. As Hall (2022) highlighted, COVID-19 offered us opportunities to showcase our agility and ability to work across departments. The need to work quickly and bring together a range of expertise and knowledge gave rise to some of our best initiatives (see, for example, McDonald and Parry, 2021; Aston, et al., 2021). During the initial months of lockdown and the switch to online learning, a number of us within the University were calling for support for students. As a Learning Developer, this was an initiative I felt our team could own. There were, of course, other interested third space professionals, all with their own areas of expertise: the technology enhanced learning team who were leading the way with the systems students would be using; the international team who were supporting students facing quarantine; and the central communications team who were responsible for liaising with students. As a newly formed working group, we worked collaboratively with our Online Course Team to create an online course, *Back to university*. Designed for all our students, it explained the new ways they would be learning, the systems that would be used and study tips to learning effectively in the online environment. The need to act quickly during the pandemic enabled us all to circumnavigate any boundaries and evidence the benefits in working in agile and unbounded ways (Whitchurch, 2009) that many of us working in third space are comfortable with (Quinsee, 2022). The fast-changing education environment requires more agile working (Menon and Suresh, 2022), and we must continue to demonstrate our willingness and ability to work in this way.

Having other third space allies also reaps rewards. Universities operate as very large organisations. There is so much to consider when implementing new strategies, so many stakeholders offering their perspective and a range of competing objectives to juggle. What may seem like a straightforward policy decision may, inadvertently, have an impact on what we do and how we operate. Being a lone voice can be both ineffective and exhausting, so finding allies in other support services such as counselling and wellbeing, careers and international student support can not only offer emotional support but also can help our voice to be heard. So, if we feel a policy decision has an impact on our service, we should consider who else may be affected, forge alliances, and make a joint case. There are also allies outside our own universities. The LDHEN email exchanges and discussions with other Learning Developers have often offered me valuable insight into how other institutions are dealing with common issues. This can present us with possible solutions or alternative approaches to propose in our own settings. There is strength in numbers and considering others' perspectives helps to support arguments; at least, that is what we tell our students.

Using University Structures

Using the university formal structures enables us, as Learning Developers, to evidence our expertise and relevance to the wider university. Within my institution we have standing invitations to all our School Boards for Teaching and Learning. Whilst there are too many meetings for us to attend them all, taking a strategic approach to such meetings can lead to some beneficial outcomes. But we must be prepared to speak out. Rather than simply a chance for us to speak to a standing item and update on our service offering, such meetings can offer the opportunity to evidence our expertise and relevance. Bringing our unique perspective of students' study experiences, we can not only offer insight as to why students might be behaving in certain ways but also offer solutions in the way of resources which could be embedded. To be effective, though, we must keep in mind that good communication requires an understanding of the audience. We need to consider the academics' aims and speak their language. This can only be achieved through an understanding of the issues they face, the culture within the School and the strategic aims. Within our University, for instance, Schools are required to write an annual teaching enhanced action plan, highlighting their priorities and actions they plan to take to meet these. Working with our academic librarian colleagues, we responded to these by offering our expertise and resources to support specific goals. Starting a dialogue and evidencing our relevance to Schools' strategic plans has allowed us to become involved in more strategic work. In addition, it has opened up conversations with academics who, perhaps, were less aware of our service, leading to exciting new collaborations. Whenever we are invited to such meetings, preparation is key. Reading the papers in advance and identifying opportunities to offer our thoughts or solutions allows us to showcase our unique insight. Such meetings are also a gateway into building those informal relationships which can lead to some rewarding collaborations and deeper understanding of each other's roles and perspectives.

As well as School meetings, there is much to be gained by joining university-wide working groups. Again, not only do these offer opportunities for us to influence strategy and offer an LD lens but the connections that are made can lead to greater understanding of our role and future collaborations. I am fortunate enough to sit on one of the university-wide teaching and learning boards where many such working groups are usually initiated, but Learning Developers without such opportunities could appeal to their department heads regarding strategic work. I have found these working groups (such as group work, academic integrity, and academic transitions) to be very rewarding. We have an invite to the table, a chance to influence policy and evidence our professional expertise, key to our long-term survival (Webster, 2022). They often lead to published documents or showcases that raise our profile and that of our service to the wider university community. Increasing the awareness and understanding of what we offer is also, of course, of benefit to the students, whom we all aim to support.

Learning Developers should not be afraid to pursue opportunities that they may feel are for the privilege of academic colleagues alone. Within our university, for instance, there are numerous funding opportunities, from small amounts given for collaborative team awards to larger amounts for innovative teaching approaches or research into teaching and learning. Applying for such funds not only affords us the opportunities to create innovative resources or deepen our research understanding in our field, but also helps us to further raise the profile of ourselves, our profession, and our service. Such funds often come with the stipulation that findings must be written up in a paper or presented at a showcase event. Such exposure, once again, evidences our expertise in a particular area of skills development and helps to initiate and develop those all-important informal relationships.

Influencing Strategy

Adapting Our Message to the Audience

If we aim to influence strategy, we must first learn to adapt our message to our audience and be cognisant of the wider strategic issues. We must consider what concerns they have, what objectives they are trying to reach, and how we can support that. Aligning the support we can offer to Schools' strategic objectives not only shows our relevance but also helps us to be part of the conversation – a team member, so to speak. And we cannot talk about strategy without discussing measurable outcomes. Whether we agree with it or not, we cannot ignore the need to demonstrate impact. I am not sure we have yet cracked this nut, but I would argue that we need to offer data to evidence our contribution to student success, retention, and progression. Our roles have clear links to these but 'proving' this remains elusive.

We may also need to consider how we 'sell' the need to be involved in strategic work and professional development opportunities to our managers. The legitimate fear is that this takes our time away from operational concerns, but being involved in strategy development can have a wider impact and return long-term benefits. We may be faced with questions as to whether we have the time to be involved in projects, so it is important to see this issue from our department's perspective. Arguably, such activity helps to raise the profile of our area, increasing understanding and awareness of not only LD but the function in which it sits. We could, for instance, offer to represent the function in meetings, feedback in meetings and ensure we bring their perspective to the table. This may also be the case with the request to attend conferences, with financial as well as time implications. Offering to present papers at conferences helps to raise the profile of our own institutions, and we can offer this benefit to support our case to attend.

Defending Our Professional Expertise

Secondly, we need to be able to evidence and defend our professional expertise. Occupying this third space can raise questions of legitimacy (Whitchurch, 2009) and we need to 'own' our area of expertise and professional identity. In this vein, we must continue to fight against the notion that we are teaching 'study skills' in a deficit way. Instead, we take an academic literacies approach, supporting students to navigate the often complex and conflicting discourses within their discipline(s) and help them to employ a range of literacy practices (Lea and Street, 1998). This latter approach requires skill and expertise. While we may wish to accept opportunities to teach new cohorts and build relationships with our academic colleagues, it is important that we maintain sound principles of embedding skills into the curriculum (Wingate, 2012, 2018; Wingate et al., 2011). Sessions should be tailored to the discipline, timely, designed in collaboration with the academic concerned, timetabled, and delivered ideally with the academic present. To this end, our team, much like London South Bank University (Thomas et al., 2022), created a staff guide on embedding academic skills. As well as hosting a series of resources which academics can embed, and teaching materials they can adapt, it also contains the principles of effective embedded teaching sessions. It clearly lays out what our academic colleagues can expect from us but also what we ask of them, such as a notice period of three weeks. We must learn to say 'no' when requests do not meet these principles and requirements. Such initiatives not only help to demonstrate our expertise but also reflect a professional service, based on sound pedagogic principles.

Self-promotion

We need to promote ourselves and our expertise. Accessing funding opportunities, which lead to the writing of reports and articles, helps to demonstrate our knowledge. Gaining academic credentials like HEA fellowship status and ALDinHE professional accreditation (Briggs, 2018) help, but there is also an element of self-promotion that is needed. Adding these to our email signatures, alongside our qualifications, publications, and awards that we have received, is one way to do this; and while we may feel uncomfortable with such self-promotion, it mirrors that of our academic counterparts. On the subject of publications, we should take up opportunities to write articles for specialised journals, like the *Journal of Learning Development in Higher Education*, or present at the annual ALDinHE conference. Not only does this help our own professional development but also supports the fight to establish LD as a profession with its own pedagogical principles.

Use Our Connections

Finally, we must harness the power of the connections we make. As well as making use of the formal structures, attending networking events, and joining working groups, we can also invite colleagues for informal catch ups, where deeper connections often form. We can work with academic, professional, and third space allies, and use these collaborations to showcase our expertise and impact. Understanding the language that they speak, their perspectives, and strategic aims and challenges will help us to find a way in to progress discussions. Getting to know other Learning Development professionals can help too. Forming alliances over common issues helps to raise not only our profile but our voice, as we share the same goal in supporting students.

Conclusion

Being a Learning Developer and operating in this third space is not without its challenges – unclear boundaries, lack of clear career progression, the potential to be undervalued and misunderstood – but we can take some benefit in being 'outsiders'. This chapter has argued that we should be confident in the expertise that we bring and say 'no' to requests for teaching that we consider would not be effective. Making use of formal and informal structures, tailoring our messages, and prioritising our own professional development are also key. These approaches have enabled me to carve out a career that embodies the LD values. It is a continual fight but one made easier by bringing people with you on the journey.

References

ALDinHE (2023). *About ALDinHE*. Available at: https://aldinhe.ac.uk/about-aldinhe/ (Accessed 25 March 2023).

Aston, S., Stevenson, M. and Inala, P. (2021) 'Facilitating connections and supporting a learning community: together', *Journal of Learning Development in Higher Education*, 22. https://doi.org/10.47408/jldhe.vi22.765

Briggs, S. (2018) 'Development of the ALDinHE recognition scheme: certifying the "Learning Developer" title', *Journal of Learning Development in Higher Education*, 13. https://doi.org/10.47408/jldhe.v0i13.461

Hall, J. (2022) 'Understanding and debating the third space: achieving strategy', in: E. McIntosh and D. Nutt (eds), *The Impact of the Integrated Practitioner in Higher Education: Studies in Third Space Professionalism*. London: Routledge, 26–32.

Johnson, I. (2018) 'Driving Learning Development professionalism forward from within', *Journal of Learning Development in Higher Education. Special edition: 2018 ALDinHE conference*, 1–29. https://doi.org/10.47408/jldhe.v0i0.470

Lea, M. and Street, B. (1998) 'Student writing in higher education: an academic literacies approach', *Studies in Higher Education*, 23(2): 157–172.

McDonald, C. and Parry, R. (2021) 'Working in partnership to deliver a skills course to social work apprentices: avoiding technological determinism', *Journal of Learning Development in Higher Education*, 22. https://doi.org/10.47408/jldhe.vi22.772

McIntosh, E. and Nutt, D. (2022) 'Introduction and literature review', in: E. McIntosh and D. Nutt (eds), *The Impact of the Integrated Practitioner in Higher Education: Studies in Third Space Professionalism*. London: Routledge, 1–18.

Menon, S. and Suresh, M. (2022) 'Assessment framework for workforce agility in higher education institutions', *Higher Education, Skills and Work-Based Learning*, 12(6): 1169–1188.

Quinsee, S. (2022) 'Leadership in the third space', in E. McIntosh and D. Nutt (eds), *The Impact of the Integrated Practitioner in Higher Education: Studies in Third Space Professionalism*. London: Routledge, 33–39.

Thomas, P., Khanom, N., Lambe, S., Adelaja, B. and Mehbali, M. (2022) 'Constructing an academic skills toolkit for embedding academic practices', *Journal of Learning Development in Higher Education*, 24. https://doi.org/10.47408/jldhe.vi24.832

Webster, H. (2022) 'Supporting third space professionals', in: E. McIntosh and D. Nutt, (eds), *The Impact of the Integrated Practitioner in Higher Education: Studies in Third Space Professionalism*, London: Routledge, 178–187.

Whitchurch, C. (2008) 'Shifting identities and blurring boundaries: the emergence of third space professionals in UK higher education', *Higher Education Quarterly*, 62(4), 377–396.

Whitchurch, C., 2009. 'The rise of the blended professional in higher education: A comparison between the United Kingdom, Australia and the United States', *Higher Education*, 58(3), pp. 407–418.

Wingate, U., 2012. 'Using Academic Literacies and genre-based models for academic writing instruction: a 'literacy' journey', *Journal of English for Academic Purposes*, 11(1), pp. 26–37.

Wingate, U., 2018. 'Academic literacy across the curriculum: towards a collaborative instructional approach', *Language Teaching*, 51(3), pp. 349–364.

Wingate, U., Andon, N. and Cogo, A. (2011). 'Embedding academic writing instruction into subject teaching: a case study', *Active Learning in Higher Education*, 12(1), pp. 69–81.

22

THE IMPACT OF LEARNING DEVELOPMENT

Kate Coulson

At the University of the East Midlands, the Head of Learning Development has been asked to join the Teaching Excellence Framework working group and is already a member of the Access and Participation working group. At the same time, a solo Learning Developer at the University of the Southwest is wondering if their tutorial approach is useful and helpful. At both institutions their work is well regarded but both Learning Developers are reflecting on their practice: What value does their work have in relation to student outcomes? Can they measure their effect? In essence: do they have impact?

Introduction

Impact, impact, impact … it is all around us. We are cajoled into thinking, talking, and writing about it in our Teaching Excellence Framework submissions, our Access and Participation Plans, institutional strategic plans, in annual reports, on social media, in serendipitous conversations with colleagues; everywhere we go, it is there. It feels like a relatively new concept that has grown out of the advent of the neoliberal university (Cannella and Koro-Ljungberg, 2017); it crept up on us without us realising, and some of us, if we stop to think, can feel the pressure to measure 'it' despite being overwhelmed with teaching, research, scholarly tasks, admin, and an increasing number of other demands on our time and sanity. That said, some of us have embraced this concept within the field of Learning Development (LD) and have focussed on impact as a research topic for many years. This research approach has been often beneficial for careers and for the teams involved; but is it valuable? What is *impact*? Why should (or shouldn't) we measure it? Can anyone just decide to measure it, *et voilà!*, there it is? What are the challenges we face if we want to measure impact? And if we work those out, how are we going to do it?

DOI: 10.4324/9781003433347-28

This chapter will discuss the *what*, the *why* (or why not), and the *how* of measuring the impact of LD. You may read this and decide to measure your impact and this chapter should give you some ideas to start; it will also suggest ways to share your findings with the larger LD community and beyond. But more importantly, reading this will create the time and space for reflection and support in answering the perennial question: do we have impact?

What Is Impact?

Acquiring an understanding as to what 'impact' means is crucial when reflecting on the nature of your practice. 'What is impact?' is a question we might ask ourselves, and one way to answer it is to find a formal definition that you feel comfortable with. In the age of the neoliberal university (and society), understanding the status quo before an intervention and then undertaking analysis after the intervention is a crude, but common, way to 'define' impact. If you are being asked to measure impact by an institution, accepting their approach and loose definition might be the easiest path forward. However, if you are considering a research project to measure the impact of your practice, you should consider analysing the potential definitions of impact that might appeal to you.

Milbourne (2015) outlines the challenges and intricacies of locating a definition and states that 'the definition of impact is still not well understood in the sector'. In fact, it can be said through personal anecdotal experience that when colleagues discuss impact in relation to institutional projects often a definition of impact is not even considered. Rarely are definitions included; however, Access and Participation Plan projects are often subject to the Theory of Change (UN, 2023), which is a theoretical framework but also arguably a wider definition and approach to social change and impact – useful to consider but not a definition per se. Hinton (2013) went so far as to proclaim that perhaps the preferred term should be 'influence' rather than 'impact' due to the 'definitional crowdedness of the term'. And Hicks (2015) follows this up by stating that there are many definitions of research impact, academic impact and educational impact, and concentrates on the fact that due to the nature of the link between causality and attribution, impact is difficult to evidence and therefore challenging to define.

Conversely, Chalmers and Gardiner (2015) have written extensively about the impact of academic practice upon teaching in higher education (mainly in an Australian context). This includes an analysis of teacher education and the impact it may (or may not) have had upon institutional culture and approach. Their definition of impact is not sophisticated or particularly lengthy, and they borrow Moon's (2004) definition: impact is 'a change appropriate to the situation'. In this definition there is no emphasis on positive change and no mention of detrimental change. The definition is succinct and clear, and perhaps one you could consider. If you do, then the premise is much clearer – does your practice make an appropriate change to the situation? For example, if you teach a cohort of first-year students how to think critically and apply that learning to their assessment, will your direct involvement elicit a change in (a) the outcome of the assessment (quantitative measurement of grade); (b) the self-reported confidence of the individual students (qualitative measurement of impact); and/or (c) a reduction in reported cohort anxiety around the assessment, according to their module tutor (also qualitative)? There could be many other ways to measure an 'appropriate change', but these examples are a good starting point. Rather than force a preferred definition it is important to reflect on your own ideological viewpoint and formulate your own useful and comfortable definition. This is your opportunity to think this through.

Why Measure Impact?

In recent years, the higher education sector in the UK has become somewhat preoccupied with counting, quantifying, measuring, and ensuring value for money. This means that there is an institutional driver to count what we do and investigate if it affects student outcomes. This is further exacerbated by sector drivers such as Access and Participation Plans (APP) and the Teaching Excellence Framework (TEF). Within these, institutions are encouraged to quantify their work and, where possible, prove its impact on the student experience and outcomes. Many Learning Developers have found themselves as members of working groups to contribute meaningfully to the construction of APPs as well as becoming important contributors to TEF returns. When Learning Developers are approached to contribute at an institutional and sector level, it is crucial that our input is meaningful and reliable and draws on research data about our practice; it ensures our contribution is effective and powerful.

Essentially, measuring impact allows us to do many things with our practice. Firstly, we can understand the nature of our work in relation to the institution and the students within it. It contextualises our contribution and ensures that we can articulate what we do, and how and why we do it. This can vary between institutions, but it allows us to create a rhetoric around our practice which has many benefits, such as how we write our AdvanceHE Fellowship applications through to advocating for the importance of our work. Secondly, it ensures that we are able to manage our provision in an informed and systematic way. Knowing what we do and the impact it has ensures that we manage the resource in the most effective way. These two aspects, when drawn together, allow us to communicate the value of LD in a clear and consistent way. This is something that Learning Developers have always had to do and by measuring impact we can equip ourselves with evidence to maximise our chances of success in what we are advocating for (this might be several things – more staff, a different institutional approach to academic skills development, funding to attend a conference, and everything in between). Measuring impact and using evidence to enhance our advocacy ensure that the institution and the sector understand and appreciate the value of LD.

There are two other significant reasons to measure impact: having (qualitative and/or quantitative) data that supports the positive outcomes related to LD work is an effective marketing tool. Internally, the data can be presented at committee meetings and incorporated into projects (APPs, TEF, and others), as well as during informal conversations with colleagues. It is a vehicle to engage in more formal dialogue across the institution with faculty, school, and departmental colleagues as well as the Students' Union. It is also a mechanism to engage with events such as internal conferences and development days.

Externally, the data can be incorporated into tweets, written up into blog posts, book chapters, journal articles, and papers to be presented at conferences and webinars. Colleagues sharing such endeavours are always warmly received by their peers and often cross-institutional projects are created after such encounters. Finally, understanding the impact of your LD provision creates a space for experimentation. For example, if an intervention has a positive impact upon student understanding, that intervention may only need some fine-tuning; however, if the research shows that an intervention isn't having the desired impact then that awareness allows us to be more agile in our approach to our practice and we can make informed adjustments.

How to Measure Impact

If you are now considering measuring impact, your thoughts will naturally turn to how you will do that. Perhaps you are already measuring impact; perhaps you are new to Learning Development and you are reading this book to understand how you approach your newfound field of expertise; perhaps you completely disagree with measuring impact or have never even considered assessing it. Wherever you are on the 'impact continuum', this section will help you work out what you could do or whether you decide to leave it well alone.

In much, if not all, LD provision there is some form of counting, be it drop-in numbers; how many tutorials you and your team have undertaken in a day, a week, or an academic year; the number of workshops delivered in a term or a semester. Each year your figures grow and grow until you reach the point of not having enough tutors to provide the teaching opportunities demanded by the institution, and then you must work out what you can continue to teach, where you might dial back and identify potential commitments that need to be relinquished. But without understanding the impact of your interventions, how do you decide?

It is important to emphasise here that impact is not the number of tutorials you have undertaken, or how busy the drop-in session was. Impact is understanding if those interventions made a change. Did they change the outcomes for the student (their grade, their feedback, their overall degree class)? Did you change their self-reported thoughts and feelings? Did they feel more confident? Did they feel able to answer a question in a class? Were they brave enough to counter a debate in a workshop?

To understand if you effected a change, you could approach it in a quantitative, qualitative, or triangulated way (Walliman, 2022). Using quantitative methods, data pertaining to LD interventions would be analysed, for example, comparing the grades of students who did not engage with LD provision with those who did within a certain period (usually near to their assessment submission or examination). This approach has been undertaken successfully in recent years; for example, Loddick and Coulson (2020) proved that LD tutorials can have a positive effect on assessment grade by two to four subgrades, by analysing large data sets.

Qualitative approaches are also useful when measuring the impact of LD. One way of collecting qualitative data might include asking students about their experiences of engaging with LD. Learning Development practitioners often ask students for feedback through a questionnaire at the end of a taught session; a more effective approach might be to interview students about their self-reported feelings immediately after an LD intervention and engage in a follow-up interview or focus group several weeks after the intervention or assessment submission. Other methods may include not linking the LD intervention to an assessment but instead asking students how their self-reported confidence may have improved (or not). By utilising both approaches within a research project, we achieve triangulation, and this has been effectively demonstrated in relation to the impact of LD by Coulson et al. (2021), who interviewed students immediately post-intervention and then some weeks later.

There are many other research approaches to successfully measure impact: auto-ethnographic approaches whereby tutors reflect and record their observed impact; interviewing faculty colleagues about their perspective; analysing large data sets of student outcomes to determine the best time to facilitate LD interventions to improve student retention; and many more. It is useful to spend time reflecting on how you might measure impact drawing on the resources and expertise available to you and your colleagues.

Does Learning Development Have Impact?

The *Journal of Learning Development in Higher Education* (*JLDHE*) is the go-to journal for Learning Developers wanting to share their research with the LD (and wider HE) community. Another effective method of sharing good practice and evidence is presenting at the ALDinHE Annual Conference, which is perhaps the largest gathering of Learning Developers in the UK each year. An analysis of the special journal issue and conference in 2022 (*Journal of Learning Development in Higher Education*, 2022) demonstrates that

Learning Developers are already measuring impact and sharing it with the community. Just in that one year, journal articles and conference papers related to the effectiveness of reading strategies (White et al., 2022); peer mentoring (Thomas and Mansfield, 2022); walking dissertation tutorials (Psaros, 2022); utilising magic to teach academic skills (Kimberley et al., 2022); student well-being (Frith et al., 2022); developing visual literacies (Bartram, 2022), and many more were presented and written by LD practitioners.

The work of Thomas and Mansfield (2022) was a direct result of research on the impact of LD undertaken by Coulson et al. (2021) in relation to the impact of student tutorials. Coulson et al. (2021) showed that students engaging with LD tutorials could improve their assessment grades from two to four subgrades. For example, a student with a D minus grade profile could improve to a C minus. The data also indicated that Black students could improve their grade by up to four subgrades which equates to an improvement from a D minus to a B minus. The home institution of Coulson et al. (2021) and Thomas and Mansfield (2022) was already very supportive of their LD practice but proving the impact with quantitative data (and followed up with qualitative data) resulted in the institution funding a peer mentoring programme to further the work of the LD provision. Proving impact directly resulted in extra funding.

The Coulson et al. (2021) research also encouraged the development of research that was perhaps more creative compared to previous endeavours. Kimberly et al. (2022) embarked upon a research project to ascertain if teaching critical thinking using magic tricks was effective. They received research funding from their institution to undertake this research and it was published in *JLDHE*, presented at the ALDinHE Conference and also shared more widely through their institutional Learning and Teaching conference as well as other HE conferences, as the implications of their work are far-ranging. And the students love learning using magic tricks!

The research outlined here is just a small snapshot of the excellent practice undertaken by LD professionals to share their practice and measure their impact. For more inspiration, start reading *JLDHE* and consider attending the annual ALDinHE conference. Learning Developers have a huge impact on the quantitative aspects of the student experience, and, perhaps more importantly, they also effect change in students' self-reported levels of confidence (Loddick and Coulson, 2020).

Conclusion

This chapter set out to outline and explore the why, the how, and the what of impact in LD. Impact is a contentious concept, and quantifying our work is challenging, time-consuming, ethically draining, and ultimately another 'wicked problem' on our 'to do' list (Rittel and Webber, 1973). Some of us can make the decision ourselves as to whether we should measure our impact.

Of those of us who have that autonomy, some will decide to embrace the approach and undertake small-scale or larger-scale research projects to ascertain the extent of any impact. And some of us will decide that other scholarly endeavours are more worthwhile and will concentrate on other important areas of LD research such as effective learning and teaching approaches, co-constructing projects with students, and everything in between. This too is worthy work and a valuable contribution to the Learning Development research canon.

Some of us will not have any choice as to whether we measure the impact of LD. The importance of sector instruments such as APPs and the TEF means that institutions are drawn to measure, quantify, and assess all facets of our work – whether we like it or not. This chapter can guide your work and act as a tool when you are designing your approach and reflecting on what you want to measure. Come back to it as you undertake your research and share it with colleagues so that they can fully appreciate the challenges, benefits, and joys of measuring the impact of LD.

For those of you who do embrace measuring the impact of LD, it is hoped that this chapter sets you on the road and encourages you to share your findings with your peers, your professional community, and beyond. And for those of you who decide to focus on other endeavours, it is hoped that this chapter guided you as you made that decision.

References

Bartram, J. A. (2022) 'Bridges and barriers to developing visual literacy', *Journal of Learning Development in Higher Education*, 25. https://doi.org/10.47408/jldhe.vi25.957

Cannella, G.S. and Koro-Ljungberg, M. (2017) 'Neoliberalism in higher education: Can we understand? Can we resist and survive? Can we become without neoliberalism?' *Cultural Studies↔Critical Methodologies*, 17(3): 155–162.

Chalmers, D. and Gardiner, D. (2015) 'An evaluation framework for identifying the effectiveness and impact of academic teacher development programmes' *Studies in Educational Evaluation*, 46: 81–89.

Coulson, K.V., Loddick, A. and Rice, P. (2021) 'Exploring the Impact of Learning Development on Student Engagement, Experience, and Learning', in: H. Huijser, M. Kek, and F.F. Padró (eds), *Student Support Services: University Development and Administration*. Singapore: Springer. https://doi.org/10.1007/978-981-13-3364-4_19-1

Frith, L., Maitland, L. and Lamont, J. (2022) 'The impact of departmental academic skills provision on students' wellbeing', *Journal of Learning Development in Higher Education*, 25. https://doi.org/10.47408/jldhe.vi25.978

Hicks, M. (2015) *Impact Evaluation of Key Themes Funded by the Office for Learning and Teaching*. Available from: https://ltr.edu.au/resources/Hicks_Secondment_report_2016.pdf

Hinton, T. (2013) 'Mapping influence: highlights from an investigation into nationally funded learning and teaching projects in Australia', in: M. Hicks (2015) *Impact Evaluation of Key Themes Funded by the Office for Learning and Teaching*. [online]. Available from: https://ltr.edu.au/resources/Hicks_Secondment_report_2016.pdf

Journal of Learning Development in Higher Education (2022) 25: Special Edition, *ALDinHE Conference Proceedings and Reflections*. Available from: https://journal.aldinhe.ac.uk/index.php/jldhe/issue/view/40

Kimberley, E., Rice, P. and West, A. (2022) 'Magic to conjure up academic skills for dissertation support', *Journal of Learning Development in Higher Education*, 25. https://doi.org/10.47408/jldhe.vi25.977

Loddick, A. and Coulson, K.V. (2020) 'The impact of learning development tutorials on student attainment', *Journal of Learning Development in Higher Education*, 17. https://doi.org/10.47408/jldhe.vi17.558

Milbourne, R. (2015) *A New National Institute for Learning and Teaching Report*. Available at: https://docs.education.gov.au/documents/newnational-institute-learning-and-teaching-report

Moon, J. (2004) 'Using reflective learning to improve the impact of short courses and workshops', *Journal of Continuing Education in the Health Professions*, 24(1): 4–11. https://doi.org/10.1002/chp.1340240103

Psaros, C. (2022) 'Walk me through your dissertation: using urban walks to develop students' thinking about research', *Journal of Learning Development in Higher Education*, 25. https://doi.org/10.47408/jldhe.vi25.968

Rittel, H.W.J. and Webber, M.M. (1973) 'Dilemmas in a General Theory of Planning', *Policy Sciences*, 4(2): 155–169.

Thomas, S. and Mansfield, S. (2022) 'Working outside the box: breaking down barriers with a Learning Development Peer Mentoring scheme', *Journal of Learning Development in Higher Education*, 25. https://doi.org/10.47408/jldhe.vi25.971

United Nations (2023) *Theory of Change: UNDAF Companion Guidance*. Available at: https://unsdg.un.org/sites/default/files/UNDG-UNDAF-Companion-Pieces-7-Theory-of-Change.pdf

Walliman, N. (2022) *Research Methods: The Basics*. 3rd edn. Abingdon: Routledge.

White, S.J., Wu, S.H., Qahtani, F.S., Warrington, K.L., Balcombe, F.O. and Paterson, K.B. (2022) 'Effects of reading strategies on reading behaviour and comprehension: implications for teaching study skills', *Journal of Learning Development in Higher Education*, 25. https://doi.org/10.47408/jldhe.vi25.970

23

LEADERSHIP IN LEARNING DEVELOPMENT

A Networked Approach

Carina Buckley

> *Leadership can be manifested in so many different and surprising ways that because I feel I'm not a typical leader, as in I don't have a leader's personality, I have to fall back on a definition that allows me some agency and to view myself as a leader in a different way. So, if I lead, I lead below the line. You know, developing good relationships, involving others in the process; that more distributed kind of model. I don't have to be in the position of visible power.*
>
> *(Research study participant)*

Introduction

Learning Development's (LD) professional values of collaboration and partnership, sharing practice and critical self-reflection (ALDinHE, 2023) can make it difficult for Learning Developers to recognise themselves as leaders. 'Leadership' is a condition often conceptualised in terms of traits, hierarchies, and transformation (Bolden, 2011) and, through its links to line management, promotion, and progression, considered synonymously with authority. In this business-oriented model, leadership relies on having a strategic vision and the resources and authority to realise it, potentially putting it out of reach for many Learning Developers. However, this takes an instrumental and narrow view of leadership at odds with its potential. A small, ethically approved research study presented in this chapter identified that leadership in LD can instead be more readily and broadly understood as a network of relations between equals, distributed through personal connections and reinforced by actions and outputs. A leader

DOI: 10.4324/9781003433347-29

is someone who works to make something better; in LD, this is someone who grows collaborations and partnerships by leveraging – organically, if not strategically – the value of their knowledge, abilities, position, relationships, and personal qualities towards achieving that aim, whilst helping others develop in a similar way. Enacting this form of leadership requires the Learning Developer to connect with new people and share ideas and experiences, making those people aware of what is possible for themselves and for their students, thus avoiding functionalist, unethical outcomes that commodify students without addressing their needs. This chapter outlines an approach to influence without authority, and argues that alongside the emphasis on networks it represents the defining feature of leadership in LD.

Leadership as a Social Activity

Leadership can be usefully understood as 'a process of social influence, which maximizes the efforts of others, towards the achievement of a goal' (Kruse, 2013, p.2, cited in Gumus et al., 2018, p.26), and which operates via the inspiration and motivation of others, collaboration, and shared goals (Arthur and Souza, 2023). By taking leadership as situated and context-dependent (Buckley, forthcoming), it frees us to concentrate on the social interactions that dynamically create and recreate it. A socially oriented view of leadership therefore offers a form of 'liberation from the self' (Syska and Buckley, 2022, p.4), as interactions with others and negotiation of meaning within a shared discourse take precedence (Ford et al., 2008; Roxå et al., 2011).

This sounds good in theory – what does it mean in practice? Firstly, a working environment should support a sense of identity, and one role of leadership is to facilitate and improve the sociability on which this rests (Ford et al., 2008). This needn't require a formal structure and the authority to implement it; it could be as simple as a semi-regular tea break that brings people together for sharing with no measurable outputs (Buckley, 2021). This, secondly, then provides the conditions for Taylor et al.'s (2022) 'social networks approach' to leadership in that relationships are built through conversation and the meaningful recognition of each other's expertise, and as a result, learning happens in and through what becomes a practice community. These 'microcultures' (Roxå and Mårtensson, 2013, p.39) are small networks of people – or even an individual – who work closely with colleagues and disseminate their knowledge and practices. A leader in this type of scenario is then someone who becomes a 'knowledge catalyst' (Fields et al., 2019, p.218), brokering conversations and prompting the construction, reiteration, and development not just of knowledge, but also beliefs, direction, and strategies. A Learning Developer empowered by the values of knowledge exchange and partnership working therefore embodies this notion of leadership, which is distributed, dynamic, inclusive, and collaborative (Fields et al., 2019).

Recognising Points of Power in Learning Development

Frameworks of leadership derived from the corporate sector often equate leadership with power, whether that resides in the leader or is deployed by that leader on behalf of or for the empowerment of others (Lumby, 2019). The leader is recognised through their position in the hierarchy, job title, and role, which is likely to include line management responsibilities – what Blanchard (2007, p.109) refers to as 'position power'. In contrast, distributed leadership emerges out of the interplay between people and their context, focussing on collaboration and social construction of knowledge to progress goals and solve problems (Gumus et al., 2018). Leadership becomes 'not something "done" by an individual "to" others' but rather a condition that 'works through and within relationships' (Bennett et al., 2003, p.3, cited in Bolden, 2011, p.251), strengthening the collective knowledge of an institution, empowering staff, and increasing their sense of ownership over their work (Arthur and Souza, 2023).

Nevertheless, steering others towards a goal remains an act of power and thereby a function of leadership (Lumby, 2019). How that power is exercised can take a variety of forms, many of them subtle. For example, Lumby's (2019) study of power in higher education identified the value of creating a favourable impression with colleagues and shaping the decision-making of others through conversation. In a top-down, one-dimensional model of leadership, these activities might not be considered as either power or leadership. However, embracing the range of forms that power can take opens leadership up beyond the roles traditionally associated with it.

For many Learning Developers, position power is challenging. However, Blanchard (2007) lists four other more accessible points of power: task, knowledge, personal, and relationship. Being able to do something, having expertise in something, our own interpersonal skills, and how we use those skills in building relationships with others are all means of effecting change and exerting influence on others. This 'unobtrusive' exercise of power (Lumby, 2019, p.1620) might be obscured even from those who exercise it, yet these points of power are essentially the foundations of leadership. Switching focus from authority to relationships, from responsibility to advocacy, and from hierarchy to mentoring, allows us to embrace collaboration opportunities and see the impact of our work more widely.

A small, ethically approved study conducted among the LD community (Buckley, forthcoming) explored the range and depth of understanding of what leadership in LD looks like. The participants, sourced through the LDHEN Jiscmail, were all self-selecting with an interest in leadership, and weren't required to have any experience of either leadership or management. Each was interviewed online about their views on collaboration, influence, dissemination, autonomy, and the values they applied to their work, and the transcripts inductively analysed for their understanding of leadership and the qualities of a good leader. Although the study participants were not asked about leadership activities explicitly, their experiences and ideas can be interpreted through the prism of Blanchard's model. By viewing LD through this lens, Learning Developers can identify pathways to leadership that accord with and are supported by the values that underpin their work.

Position Power

Position power refers to the authority that comes with a job title or a role; in LD this tends to be implicit, rather than explicit, and is not necessarily exercised with authority. However, an LD role can be viewed as being an authority, as Participant 3 attests: 'We're kind of like in-house consultants in a way. We'd get brought into different projects to consult from a pedagogy perspective'. This also applies to working with students, and the participants recognised that authoritative balancing act:

> Influence probably first and foremost is with students. Influence doesn't quite feel like the right word … you offer something, and the student can take it or leave it or take it and try it.
>
> (Participant 4)

> I don't think that influence is the right word when I think about the students because I don't want it to be like that hierarchy. But I think we have a way of connecting with our students, which I think is quite unique and I love it.
>
> (Participant 11)

Nevertheless, sometimes position power is more explicit, both in how it is recognised and in what its accrued benefits can mean for how LD is seen:

> I knew that I had a real breadth of experience through the projects that I've done, but my name badge didn't say that. So a lot of doors were like, no, you can't come through this door, because you don't really know what you're talking about. But now I have a different job title. I'm still the same person, but I get access now.
>
> (Participant 8)

Task Power

Translating position power into something more tangible can be done by taking the qualities or capabilities of the LD role and leveraging them as a form of task power, which comes from 'being able to help others with a process or procedure' (Blanchard, 2007, p.109). While this might most immediately relate to working with students, it is equally applicable to building and maintaining relationships with colleagues. For example, Participant 13 responded to a request from a course team with a counter request, putting conditions on them before they could or would receive any help:

> I've got a meeting shortly with one course team to show them the difference between a bespoke session for their faculty and one of our generic central ones so they know they're not just being taken off the shelf, that we need something from them to create something.
>
> (Participant 13)

When both Learning Developer and subject lecturer are invested in the task, the need for task power is lessened or perhaps rendered invisible; although the task is in the gift of the Learning Developer, the overriding feeling is one of collaboration. This was experienced by one participant, who had built up familiarity with one course team and understood what they valued, and which then helped create an impetus and importance around the task: 'The lecturers in that field … really value academic writing. It's got a high value, [so] the message goes out to students: this is something that's very important' (Participant 15).

Unfortunately, the same participant had also experienced what might be considered the other side of task power – when a task is reduced to an instrumental act, and the power involved is misunderstood: 'Some lecturers I suppose simply want you to come and, you know, almost like a plug, you'll give them the academic writing. Then they'll magically have it and everything will be alright' (Participant 15). In this situation, the lecturer has failed to acknowledge the task power of the Learning Developer, seeing it instead in the way one might view the taking of a pill. This serves to highlight the value of knowledge power in reinforcing and forging Learning Developers' task power.

Knowledge Power

Knowledge power rests on expertise and skills, and can be formalised (and made transferable and transparent) through certification and qualifications (Blanchard, 2007). However, knowledge power can also be tacit; it just needs to be recognised by others. The Learning Developer can fully exploit this point of power as it can visibly and measurably (certainly qualitatively if not quantitatively) be applied to a wide range of stakeholders, and thus offers the most opportunities for its use.

First, within a team of Learning Developers, one can exercise knowledge power where there is variation in each member's prior experience. After joining a new institution, Participant 12's strong background in teaching was soon noticed:

> My colleagues recognise [my experience] and ask me what they should do in certain situations because some of them have not had so much experience ... things like managing your class, coping with the different demands that students have.
>
> (Participant 12)

Outside the immediate team, academic colleagues can also be engaged through knowledge power, as the knowledge that the Learning Developer holds of students and their experiences of learning is from a different perspective to the subject teaching staff:

> Three students might come to me with the ... same misunderstanding of the same assignment, and I'll be knocking on the door of the person who's set the assignment... I'll be going, you've got a problem coming down the tubes ... Shall we think about what we might be able to do now? And how about next year?
>
> (Participant 7)

Similarly, several participants reported on how they were able to push their subject teaching colleagues further than they had expected or intended to go, or to guide them in a more appropriate direction for the benefit of the students:

> We'll often get asked by a member of faculty staff, 'Can you do something on criticality concerning X?' We look at the brief and we go yeah, it's criticality. But what about reflection? Because that's what this is asking for ... We make them realise what it is that they're asking students to do.
>
> (Participant 13)

The knowledge power of the Learning Developer can reach colleagues around the university, if they are aware of what the Learning Developer knows. Participant 4 invited Counselling colleagues to a team meeting so they could learn more about how to title workshops in an appealing way. And the 'insight that I have from my student-level work' and its connection to getting 'student information about the student experience' was a valuable link to senior management for Participant 16.

Ultimately, the most common and perhaps most impactful use and recognition of knowledge power comes from direct contact with students, as expressed memorably by Participant 20: 'I quite like to describe my job as being a midwife to thoughts occasionally. It's not my thoughts, but I can help get them out'. Knowledge power is vital, but, as these examples show, its success depends on how well the Learning Developer works with others. Knowledge alone is not enough to lead in LD.

Personal Power

Working closely with someone is achievable for most people; to do so successfully may be the result of personal power, which, as Blanchard (2007, p.109) claims, has at its root the idea that 'people like to be around you'. This might be because of 'personal attributes such as strength of character, passion, inspiration, or wisdom'. If these feel too much or too unattainable, then it also derives from and is 'enhanced by strong interpersonal skills, such as the ability to communicate well and be persuasive', which are part of the skillset that Learning Developers bring to their role. Learning Developers commit to partnership working, collaboration and critical self-reflection (ALDinHE, 2023), making personal power a useful tool in their practice. As noted previously, this can be effective with colleagues as well as students. Participant 16 felt that LD had a role in 'demystifying processes so that [students] can become integrated and it's trying to make university … be us all together. And I think that that's my approach to working with colleagues as well'.

Participant 7 takes an open and inclusive approach to colleagues, describing it as being as 'friendly with everybody' and advocating 'meeting people, … going for a coffee with people', not just for its own sake but because it is clear that

> that level of personal relationship interaction is probably the best starting point because I think that it lubricates everything else. People who know and like me will tend to come to the things that I'm doing that might be about my work and tend to get it in the way that it's intended.
>
> (Participant 7)

The value of personal power was summarised elegantly by Participant 8, whose career had seen progression through the institution: 'I think the biggest thing I learned was, you have to get them on side. If they don't like you, they won't follow you'.

Relationship Power

The final point of power, that of relationship power, is strongly linked to the other four points of power and can be derived from them, simply because 'Someone has to be willing to be influenced … for you to have that influence. So it's building that relationship where you can influence people' (Participant 2). By 'cultivating a relationship', 'understanding a colleague' or 'building a friendship', or even, more strategically, 'knowing someone who owes you a favour' (Blanchard, 2007, p.110), it is possible to draw and exert power (or influence) via association. Participant 19 described this as 'critical allyship', which is explained as understanding and being able to show you understand where people are trying to get to with what they're doing and having respect for why they're trying to get there ... And then from that basis of solidarity with those objectives, starting to push and nudge and cajole, and hopefully inspire.

(Participant 19)

However, this participant stressed the need for authenticity: these are 'alliances', a partnership, rather than a mechanistic means of getting something done – even when the goal is to get something done. For Participant 1, the aim is to recognise and overcome the siloed teams inevitably found in a large organisation:

That's what we're doing with the transition project ... we're owning it, but we've got people from the faculties, we've also got WP and outreach and marketing and careers ... so trying to make those kinds of connections.

(Participant 1)

Despite this obvious organisational benefit, the primary focus of relationship power remains on the people involved and what they can learn from each other, from 'being in the presence of other people and learning from them' (Participant 2), 'asking how are things going, what do you need?' (Participant 6), and feeding 'a very proactive curiosity around what other people are doing' (Participant 5), since 'it's inevitable that things go on that you're interested in' (Participant 12). Enjoying these broad boundaries, relationship power is therefore within the reach of any Learning Developer keen to learn more about their colleagues and their activities.

A Networked Approach to Leadership

LD is a situated practice, and Learning Developers are situated practitioners 'in dialectical relation with the surrounding world' (Roxå and Mårtensson, 2009, p.548). Through conversation, social contact, and the building of trust, Learning Developers can guide and influence the scope and visibility of the field, and contribute to the ongoing negotiations around the nature of higher education and its purpose. In this type of generous reciprocity, Learning Developers can take a leadership role by capitalising on one or more of the five points of power that best suits their context. They can bring fresh perspectives to established interactions and position themselves as a hub for sharing knowledge and expertise, focussing if necessary on one relationship, one task or one experience at a time. In a field without clear paths of progression, where most promotion opportunities sit firmly outside LD, we can embrace the 'human doings' outlined in these illustrations of the five points of power as part of our relationships with 'human beings' (Taylor et al., 2022). This may be the most effective way for Learning Developers to fulfil their potential as leaders.

References

ALDinHE (2023) *About ALDinHE*. Available at: https://aldinhe.ac.uk/about-aldinhe/ (Accessed: 31 March 2023).

Arthur, L. and Souza, A. (2023) 'All for one and one for all? Leadership approaches in complementary schools', *Educational Management Administration and Leadership*, 51(1): 245–263. https://doi.org/10.1177/1741143220971285

Blanchard, K. (2007) *Leading at a higher level: Blanchard on leadership and creating high performance organisations*. Harlow: Financial Times Prentice Hall.

Bolden, R. (2011) 'Distributed leadership in organizations: A review of theory and research', *International Journal of Management Reviews*, 13: 251–269. https://doi.org/10.1111/j.1468-2370.2011.00306.x

Buckley, C. (forthcoming) 'Leadership in learning development paper', *Journal of University Teaching and Learning Practice*.

Buckley, C. (2021) 'Performing community: An online tea break as a radical act', *Journal of Learning Development in Higher Education*, 22. https://doi.org/10.47408/jldhe.vi22.761

Fields, J., Kenny, N.A. and Mueller, R.A. (2019) 'Conceptualising educational leadership in an academic development program', *International Journal for Academic Development*, 24(3): 218–231. https://doi.org/10.1080/1360144X.2019.1570211

Ford, J., Harding, N. and Learmonth, M. (2008) *Leadership as Identity: Constructions and Deconstructions*. Basingstoke: Palgrave Macmillan.

Gumus, S., Bellibas, M.S., Esen, M. and Gumus, E. (2018) 'A systematic review of studies on leadership models in educational research from 1980 to 2014', *Educational Management Administration and Leadership*, 46(1): 25–48. https://doi.org/10.1177/1741143216659296

Lumby, J. (2019) 'Leadership and power in higher education', *Studies in Higher Education*, 44(9): 1619–1629. https://doi.org/10.1080/03075079.2018.1458221

Roxå, T. and Mårtensson, K. (2009) 'Significant conversations and significant networks – exploring the backstage of the teaching arena', *Studies in Higher Education*, 34(50): 547–559. https://doi.org/10.1080/03075070802597200

Roxå, T. and Mårtensson, K. (2013) *Understanding Strong Academic Microcultures: An Exploratory Study*, CED, Centre for Educational Development, Lunds Universitet. Available at: https://lucris.lub.lu.se/ws/files/55148513/Microcultures_eversion.pdf (Accessed: 31 March 2023).

Roxå, T., Mårtensson, K. and Alveteg, M. (2011) 'Understanding and influencing teaching and learning cultures at university: a network approach', *Higher Education* 62: 99–111. https://doi.org/10.1007/s10734-010-9368-9

Syska, A. and Buckley, C. (2022) 'Writing as liberatory practice: unlocking knowledge to locate an academic field', *Teaching in Higher Education*, 28(2): 439–454, https://doi.org/10.1080/13562517.2022.2114337

Taylor, K.L., Kenny, N.A., Perrault, P. and Mueller, R.A. (2022) 'Building integrated networks to develop teaching and learning: the critical role of hubs', *International Journal for Academic Development*, 27(3): 279–291. https://doi.org/10.1080/1360144X.2021.1899931

24

PROFESSIONAL DEVELOPMENT AND RECOGNITION IN LD

Steve Briggs

During a collaborative keynote at the 2017 Learning Development Conference to explore what the Learning Development community considered made someone a professional 'Learning Developer', it became clear there was a consensus that Learning Development professionals could have different roles, qualifications and experiences. Despite such diversity, shared values associated with working as a Learning Development practitioner were clear. These values have since become the foundation for guiding professional development opportunities and developing pathways to formally recognise expertise within the Learning Development community.

Introduction

Educational disciplines will often have well-established professional development and recognition pathways aligned to qualifications and/or chartership. However, at the start of the 2010s the Learning Development (LD) field had very limited bespoke continued professional development (CPD) opportunities and no formal recognition opportunity for practitioners. Discipline-specific professional development ensures that practitioners have regular opportunity to disseminate and discuss best practices and/or emergent issues with peers, which is crucial in terms of teaching and learning innovation and excellence. From an individual perspective, professional recognition provides structured opportunities for a practitioner to undertake critical reflection on their practice and serves to support career progression aspirations (for instance, recognition status could be essential or desirable criteria in a future job application). Collectively, achieving greater recognition as a community will serve to raise both awareness and the status of the field per se.

DOI: 10.4324/9781003433347-30

This chapter provides an overview of how LD CPD opportunities in the UK have progressively emerged in terms of discipline-specific professional development opportunities. It then details professional recognition routes open to Learning Developers, both within the field and beyond, to evidence acquisition of specialist Learning Development skills and knowledge.

Professional Development Events

A calendar of the professional development events discussed in this section is available via the ALDinHE website (see ALDinHE, 2023a).

Learning Development Conference

The inaugural Learning Development conference took place in 2003 and became an annual event from 2005 (except for 2020 when a programme of LD@3 events was delivered instead – discussed later). From 2005 to 2019 the conference took place in person, was delivered online in 2021, and in 2022 assumed a hybrid format. Previous conferences centred on the core themes pertinent to the LD community and comprised keynotes, workshops, and poster presentations. Up until 2014, the ALDinHE conference acted as the primary vehicle for providing a regular professional development offer in terms of in-person training and networking.

The annual conference provides a host of professional development opportunities for Learning Developers. There are typically around 150 attendees from across UK universities (and some international representation) which ensures excellent networking opportunities during the event. The event comprises highly interactive parallel sessions and keynotes that address topical Learning Development issues. ALDinHE provides scaffolded support for new presenters through offering mentorship for abstract and conference session preparation. There is also a conference buddy scheme to support Learning Developers who are attending for the first time.

The conference is arranged by a Conference Working Group (see ALDinHE, 2023b) which provides potential developmental opportunities around event planning and promotion for volunteer members. As discussed later in this chapter, engagement in such working groups provides excellent prospects for Learning Developers to build evidence to support professional recognition applications.

Regional Events

Given the finite nature of university staff development budgets, attendance at ALDinHE conferences was often restricted and many Learning Development professionals had limited access to the wider community beyond online mailing lists. It was within this context that the demand for access to more frequent CPD opportunities tailored to LD professionals began to be explored by the ALDinHE Steering Group in 2014.

ALDinHE responded by providing funding to support LD teams to host one-day regional networking events. These events were aligned to a topical theme (such as impact evaluation, critical practices, and employability) and an open invitation extended to any LD practitioner who wanted to attend (as a presenter and/or attendee). The first event was held at the University of Bedfordshire in 2014, with subsequent events held across the UK including York, Anglia Ruskin, Bradford, East Anglia, and Leicester. Momentum was built through sessions at ALDinHE conferences to encourage and support members of the LD community to host and attend events (Livesey et al., 2017; Briggs and members of Professional Development Working Group, 2016; Briggs, Kukhareva and Mathew, 2015). ALDinHE regional events were also hosted in collaboration with other professional associations. For example, ALDinHE and BALEAP co-hosted an academic literacies event (BALEAP, 2018), and ALDinHE and the Sma Network have co-hosted an event related to providing maths support. Regional events usually attracted at least 20 attendees and, as intended, acted as an effective bridge between conferences.

The regional events scheme resulted in a significant expansion in the frequency and accessibility of in-person professional development available to Learning Development practitioners. This was evident in the increased number of events that ran between 2014 and 2019. However, in the post-pandemic world, in-person regional events have been somewhat superseded by online events and now occur less frequently. As such, Learning Developers should aim to prioritise their attendance whenever local in-person regional events occur.

LD@3

As the ALDinHE 2020 conference approached, the severity of the pandemic was becoming clearer, and the ALDinHE Co-Chairs and Conference Leads made the difficult decision to cancel just before the first UK national lockdown. Given that a full conference programme was in place, the ALDinHE Executive decided to invite conference presenters to deliver their sessions online. These would be offered on an open-access basis to provide inclusive support for the LD community during this challenging and uncertain time. In the first instance, mini-keynote presenters were invited, and the offer then extended to all participants. ALDinHE also reached out to the Librarians Information Literacy Annual Conference (LILAC, 2020) organisers to invite their presenters to participate, given their conference had also been cancelled. To provide some much-needed structure and consistency at a very uncertain time, it was decided that webinars would run at the same time each day, at 3 pm, and LD@3 was born. Uptake exceeded all expectations, and a daily LD@3 webinar ran for almost two months between April and June 2020. These original LD@3 sessions were typically attended by upwards of 50 participants.

Subsequently, LD@3 has become an ongoing ALDinHE professional development offer. Frequent webinars continue to be offered and – to promote inclusivity – have remained open access. As such, LD@3 sessions provide both an excellent and a highly accessible professional development opportunity for Learning Developers in relation to keeping up to date with contemporary issues and innovative new practices.

Other Professional Development Opportunities

There is a range of other professional development opportunities available to Learning Developers through ALDinHE. For instance:

Journal of Learning Development in Higher Education (*JLDHE*) (see ALDinHE, 2023c). The *JLDHE* provides an excellent source of professional development for readers and is a source of recognition for authors. The *Journal* also runs a *JLDHE* Reading Club (ALDinHE, 2023d) to support wider community engagement and discussion.

Steering Group and/or Working Group membership (see ALDinHE, 2023b). Learning Developers can volunteer to join working groups related to ALDinHE activities (including the conference and LearnHigher). Many members of working groups are also members of the Association Steering Group (which has a self-nomination application process). As discussed later in the chapter, such participation can provide an excellent professional development opportunity in terms of acquiring experience needed for specific teaching excellence recognition applications.

Communities of Practice (see ALDinHE, 2023e). At the time of writing there were five communities of practice (Research and Scholarship, Peer Mentoring, Neurodiversity/Inclusivity, Leadership, and Health and Social Care). These meet throughout the year and provide the opportunity for focussed professional development discussions and networking. Practitioners can also propose new communities of practice to ALDinHE.

Professional Recognition Opportunities for Learning Development Practitioners

ALDinHE Recognition

A Need for Recognition

Pre-2017 there was no bespoke qualification or professional recognition associated with working in Learning Development. Rather, professional standing could be attributed to tenure in a role or proxy qualifications (such as a teaching, librarianship, or English as a Second or Other Language recognition) (Shahabudin and Coonan, 2015). Such indicators were often used inconsistently and in contradictory ways across the LD community. This was a significant concern to ALDinHE in terms of ensuring that expertise and professional standing amongst its members were being appropriately recognised.

In 2017, ALDinHE launched a dedicated recognition scheme for LD practitioners (see Briggs, 2018a, 2018b, 2019). The scheme was informed by the collaborative keynote referenced at the start of this chapter (Buckley and Briggs, 2017). During this session, circa 120 ALDinHE conference attendees worked in groups to identify common characteristics associated with LD practitioners. It was established that although members of the LD community had diverse qualifications, subject specialisms, and work experience, they shared common values, which have since become the basis for the recognition scheme.

Application Pathways and Reviewing

Recognition is awarded based on evidence of commitment to ALDinHE professional values. There are two pathways – Certified Practitioner (CeP) and Certified Leading Practitioner (CeLP) (ALDinHE, 2023f). CeP is aimed at Learning Development practitioners working within an institution. Applicants evidence commitment to the ALDinHE values in relation to three dimensions: work history; value statement; and supporting reference. CeLP is aimed at Learning Development practitioners working both within and beyond an institution. Applicants demonstrate commitment to the ALDinHE values in relation to four dimensions: work history; value statement; community engagement impact statement; and a supporting testimonial.

Applications are designed to promote critical reflection around Learning Development practices. Applicants have previously been supported to apply for recognition through sessions at the ALDinHE conference (Briggs, Koulle and Carter, 2019; Briggs et al., 2018c; Briggs et al., 2018d), along with dedicated writing retreats (Briggs and Koulle, 2019). Recognition scheme applications are independently reviewed by two reviewers who make awarding recommendations to the ALDinHE Professional Recognition Panel. Applicant professional development is further supported through application feedback.

Between 2017 and March 2023, 121 ALDinHE recognitions (84 CeP and 37 CeLP) have been awarded. Applicants have been received from over 30 universities. Notably, applications have been received from academic skills tutors, lecturers, librarians, dyslexia tutors, EAL tutors, and learning technologies, reflecting the diversity of the LD community – as was evident at the 2017 collaborative keynote.

Networking and Expertise Directory

As the ALDinHE recognition scheme became established, a networking and expertise directory was added to the ALDinHE website (ALDinHE, 2023g). This included details of CeP and CeLP recipients and is searchable based on keywords reflecting areas of expertise. This supported professional networking and informal mentoring within the LD community by providing an open and central list of certified LD experts. From 2023, the directory will be updated every two years to ensure it remains up to date.

Mentoring

At the start of the 2020s, further developmental opportunities for UK Learning Developers emerged through the introduction of ALDinHE mentoring opportunities (ALDinHE, 2023h). Mentoring covers a range of developmental opportunities, including submitting an ALDinHE Conference proposal, writing for *JLDHE* or creating a resource for *LearnHigher*. The ALDinHE Mentoring Scheme (ALDinHE, 2023i) was formally launched at the 2023 Learning Development Conference and includes the opportunity for mentors to obtain additional recognition (ALDinHE Certified Mentor (CeM) status) for their contributions.

Sector Recognition

AdvanceHE Fellowships

To evidence transferability of skills and knowledge and support future career progression, it is essential for LD professionals to seek recognition for their teaching and learning expertise across the wider higher education sector. LD practitioners should therefore be encouraged to consider applying for AdvanceHE fellowship status commensurate with their responsibilities and experiences. Many LD professionals will be eligible to work towards FHEA on the basis that they have substantive teaching and learning support roles. Experienced LD professionals with responsibility for leading, managing, or organising areas of work would likely also be eligible to apply for SFHEA. As more LD professionals advance in their careers and enter strategic leadership roles, there will also likely be a progressive increase in PFHEA recipients who have an association with LD.

Teaching Excellence Awards

There have been a number of previous AdvanceHE National Teaching Fellowships (NTFs) awarded to staff working in (or from) a Learning Development background. Such winners include John Hilsdon (2005), Debbie Holley (2014), Jennie Blake (2018), Helen Webster (2019), Steve

Briggs (2020), and Kate Coulson (2022). Similarly, an LD Team (Lancaster University in 2022) has been recognised through AdvanceHE's Collaborative Awards for Teaching Excellence (CATE). It is particularly notable that there has been an LD-associated NTF winner in four of the last five years with the addition of a CATE winner in 2022. This would align to the expansion of the LD community and increased opportunities for professional development afforded to those working in this field.

Navigating Learning Development Recognition

The nature of opportunities afforded to LD practitioners through previous and current work experiences will determine if/when they are able to obtain the recognitions outlined in this chapter. The following provides guidance to help prospective applicants to start to consider what recognition opportunities might be possible at different stages of an LD career.

Creating Opportunities to Work Beyond Your Institution

LD practitioners who have received NTFs have typically been actively involved in national work related to the LD field. For example, John Hilsdon and Steve Briggs were ALDinHE Chairs/Co-chairs; Kate Coulson was the ALDinHE Secretary; and Debbie Holley and Helen Webster were ALDinHE Steering Group members. In most cases, each started as an ALDinHE working group member and then progressed to a Steering Group and/or executive position which afforded them opportunities to lead national work related to LD. This highlights the significant benefits associated with working beyond institutional roles. Such engagement both supports professional development and generates evidence for recognition applications. In many instances, such involvement will support an LD practitioner to apply for a higher level of recognition than if they were to just rely on evidence associated with undertaking their primary job given the wider range of responsibilities and opportunities afforded.

Applying for CeP and CeLP

An LD practitioner needs to be a member of ALDinHE (either an individual membership or work at an institution that is a member) to apply for recognition. Table 24.1 indicatively maps LD-related positions and ALDinHE working group roles (this list is not exhaustive and other educational association engagement would potentially also correspond if there was a clear LD focus) that are likely to be commensurate with evidence needed to apply for CeP or CeLP recognition.

TABLE 24.1 Examples of learning development roles and activities aligned to CeP and CeLP recognition

Recognition	Examples of related learning development roles/activities
CeP	• Lecturer with academic skills responsibilities • Academic Skills Tutor • Learning Technologist • Librarian • ALDinHE Working Group member
CeLP	• Learning Development operational and/or strategic leader (e.g., Senior Tutor / Learning Development Manager) • ALDinHE Steering Group Member and Working Group Chair/Co-Chair • ALDinHE Executive Role (e.g., ALDinHE Co-Chair/ALDinHE Secretary)

In each case, it would be necessary for a prospective applicant to be experienced in a role/position prior to application; typically, this would involve upwards of two years' experience.

Applying for AdvanceHE Fellowships

AdvanceHE's (2020) Fellowship Category Tool can be used to self-assess which category of fellowship is right for potential applicants. This involves selecting statements that are commensurate with previous and current teaching and learning experiences. Upon completion, feedback is provided in terms of which fellowship category is most appropriate. Most universities will have an academic development unit that should be able to provide guidance and support around how to apply for AdvanceHE recognition (depending on the institution, this could be via a direct application to AdvanceHE and/or through an AdvanceHE accredited institutional fellowship recognition scheme).

Table 24.2 indicatively maps LD positions and ALDinHE working group roles to AdvanceHE fellowships. This further illustrates how it is possible for Learning Developers who do not work in managerial and/or strategic positions within their institution to collate evidence for SFHEA or PFHEA through engagement with an external organisation, such as ALDinHE. Please note that this is intended to be illustrative rather than definitive, and it is recommended that prospective applicants always check eligibility via the AdvanceHE Fellowship Category Tool.

TABLE 24.2 Examples of Learning Development roles and activities aligned to AdvanceHE fellowship recognition

Fellowship	Examples of Learning Development positions	ALDinHE activity
AFHEA	• Graduate Teaching Assistant • Doctoral student • Peer Assisted Learning Supporter	• LDHEN participation • ALDinHE event engagement
FHEA	• Lecturer • Academic Skills Tutor • Learning Technologist • Librarian	• ALDinHE Working Group member
SFHEA	• Learning Development operational manager (e.g., Learning Development Team Leader)	• ALDinHE Steering Group Member and Working Group Chair/Co-Chair
PFHEA	• Strategic leader position (e.g., Director of Teaching and Learning with a Learning Development background)	• ALDinHE Executive Role (e.g., ALDinHE Co-Chair / ALDinHE Secretary)

Conclusion

The 2010s were a transformational period in terms of the range of professional development opportunities available to LD practitioners. Led by ALDinHE, the community has progressively reclaimed the 'Learning Developer' title and defined what it means to be a professional in the LD field. Looking ahead, I anticipate that these foundations will eventually lead to the introduction of undergraduate and postgraduate qualifications related to LD, at which time it may be that ALDinHE will become a Professional Standard Regulatory Body for universities where LD qualifications are taught. That withstanding, when formal qualifications do emerge, I also foresee future debates around the merits of the current values-based recognition scheme (Cep and CeLP) relative to awarded LD HE qualifications.

References

ALDinHE (2023a) *Events*. Available at: https://aldinhe.ac.uk/events/ (Accessed: 24 March 2023).

ALDinHE (2023b) *Join a Working Group*. Available at: https://aldinhe.ac.uk/join-aldinhe-community/join-a-working-group/ (Accessed: 22 March 2023).

ALDinHE (2023c) *Publish in Our Journal*. Available at: https://aldinhe.ac.uk/research/publish-in-our-journal/ (Accessed: 24 March 2023).

ALDinHE (2023d) *LD Reading Groups*. Available at: https://aldinhe.ac.uk/ld-reading-groups/ (Accessed: 24 March 2023).

ALDinHE (2023e) *Communities of Practice*. Available at: https://aldinhe.ac.uk/networking/communities-of-practice/ (Accessed: 24 March 2023).

ALDinHE (2023f) *ALDinHE Recognition Scheme*. Available at: https://aldinhe.ac.uk/aldinhe-professional-accreditation (Accessed: 24 November 2022).

ALDinHE (2023g) *Networking and Expertise Directory*. Available at: https://aldinhe. ac.uk/support/expertise-directory/ (Accessed: 24 November 2022).

ALDinHE (2023h) *Mentoring*. Available at: https://aldinhe.ac.uk/support/ mentoring/ (Accessed: 06 December 2022).

ALDinHE (2023i) *ALDinHE Mentoring Scheme*. Available at: https://aldinhe.ac.uk/ support/mentoring/aldinhe-mentoring-scheme/ (Accessed: 23 March 2023).

AdvanceHE (2020) *Which Category of HEA Fellowship is Right for You?* Available at: https://www.advance-he.ac.uk/form/fellowship-decision-tool-2011 (Accessed: 22 March 2023).

BALEAP (2018) *BALEAP PIM – Academic Literacies and EAP: Same or Different?* Available at: https://www.baleap.org/event/academic-literacies (Accessed: 24 November 2022).

Briggs, S. (2019) 'The best way of getting recognised: The ALDinHE recognition scheme', *Take 5*, 31. Available at: https://lmutake5.wordpress.com/2019/03/20/ take-5-31-the-best-way-of-getting-recognised/ (Accessed: 24 November 2022).

Briggs, S. (2018a) 'Development of the ALDinHE recognition scheme: Certifying the "Learning Developer" title', *Journal of Learning Development in Higher Education*, 13. https://doi.org/10.47408/jldhe.v0i13.461

Briggs, S. (2018b) 'Opinion piece – Moving from Learning Developers to Learning Development Practitioners', *Journal of Pedagogic Development*, 8(3), Available at: https://www. beds.ac.uk/jpd/volume-8-issue-3-november-2018 (Accessed: 22 November 2019).

Briggs, S., Carter, A., Koulle, K. and Rafferty, V. (2018c) 'An introduction to the ALDinHE Certified Practitioner (CeP) Recognition Scheme', *ALDinHE 2018: The Learning Development Conference*, University of Leicester, Leicester, 26–28 March.

Briggs, S. and Koulle, K. (2019) 'The best way to write an ALDinHE recognition scheme application?' *Take 5*, 33. *Available at*: https://lmutake5.wordpress. com/2019/05/21/take5-33-the-best-way-to-write-an-aldinhe-recognition-scheme-application (Accessed: 22 November 2019).

Briggs, S., Koulle, K. and Carter, A. (2019) 'ALDinHE recognition scheme: An introduction', *ALDinHE 2019: The Learning Development Conference*, University of Exeter, Exeter, 15–17 April.

Briggs, S., Kukhareva, M. and Mathew, D. (2015) 'Developing ALDinHE local networks: examples and ideas for regional events', *ALDinHE 2015: The Learning Development Conference*, Southampton Solent University, Southampton, 30 March–1 April.

Briggs, S. and Members of Professional Development Working Group (2016) 'Your ALDinHE regional networks,. *ALDinHE 2016: The Learning Development Conference*, Heriot-Watt University, Edinburgh, 21–23 March.

Briggs, S., Webster, H., Buckley, C. and Pritchard, C. (2018d) 'An introduction to the ALDinHE Certified Leading Practitioner (CeLP) Recognition Scheme', *ALDinHE 2018: The Learning Development Conference*, University of Leicester, Leicester, 26–28 March.

Buckley, C. and Briggs, S. (2017) 'Community keynote – the future of Learning Development', *ALDinHE 2017: The Learning Development Conference*, University of Hull, Hull, 10–12 April.

LILAC (2020) *The Information Literacy Conference*. Available at: https://www. lilacconference.com/ (Accessed: 22 March 2023).

Livesey, L. and Members of the ALDinHE Events Working Group (2017) 'You can too: how to put on a regional symposium', *ALDinHE 2017: The Learning Development Conference*, University of Hull, Hull, 10–12 April.

Shahabudin, K. and Coonan, E. (2015) 'Dilemmas of difference in an age of convergence: co-working for librarians and Learning Developers', *ALDinHE 2015: The Learning Development Conference*, Southampton Solent University, Southampton, 30 March–1 April.

25

RAISING THE PROFILE OF LEARNING DEVELOPMENT IN HIGHER EDUCATION

Institutional and Sector Perspectives

Helen Webster

You are a fly on the wall in a meeting of senior leaders from Higher Education institutions and agencies around the country. They discuss the support needs of students in the modern university: re-engaging students with their learning post-pandemic, the increase in students reporting poor wellbeing, low sense of belonging and academic confidence, a rise in contract cheating and use of AI, the challenges of embedding provision in the curriculum, the implications of learning analytics and a data-driven approach to targeting support ... What to do?

'Wait', you think, 'there's a profession which can help understand and address these issues ... have you spoken to your Learning Developers?'

In the context of the Widening Participation agenda of the early 2000s and increasing internationalisation of Higher Education (HE), universities began to employ study skills practitioners to offer these supposedly 'weaker', 'struggling' non-traditional students additional support in those requisite skills which they were felt to lack, to improve retention and help them catch up and keep up with their traditional peers. Over time, that remit was broadened to encompass all students, as it was increasingly the view that schooling did not provide students with the skills they allegedly should have, to be fully prepared for university. However, the Learning Development (LD) community of practitioners which coalesced in the early 2000s rejected this view and established a practice influenced by Academic Literacies theory (Lea and Street, 1998), a non-deficit approach rooted in principles of emancipation, social justice, and critical pedagogy, recognising the role of cultural capital and systemic privilege which disadvantaged those students who did not share the middle-class, white, Western, non-disabled discourses dominant in UK HE. This foundation is

DOI: 10.4324/9781003433347-31

now codified in the ALDinHE values, in which a certified practitioner must demonstrate a commitment to emancipatory practice and working alongside students to help them make sense of higher education (Briggs, 2018).

Perceptions of LD

From the very beginning, LD has had to negotiate a difficult tension between what our institutions have employed us to do, and what we perceive our roles to be. The problem that our employers and managers hired us to solve is not the problem as we see it: a far bigger, more complex one, located as much in the discourses and practices of the discipline and the institution as in the students. The very premise of our employment is, from our perspective, often highly flawed, which creates difficulties as we seek to establish ourselves as a new, hybrid 'third space' profession (Whitchurch, 2013) within the context of learning, teaching, and assessment, and influence wider educational policy and practice. And we are not asserting this from a position of much power (Blythman and Orr, 2006; Barkas, 2011b; Murray and Glass, 2011; Webster, 2022); the low status of LD and its vulnerability to being over-absorbed within or subordinated under other functions or professions, positioned away from learning and teaching in a student service delivery capacity, often does not leave us much capital to influence discussions about student learning and success within our own institutions, let alone across the sector. This chapter articulates the valuable perspective that LD can offer the higher education sector, but also explores how we are perceived within the learning and teaching landscape, how we might understand ourselves within that context and, looking from the outside in, opportunities to shape that perspective and position our contribution more strategically.

We must articulate our distinct value to the sector in terms that speak to strategic priorities and agendas. LD is a third space profession in a number of respects (Whitchurch, 2013), from which we derive our unique boundary crossing value and which is in many ways a source of freedom, allowing us to operate 'under the radar' and 'in the cracks'. However, several Learning Developers have drawn attention to an additional, unique aspect of our third space positioning, namely our ability to open up a neutral, liminal space within and beyond the curriculum, shaped by our non-judgemental, emancipatory, person-centred values, in which we can facilitate students to explore their own learning (Blythman and Orr, 2006, p.6; Johnson, 2018, p.9; Abegglen, Burns and Sinfield, 2019; Webster, 2022). An Academic Literacies approach is inherently a dialogic one, and through our work with students, we gain a privileged access to the student voice in all its diversity, which is not fully accessible through other mechanisms such as student surveys, educational research, or Student Union representation. Our perspective on how students experience their learning 'in real time' on the ground can enrich curriculum design, inform student support initiatives and projects, policies and strategies, contribute to quality assurance and enhancement, and give early warning of the impact on students of issues from minor changes in assessment design to major ones such as the pandemic. We can be an invaluable 'critical friend' to help interpret student responses to surveys such as the NSS, PTES, or PRES, unpack sticking points within curricula or the student journey, and helpful partners in designing and implementing solutions. As third space professionals, we occupy 'mediating roles between the experience of students, the goals of academics, and the wider ambitions of our HE institutions' (Hilsdon, 2011, p.24), and as such, we sit at a nexus of a number of agendas, from the Widening Participation and internationalisation drive from which our roles often arose, but also initiatives to address attainment and awarding gaps, enhance student wellbeing, belonging and success, implement inclusive curricula and student partnership approaches to enhancing the student learning experience.

Yet our third space positioning is also a source of vulnerability. Unfortunately, understanding of LD, indeed awareness of LD as a coherent profession and even the term itself, continues to be poor across our institutions and across the sector. A deficit model still prevails in the perspectives of senior leadership and management (Wingate, 2015), and the term Learning Development has never gained traction outside the community, as is evident in the range of job and service titles we are given. It is easily confused with 'Learning *and* Development' (i.e., non-educational staff development, a Human Resources function), learning design, or learning technology. Indeed, this lack of consistent terminology is compounded by our own difficulty in articulating what we do (Hilsdon, 2011) and by a lack of internal consensus not only about what Learning Developers are called and do, but what Learning Development *is*. Murray and Glass (2011) reported that there was a poor understanding of LD in practitioners' institutions, with other authors voicing concern at the resulting perception as low-skilled 'support' work rather than teaching (Barkas, 2011a; Blythman and Orr, 2006; Johnson, 2018; Webster, 2022). An informed understanding of our remit, approach, and expertise is still lacking among our management and senior leadership, and this is reflected in how they have constituted and located our roles, choices which can constrain how we enact them to the benefit not just of students but to our institutions and the wider sector. The flexibility and diversity of LD is a positive feature, with provision being constituted in various ways to suit the organisational structure and culture of different institutional contexts, but equally this lack of consistency may have obscured LD's presence. LD is accordingly all but invisible in sector-level discussions of student educational experience and success. Wingate (2015, p.12) noted the 'lack of a strong unified voice calling for change and convincing university managers and academics of the need for change', and indeed what voice we have has to date been fragmented, underconfident, and inward-looking. LD is often absent from high-level strategic conversations at sector and institution levels about highly relevant matters such as student success, recent examples including student wellbeing, belonging, access and outreach work, 'whole institution approaches', embedding support into the curriculum, and navigating the return to the 'new normal' following the pandemic, in which we have a useful role to play or valuable insights to share.

Repositioning Learning Development

If you believe as I do that LD is a force for good in HE, and has much to offer the sector as well as students, then we must more visibly, effectively, and assertively locate ourselves within the broader landscape of learning and teaching in HE, within our institutions and the sector as a whole. It is true that a certain invisibility has allowed us to determine our own practices and values, and that the more visible LD has become, the more it is in danger of being co-opted or constrained by more managerialist agendas. Yet the converse has impacted on our ability to capitalise on our distinct praxis, both to consolidate our profession and to position it in a more influential way in our institutions and the sector. Putting our heads above the parapet comes with risks, but continuing to operate under the radar is not without implications; apart from lost opportunities to influence and contribute to sector agendas, invisibility makes it easier to undervalue, under-resource, and cut professional Learning Development teams and absorb 'study skills' delivery as a lesser priority into other functions.

Currently, we are often not well integrated within the formal architecture of teaching and learning structures and processes in our institutions, positioned more as student service delivery than as part of the educational landscape, as 'giving advice and guidance' rather than teaching. To change this, we need to raise our profile and expectations of what we can do. Learning Developers have successfully built relationships with individual module or programme leaders, advocating for provision to be embedded in subject teaching and gaining access to timetabled slots in key modules to offer bespoke sessions using authentic materials from the discipline. However, this bottom-up progress has its limitations; we have managed to push back against central generic 'bolt-on' provision, but have often had to settle for what I would term 'wheel-in' provision, where a Learning Developer is brought into the timetable for a one-shot session which is not truly integrated into the programme curriculum in a meaningful sense, with little opportunity to iterate and build on provision and only a superficial sense of how it hooks more broadly into student progress and a course's wider disciplinary culture, let alone influence it. We could push for more ambitious, perhaps top-down models of embedding LD, for more systemic change in addition to our focus on the individual learner. This might be CPD to enhance our academic colleagues' practice or 'critical friend' consultancy, a more meaningful integration within the whole curriculum via a more formal contribution to programme and module development and review, curriculum and assessment design, quality assurance, and enhancement mechanisms, beyond what we have envisaged and achieved so far. To do this, we need to work sensitively not just with academic and administrative but also Educational Development colleagues, but the more clearly we can articulate and delineate the distinct expertise we can bring, and how it complements theirs, the better we can collaborate. Educational Development is in many ways the flipside of Learning Development; where we work with students, they work with staff, and where we work with education as it currently is and as students experience it, they work with education as it could and should be. Educational Development can help us to bring about lasting, more systemic change, and we can bring an emergent, 'chalk-face' perspective to their work. Similarly, we might push for a more established presence on teaching and learning committees, not just at department or faculty level but at the institution level to bring our perspective and expertise to bear on education policy and strategy development in addition to reporting on our own services and highlighting trends we are spotting. One difficulty here is the lack of seniority of most LD roles; even service heads are often not employed on a grade which gives us access to these forums. We are frequently therefore reliant on working through those professions in whose divisions our provision is located, through layers of management, or as individuals gaining a prominence that affords us this access (for example, through teaching awards), which does not formalise the profession's status in these spaces.

Learning Development at Institution and Sector Levels

One place to start gaining traction is to more proactively and agentically consider the regulatory processes which generate strategic priorities and drivers for our institution, beginning with familiarising ourselves with the institution's strategic plan for education, Access and Participation Plan, or NSS results. For example, it is common that a strategic plan might be disseminated to us in terms of management-set objectives, or only the NSS results which pertain to the student services we are located in are fed back to us for comment and improvement in service delivery. However, our third space, student-centred positioning may allow us a broader perspective on how we might align our goals with strategic initiatives in ways which might not be obvious to our senior leadership. For example, many of the questions in the NSS are ones which we could help to interpret and advise on, including the new question on freedom of expression (highly relevant to an Academic Literacies or Students as Partners approach), or feedback, an area which rarely scores satisfactorily and which we have a privileged insight into, working with it as we do in our one-to-one practice. Other regulatory frameworks to which we could fruitfully contribute ideas as well as data might include the OfS's Access and Participation Plans in England and Wales, or implementation of charters such as the AdvanceHE Race Equality Charter or Student Minds University Mental Health charter, which explicitly mention areas directly relevant to LD without quite being aware of its existence.

If we have a more established place within the educational landscape of our institutions, we are better positioned to help them respond to new drivers and agendas as they arise. To inform our work at this institutional level, we need to be aware of current national agendas, developments, and news relating to HE. This not only helps us to contextualise our own work in the sector, and understand and anticipate the impact of these drivers on us, but also offers us the opportunity to deliberately position our provision in those terms and clarify how we might play a role in our institutions' responses to those drivers. This is not to say that we always support those agendas and unquestioningly align our work with them; rather, that we can be more proactive and vocal in our stance on them, contribute to and shape our institutions' responses to them, or connect issues in an intersectional way which might otherwise seem unrelated. The COVID-19 pandemic was one example where Learning Developers found themselves at the forefront of student support, but the cost-of-living crisis is also relevant to learning. An upcoming agenda is learning analytics; universities are now in possession of large quantities of data about students' learning, and therefore under an obligation to act on it. This response could far too easily become a deficit approach, targeting those students deemed 'at risk' with 'study skills' approaches, whereas an LD perspective might be able to suggest more empowering and theorised data-driven approaches to supporting students. The evidence-based 'What Works' turn in government education policy and regulation has highlighted the paucity of evidence on interventions to enhance student success, particularly in terms of wellbeing, inclusion, and attainment. Scholarship is rarely built into LD roles – many of us conducting what research we can on an individual basis on the margins of our role, using customer satisfaction models to evaluate our practice – but a more strategic and scholarly approach to capturing what we do would greatly contribute to this piece of work as well as giving us the leverage we might need to argue for more effective forms of provision. The debates about how assessment practices should respond to AI-authored text and contract cheating would benefit hugely from a more prominent LD voice, and 'whole institution' approaches to student wellbeing and belonging have clear links to building students' academic confidence, agency, and success. We might begin by keeping abreast of sector news, via channels such as *WONKHE*, *THE*, and the *Guardian Higher Education* section (the *WONKHE* weekly roundup email and podcast is especially useful), subscribing to JISCMail lists of organisations and professions other than LDHEN, and keeping an eye on what sector agencies are doing. These might include the relevant Government department; quality and regulatory bodies such as DfE, QAA, or OfS; sector agencies such as UUK, AdvanceHE, Jisc, UCAS,

TASO, or Student Minds; or related professional bodies such as SEDA, BALEAP, CILIP, AMOSSHE, BACP, UMHAN, UKAT, or ADSHE. Community forums such as the LDHEN list, ALDinHE regional events, and webinars are good spaces to discuss the implications for LD, and the opportunities these developments might pose.

We might also aim for greater visibility across the sector to raise the profile of LD more generally, contributing to conversations on a wider scale. To do this, we need to position ourselves as experts with something distinct and valuable to offer, outside our own community, which demands a level of confidence that many of us may find uncomfortable. Yet we are well placed to offer informed and insightful commentary on a range of sector issues and developments and share innovative approaches, and should look beyond our own community to do so. Visibility for the profession as well as the individual can also be achieved by professional recognition, and it is encouraging that several Learning Developers have achieved National Teaching Fellowships in recent years, which gives not just prominence but access to networks beyond LD. Contributing to sector discussions via social media and commenting on articles and blogs beyond the ALDinHE community might be a step towards beginning to write opinion pieces for journalistic outlets such as *WONKHE* or *THE*, or guest posts for the blogs of sector agencies such as AdvanceHE or, equally importantly, writing responses to stories in these outlets which have either misrepresented or overlooked LD. Whether writing in our own capacity or on behalf of the community, we can foreground our distinct perspective as Learning Developers and establish that this is located within the wider collective perspective of our profession. To a great extent though, raising awareness of what we do and how and why we do it among our own senior leadership will also improve our prominence across the sector, as it is our Vice Chancellors who collectively form so many of the representative and consultative groups shaping HE.

LD has so much to offer our institutions and the sector as a whole, beyond the value we add to each student's success. We have a distinct perspective on the student experience through our work, enhanced by our specific professional values and theoretical basis, which can help our institutions' education and student experience strategy and inform discussions of key agendas and drivers at sector level. However, our visibility has been impacted by a number of factors; the low status and lack of wider understanding of our work is perhaps compounded by our own lack of consensus and professional confidence and an inward-looking tendency amongst our community rather than reaching beyond it. Flying under the radar has served us well in building and establishing our practices, but to fully realise our potential, we need to have belief in our expert status, confidence in the value of what we have to offer, and assertiveness in making our voices heard in new spaces. After all, isn't this what we teach our students?

References

Abegglen, S., Burns, T. and Sinfield, S. (2019) 'It's Learning Development, Jim – but not as we know it: academic literacies in third-space', *Journal of Learning Development in Higher Education*, 15. https://doi.org/10.47408/jldhe.v0i15.500

Barkas, L.A. (2011a) '"Teaching" or "support"? The poisoned chalice of the role of Students' Skills Centres', *Journal of Further and Higher Education*, 35(2): 265–286. https://doi.org/10.1080/0309877X.2011.558889

Barkas, L.A. (2011b) *The Paradox of Skills: Widening Participation, Academic Literacy and Students' Skills Centres*. Rotterdam: Sense.

Blythman, M. and Orr, S. (2006) 'Mrs Mop Does Magic', *Zeitschrift Schreiben (European Journal of Writing)*, 1–8.

Briggs, S. (2018) 'Development of the ALDinHE recognition scheme: Certifying the "Learning Developer" title', *Journal of Learning Development in Higher Education*, 13. https://doi.org/10.47408/jldhe.v0i13.461

Hilsdon, J. (2011) 'What is learning development?', in P. Hartley et al. (eds) *Learning Development in Higher Education*. Basingstoke: Palgrave MacMillan, 13–27.

Johnson, I.P. (2018) 'Driving learning development professionalism forward from within', *Journal of Learning Development in Higher Education*. https://doi.org/10.47408/jldhe.v0i0.470

Lea, M.R. and Street, B.V. (1998) 'Student writing in higher education: An academic literacies approach', *Studies in Higher Education*, 23(2): 157–172. https://doi.org/10.1080/03075079812331380364

Murray, L. and Glass, B. (2011) 'Learning Development in Higher Education: Community of Practice or Profession?', in P. Hartley et al. (eds) *Learning Development in Higher Education*. Basingstoke: Palgrave MacMillan, 28–39.

Webster, H. (2022) 'Supporting the Development, Recognition and Impact of Third Space Professionals', in E. McIntosh and D. Nutt (eds) *The Impact of the Integrated Practitioner in Higher Education: Studies in Third Space Professionalism*. Abingdon: Routledge, 178–187.

Whitchurch, C. (2013) *Reconstructing Identities in Higher Education: The Rise of Third Space Professionals*. Abingdon: Routledge.

Wingate, U. (2015) *Academic Literacy and Student Diversity: The Case for Inclusive Practice. Multilingual Matters*. Bristol: Multilingual Matters.

26

THE FUTURE OF LEARNING DEVELOPMENT

Two Visions

Ed Bickle, Steph Allen and Marian Mayer

> *A Learning Developer walks into a crowded room. There is no need to explain to anyone what they do as their occupation; after all, everyone recognises a Learning Developer, why wouldn't they? Everybody knows the vital role a Learning Developer plays in developing the core academic skills of Higher Education students to help them succeed and thrive in their studies. In fact, only the day before, the Learning Developer has been a guest on morning television, discussing the vital role that Learning Developers play in shaping the debate on the growing use of Artificial Intelligence within Higher Education.*
> *Welcome to the future.*

Introduction

In the first book about Learning Development (LD), published in 2011, the field of LD was identified as a work in progress (Hilsdon et al., 2011), reflecting the differing modes of being and working with the teaching and learning community. Provision has been variable and patchy within institutions, according to establishment attitudes, student numbers, funding, resources, staff expertise, and training of Learning Developers to support students in the post-16 education sector. LD was described as 'flying under the radar of government policies and senior management concerns' (Hilsdon et al., 2011, p.253), and, despite best efforts, it still is. Although Learning Developers have been left to establish themselves institutionally, nationally, and internationally, and have not necessarily been shy about their role and impact, many are not visible, having been subsumed into multidimensional education spaces and categorised under sweeping generalisations of the noble librarian or indistinct 'learning hubs'.

DOI: 10.4324/9781003433347-32

This lack of recognition has not best reflected the pedagogical importance of the LD community. So where does this leave LD, and what does the future hold? The first step in understanding what the future may hold occurred at the 2022 ALDinHE annual conference in Northampton. In a workshop entitled 'Learning Development 2030' (Bickle et al., 2022), conference colleagues were free to set out their future directions for the profession. Participant discussions focused on issues such as the growing importance of technology and the ways in which LD can harness these technological developments. Others focused on commercial funding and sponsorship, yet all outlined ways in which the profession can become more widely recognised, labelling LD practitioners as the 'change makers', 'breaking down borders', describing the essential role LD plays in guiding and supporting students (Bickle et al., 2023). It was evident that practitioners see the need for change, that LD cannot sit still. In this chapter we present two differing visions of the future: a dystopian, technology-led future; and a utopian, humanistic one in which LD thrives.

Dystopia: Deus ex machina

> An imagined world or society in which people lead wretched, dehumanized, fearful lives.
>
> (Merriam-Webster, 2023a)

During the COVID-19 pandemic, institutions, pushed to evidence student support, celebrated the newly promoted 'golden goose' LD provision as the front liners. Institutions had no choice but to advance education delivery to online platforms, forcing Learning Developers to rapidly adapt to the synchronous and asynchronous formats with varying degrees of success. This was an opportunity to reconsider the resources for working online, then later in hybrid formats, highlighting the innovative creativity and experimentation bursting across the sector. Later, the technology sector released an explosive and revolutionary changemaker that would impact upon the fundamental way in which LD is taught, that of the rapid growth of artificial intelligence (AI) within higher education (HE).

The use of AI technology has been both controversial and, arguably, essential within the education sector. Whilst old school academics might contend that students should enter HE with well-rounded English language and grammatical skill sets, others would counter that there is a greater need for creativity or practical skills, however they are expressed in writing. Those who have been teaching and marking recognise that these arguments are unlikely, in the near future, to disappear. Despite the academic communities' best efforts to prepare students for the (written) working world – those entering the legal, media and communication, medical, and other critical professions – the ability to communicate effectively is still desirable within industry.

Since 2011, new and widely accessible software has become available. These range from programmes that assist with small tasks, for example, spell check, grammar check, encyclopaedic information, and library functions such as finding books – all tools to assist in researching, writing, editing, and checking – to support the student in communicating their thoughts and ideas at the end of an assessed unit of study. In late 2022, a 2015 technological piece of software was released to potential users called ChatGPT. The launch of the software, an early AI tool based on a large language model filled with predicted text narrative for users to engage with, changed the landscape for writers at all levels. Within weeks, trial user accounts were being exploited to test, even train, the software to carry out a range of academic and scholarly tasks. The capabilities of the AI included elements of information retrieval, sentence structuring based on essay formats, answer formatting, 'informed opinion', guidance, and other pre-programmed and human intervention input. According to Lancaster (2023, cited by Weale, 2023), a leading UK computer scientist and Academic Integrity, Plagiarism, and Contract Cheating researcher, ChatGPT was a game changer and '[universities] have to adapt sooner rather than later to make sure that students are assessed fairly, that they all compete on a level playing field and that they still have the skills needed beyond university'.

As well as contending with practical benefits for students who are not natural writers, and those whose character leans towards what Cain (2013) considers to be 'quiet introverts' not inclined to connect with others, the software appears to be attractive. Webb (2023, cited by Weale, 2023) argues that we should look at such software as 'the next step up from spelling or grammar checkers: technology that can make everyone's life easier'.

Early AI users with access to the various software have experienced a range of responses to prompted queries. For example, testing the software for legal examinations resulted in near-perfect answers (Weiss, 2023), yet individuals using ChatGPT for self-diagnosis have had worrying recommendations. As of mid-2023, the software was unable to ask humans the right questions to assess and determine multiple potential avenues for treatment. In one reported situation, where software was incapable of asking nuanced questions with potentially nuanced responses of a patient, had the individual followed the (mis)diagnosis they could have been in mortal danger (Tamayo-Sarvo, 2023). This is a warning to medical students who might be tempted to rely on the emerging technology rather than learn the craft of clinical medicine.

As Eaton (2022) pointed out, if there are concerns around an explosion of cheating because of 'new technological advances … technology isn't the problem', which leads us to understand that, perhaps, education and how it is delivered and assessed may play a part too. What could this mean for LD? The role and identity of Learning Developers may well evolve into new jobs, activities, responsibilities, and titles. With the turning point of greater access to AI, digital information and its role in education, LD and Learning Developers may become more aligned to what we envisage as 'Integrated Learning Development' – a blend of traditional skill sets and the demands arising from machine enhancements. Learning Developers of the future may become:

- Retrained as AI prompters to guide students how to ask software relevant questions to gain relevant responses in order to avoid the Garbage In Garbage Out (GIGO) information delivery.
- Reality-based experiential education explainers to help differentiate AI responses and reality, reinvigorating and empowering students around the notion of what it means to be a human writer.
- Assessment designers who review or produce assignments that develop higher-order thinking through authentic experiential learning via real-time in-person collaborative makerspaces.
- Advisors on how to analyse and critique AI responses to both test AI and student critical thinking and how to evaluate information provided.
- Involved in monitoring, assessing, and evaluating the impact of AI on social constructivism, for example, beyond being a passive knowledge receiver but a constructor or reconstructor of that knowledge.
- Developers of novel pedagogy and practice in order to navigate the digital world such as tasks with no grades to encourage engaged, deep, and risk-free learning.
- Differentiated advocacy supporters around and for Academic Integrity.
- Centrepoints for networking, lifelong learning, and community engagement, potentially creating and offering innovative services.
- Sponsored AI software promoters with a focus on differentiated learner needs by involving students to improve the software through critique of its approach to equity, diversity, accessibility, and inclusion.
- Leaders and catalysts for the societal withdrawal from internet usage. In an age of hackers and privacy concerns, individuals decline a digital footprint.
- No longer required in the education sector at all – the user has become the expert.

Noting the changes within the education sector, and what is predicted to be increasing numbers of students in the UK university sector, as Learning Developers we will have to step fully outside our comfort and knowledge zones to work with students and colleagues for developments we cannot yet predict. We look forward to reviewing this chapter in several years' time to see how our predictions play out. What we do know, though, is that it is a Brave New World and Learning Developers will need to either rise to the challenge or shape the direction of travel.

A Utopia: A True Understanding of LD

> A place of ideal perfection especially in laws, government, and social conditions.
>
> (Merriam-Webster, 2023b)

Like most sectors, the world of HE has undergone significant disruption over the past three years while we have adjusted to the impacts of COVID-19 on learning and teaching. It is hard to forget how immobilising, impairing, and incapacitating the experience was for those who lived and worked through that era. As we evolve into a rapidly evolving 'new normal', we must ask ourselves where we as Learning Developers sit within the new environment. With the pivot to the online and hybrid working world, we must ask ourselves:

- Have students become accustomed to LD being seen as primarily an online activity?
- Do we need to ensure LD has a greater physical space on campus?
- Is the need for LD support greater than it has ever been?
- In this reshaped environment, and where resources in terms of budgets and staff availability are limited, how do we encourage students to maximise their engagement with LD?

There are no easy answers to these questions, and addressing them will vary at a local level depending on, for example, the positioning of LD as a central or faculty-based team (or indeed both). What remains the case is that students must be at the heart of LD practice. The hybrid era provides new opportunities to offer a greater amount of flexibility for ways in which students are able to engage with LD.

With this in mind, we began this chapter with an epigraph in which we laid out the raison d'être of LD: that the role of Learning Developers within HE is fully understood. Chapter 25, for example, outlined the vulnerability of LD being positioned in 'third space', discussing issues with the term LD itself and how perceptions and understanding of LD remain poor within institutions. In our utopia, LD practitioners practise in a world in which they no longer need to explain and justify their existence (Syska and Buckley, 2022). To address this, we start with the words of Verity and Trowler (2011). Written over ten years ago, they suggested the idea of 'the integration of Learning Development with academic provision to provide a seamless experience for all students, who would learn subject content and become skilful in their academic practices simultaneously' (p.248).

Whilst we see an integrated approach as the 'ideal', we do so whilst being mindful that LD can, and should, still be seen as something unique, with students being able to identify LD practitioners as different to their course lecturers and tutors. In this sense, LD practitioners should always be seen as offering a 'safe space'. A seamless integration is crucial to the utopian path of LD, although we acknowledge it suggests that progress is slow in respect of this proposed integration (Johnson, 2022). In 2011, Verity and Trowler suggested that the role of LD remains remedial, with it being relevant only to a subsection of the student population. This could also be described as a failure-based approach (Pritchard, 2022). In our utopian future, LD is no longer seen in this light, having moved away from any connotation of a deficit model to teaching, with staff and students alike recognising LD as a practice that benefits the entire student population, moving past the idea that LD is purely to help students pass an assignment. In future, we suggest LD practitioners will:

- Play an increased role in policymaking processes and effective task and finish working groups.
- Lead on discussions around the use of AI and Academic Integrity.
- Be increasingly encouraged and inspired to join professional practice groups such as ALDinHE.
- Build closer partnerships with teaching and support staff, including co-creation of lectures, and learning materials.
- Lead on inviting and hosting subject specific guest speakers to the institutional community.
- Be relentless in promoting the benefits of LD to the HE community, particularly to those in decision-making positions.
- Publish on institutional blogs about advances in LD.

The question remains, however, how LD can become more instantly recognisable in the future. How do we 'persuade, manoeuvre and alter perceptions among real people' (Verity and Trowler, 2011, p.244)? In terms of best practice, there has been an increase in demand for recognition through informal networking and training routes, as well as recognition through the professional sector such as ALDinHE, which identifies that since its launch in 2017, its professional recognition scheme has awarded CEP and CELP status to over 120 Learning Developers (see Chapter 24). Whilst this is encouraging, as yet there are still no formal funded training routes available to those joining the profession. This is perhaps a potential new route for LD, with fully accredited entry routes into the profession, akin to entry routes into librarianship, for example. Creating such routes would provide new staff with a firm theoretical and practical underpinning as to the role of LD and its location within HE. As well as demystifying the role for newcomers, it could potentially assist with career progression, and lead to greater recognition within the wider HE ecosystem as to the unique role of the Learning Developer. This is especially critical given the lack of progression opportunities that currently exist for many Learning Developers, particularly those not on academic career pathways. We suggest that expanding informal networks may also be possible in the future, such as regional knowledge exchange forums/programmes and working groups, examining opportunities such as a cross-sector induction programme for new LD staff.

In Chapter 17 the authors outlined that LD practitioners often work to contracts that preclude the requirement to conduct research, resulting in minimal levels of engagement with research for many practitioners. Whilst the LD community continues to thrive through networking events, discussing, and debating the skills required for Learning Developers and sharing ideas for professional skills and student experience, a utopian position would involve research being written into all LD job descriptions. This, however, is perhaps pushing the boundaries of realism, given the wide variety of roles that LD practitioners work in. It is unrealistic, for example, to expect that in the future, every LD role across the sector will be positioned within an academic contract. Nor should every Learning Developer be in a position where research is a compulsory element of their contract. Rather, in a utopia we envisage that Learning Developers who have the wish and desire to engage in research are given the financial and workload planning freedom and opportunity to do so. Crucial to this will be the development and promotion of a culture of robust research, in order to further the field (Syska and Buckley, 2022). In summary, an LD utopia involves:

- Greater recognition of LD from the wider HE sector, where Learning Developers no longer need to justify their role.
- Fully accredited entry routes into the profession as well as clear progression opportunities.
- Closer engagement/integration into core teaching practices.
- No longer thought of as a 'deficit' approach.
- Freedom to conduct research for those who so wish.

Final Thoughts

Since 2011, when the foundational book on LD was published, the profession and practice of LD has evolved within the educational ecosystem, with Learning Developers establishing themselves as knowledgeable, experienced, expert practitioners, passionate about the discipline. Many of Hilsdon et al.'s (2011, p.257) observations remain true today:

> A Learning Development approach is not designed merely to provide support for the 'needy' and does not see students as deficient or in need of remediation. Rather, it is a response to the need for a higher education

which is accessible and relevant to all with the ability to benefit. It is therefore applicable to all students, not just groups seen as vulnerable, and it requires flexible and multi-faceted modes of practice.

Whilst within this chapter we have presented two differing visions of the future, the reality is likely to be less clear-cut. At a time of genuine unprecedented change in technology for society, the LD community will need to consider the applications of AI and the potential uses for creating and guiding practical and authentic development opportunities that students can meaningfully engage with, for and beyond their educational experience. Whilst there is enthusiasm amongst the academic development community, the journey for all to engage with and adapt to the technology to produce teaching and learning that remains human in nature will be a voyage that will be a cause for reflection in the next iteration of this book.

If LD is to continue to thrive, it must strengthen and consolidate its position within HE. LD practitioners must be at the forefront of this change. We must take it upon ourselves to promote the benefits of LD to students, colleagues, and key decision-makers: as teams we must drive the LD agenda within our own institutions. We must collaborate and work closely with HE colleagues to embed LD into day-to-day teaching practices, so that we become relevant and valued. At the same time, LD must develop its own professional recognition as well as academic identity through innovative, robust, research.

Learning Development remains a work in progress.

References

Bickle, E., Allen, S. and Mayer, M. (2022) 'Learning Development 2030', *Journal of Learning Development in Higher Education, Special Issue 25: ALDinHE Conference Proceedings and Reflections.* https://doi.org/10.47408/jldhe.vi25.972

Bickle, E., Allen, S. and Mayer, M. (2023) 'Learning Development 2030: A time for change?', *Take5*. Available at: https://lmutake5.wordpress.com/2023/01/26/take5-80-learning-development-2030-a-time-for-change/ (Accessed: 14 February 2023).

Cain, S. (2013) *Quiet: The Power of Introverts in a World That Can't Stop Talking.* London: Penguin Books.

Eaton, S.E. (2022) 'Sarah's Thoughts: Artificial Intelligence and Academic Integrity', *Learning, Teaching and Leadership.* Available at: https://drsaraheaton.wordpress.com/2022/12/09/sarahs-thoughts-artificial-intelligence-and-academic-integrity/ (Accessed: 21 February 2023).

Hilsdon, J., Keenan, C. and Sinfield, S. (2011) 'What is Learning Development?', in: P. Hartley, J. Hilsdon, C. Keenan, S. Sinfield and M. Verity (eds) *Learning Development in Higher Education.* Basingstoke: Palgrave Macmillan, 253–258.

Johnson, I. (2022) 'To embed, not to embed, how to embed', *Journal of Learning Development in Higher Education, Special Issue25: ALDinHE Conference Proceedings and Reflections.* https://doi.org/10.47408/jldhe.vi25.966

Merriam-Webster (2023a) *Dystopia*. Available at: https://www.merriam-webster.com/dictionary/dystopia (Accessed: 3 April 2023).

Merriam-Webster (2023b) *Utopia*. Available at: https://www.merriam-webster.com/dictionary/dystopia (Accessed: 3 April 2023).

Pritchard, C. (2022) 'Learning Developers as their own cultural critics?' *Journal of Learning Development in Higher Education, Special Issue25: ALDinHE Conference Proceedings and Reflections*. https://doi.org/10.47408/jldhe.vi25.967

Syska, A. and Buckley, C. (2022) 'Writing as liberatory practice: unlocking knowledge to locate an academic field', *Teaching in Higher Education*, 28(2): 439–454. https://doi.org/10.1080/13562517.2022.2114337

Tamayo-Sarvo, J. (2023) 'I'm an ER doctor: Here's what I found when I asked ChatGPT to diagnose my patients', *FastCompany*. Available at: https://www.fastcompany.com/90863983/chatgpt-medical-diagnosis-emergency-room (Accessed: 25 March 2023).

Verity, M. and Trowler, P. (2011) 'What is Learning Development?', in P. Hartley, J. Hilsdon, C. Keenan, S. Sinfield and M. Verity (eds) *Learning Development in Higher Education*. Basingstoke: Palgrave Macmillan, 241–252.

Weale, S. (2023) 'Lecturers urged to review assessments in UK amid concerns over new AI tool', *The Guardian*, 13 January. Available at: https://www.theguardian.com/technology/2023/jan/13/end-of-the-essay-uk-lecturers-assessments-chatgpt-concerns-ai (Accessed: 20 February 2023).

Weiss, D. (2023) 'Latest version of ChatGPT aces bar exam with score nearing 90th percentile', *ABA Journal*. 16 March. Available at: https://www.abajournal.com/web/article/latest-version-of-chatgpt-aces-the-bar-exam-with-score-in-90th-percentile#:~:text=The%20latest%20version%20of%20the,of%20273%20set%20by%20Arizona (Accessed: 3 April 2023).

OPENING

Carina Buckley and Alicja Syska

For me, it's about thinking with other people.

(Survey respondent)

Our aim with this book was to take our readers on a discursive, winding, and tangential journey through Learning Development, one circumscribed only by the current configuration of the field. However, unlike most journeys, this is one without a final destination; rather, there is a multiplicity of options, offered as fleeting glimpses along the path through these chapters, each one acting as a junction rather than a terminus and serving to give a 'sharpening of attention … to something coming into existence', as Kathleen Stewart (2010, p.340) writes. This book therefore represents both our questioning and our understanding of what it is that is coming into existence; in asking, 'How to be a Learning Developer in higher education', we are asking what difference our attention makes, to the field and to ourselves. In asking *how to be*, we are aiming to clarify not just *who we are*, but also *who we might become*.

Learning Development is a field of movement and momentum, a 'fluidity of becoming' (Gale and Wyatt, 2022, p.80) built on repeatedly inscribed structures, thoughts, and praxis that are not stable and fixed but rather a dynamic 'gathering of experience' (Stewart, 2010, p.340), subject to its own movement and momentum. This gathering – an enmeshing of ideas, practices, concepts, and frameworks, of ways of being and ways of doing – is also affective and relational; it is essentially about people, in relation to each other and the structures in which they operate. We are 'making kin' (Haraway, 2016, cited in Gale and Wyatt, 2022, p.81) with the field and with each other in the field, building connections and following lines of potential, whilst

DOI: 10.4324/9781003433347-33

acknowledging that this might be unplanned, non-strategic, ad hoc; Learning Development is thus a 'bloom space' (Stewart, 2010, p.340) wherein anything can happen and may, if we are awake to its possibility.

The essays in this volume demonstrate a 'collective attunement' (ibid.) to the possibilities offered by and for Learning Development. There are challenges along the road and neoliberal diversions that might threaten to pull us off track. We must take stock of the field and what it can offer to a sector overly enamoured with research. We are called upon to measure its impact and quantify its value whilst somehow performing the mental gymnastics that allow us to remain true to the fundamental values that guide our practice. We push for the much-needed reorientation of HE towards inclusivity and decolonisation whilst also defending against our own marginalisation. Above all, we are compelled to critique, interrogate, and reconstitute a system whose structures, processes, and drivers make Learning Development so necessary.

However, while there are missions to tackle, there are also opportunities. Each contribution in this book represents a space of potential in flux, a 'not-yet-ness' (Gale and Wyatt, 2022, p.80) ready to be claimed. Learning Development is a key function of Learning and Teaching; Learning Developers have unique insights to offer. We cannot wait for permission to contribute but instead must make that offer, generously, pre-emptively, and confidently, supported and sustained by the lines of attachment that connect us to this wider community. The fluidity of becoming depends upon people, ideas, and praxis in motion. When we ask what Learning Development could be, we must begin with what it already is: open, integrated, and connected. What it could become depends on us. This is your invitation to join and grow that conversation.

References

Gale, K. and Wyatt, J. (2022) 'Making trouble with ontogenesis: Collaborative writing, becoming, and concept forming as event', *Qualitative Inquiry*, 28(1): 80–87.

Stewart, K. (2010) 'Afterword: Worlding refrains', in: M. Gregg and J.G. Seigworth (eds), *The Affect Theory Reader*. Durham, NC: Duke University Press, 339–353.

INDEX

Pages in *italics* refer to figures and pages in **bold** refer to tables.